The Formation of Ḥanbalism

Piety into Power

CULTURE AND CIVILIZATION
IN THE MIDDLE EAST

Series Editor

Ian R. Netton
University of Leeds

This series studies the Middle East through the twin foci of its diverse cultures and civilisations. Comprising original monographs as well as scholarly surveys, it covers topics in the fields of Middle Eastern literature, archaeology, law, history, philosophy, science, folklore, art, architecture and language. While there is a plurality of views, the series presents serious scholarship in a lucid and stimulating fashion.

The Formation of Ḥanbalism

Piety into Power

Nimrod Hurvitz

Routledge
Taylor & Francis Group
NEW YORK AND LONDON

First Published in 2002
by Routledge

This edition by Routledge:

Routledge
Taylor & Francis Group
711 Third Avenue,
New York, NY 10017

Routledge
Taylor & Francis Group
2 Park Square
Milton Park, Abingdon
Oxon OX14 4RN

First issued in paperback 2011

British Library Cataloguing in Publication Data
A catalogue record of this book is available from the British Library

Library of Congress Cataloguing in Publication Data
A catalogue record for this book has been applied for

ISBN10: 0–7007–1507–X (hbk)
ISBN10: 0–415–61641–7 (pbk)

ISBN13: 978–0–7007–1507–7 (hbk)
ISBN13: 978–0–415–61641–6 (pbk)

Publisher's Note
The publisher has gone to great lengths to ensure the quality of this reprint but points out that some imperfections in the original may be apparent.

For Dina, Yaara and Hagar

Contents

Acknowledgements

This book grew out of a dissertation under the supervision of Michael Cook, to whom I owe a great debt for the time and patience with which he introduced me to the history of medieval Islam. His guidance during my graduate studies and his meticulous reading of later drafts have made me rethink many ideas, saved me from numerous pitfalls and greatly improved this study.

Conversations over the years with Nurit Tsafrir contributed to the growth of numerous ideas, several of which appear in this book. I would like to thank her for the time she took to read an early draft and the corrections she made.

Several friends and colleagues have read and commented about parts of earlier drafts. I would like to thank Haim Haimes, Sumaiya Hamdani, Israel Gershoni, Sam Kaplan, Yoram Meital, Ehud Toledano and Dror Zeevi, for their remarks, thoughts and criticism.

My gratitude to my family is obviously beyond words. Still, I must thank my parents, Haggai and Adina, for instilling in me the love of books, ideas and intellectual dialogue. My wife and daughters, Dina, Yaara and Hagar, have helped in many ways, but most importantly in placing this project in its right proportions.

I would like to thank the Herzog Centre for providing financial aid in the final stage of this project. I am also grateful to Brenda Malkiel who improved the clarity of this work and Lia Moran who prepared its indices.

Transliteration and Dates

The transliteration follows the system of the *Encyclopaedia of Islam* with the exception of q in the place of ḳ and j in the place dj. The dates in the text are in accordance with the Hijri calendar.

Introduction

'Allah strengthened this faith [Islam] with two men and no other compares with them, Abū Bakr al-Ṣiddīq on the day of the *ridda* [war of apostasy] and Aḥmad ibn Ḥanbal on the day of the *miḥna* [Inquisition].'[1]

This flattering remark was made by 'Alī b. al-Madīnī (d. 235) who, along with Aḥmad b. Ḥanbal (d. 241), was one of the leading scholars of his generation when the caliph al-Ma'mūn initiated a wave of interrogations known as the *miḥna* (218).[2] When the persecutions ceased fifteen years later, Ibn Ḥanbal was the leading spiritual authority of his day, owing to his resistance to the *miḥna*'s administrators and Ibn al-Madīnī was a disgraced pariah because he collaborated with them. Guilt, or maybe an attempt to stage a comeback to favor, prompted Ibn al-Madīnī to compare Ibn Ḥanbal to Abū Bakr (d. 13), the Prophet's political heir. Although the comparison between a scholar and a political leader is a little surprising, Ibn Ḥanbal and Abū Bakr do have something in common: Both are remembered as strong-willed individuals who saved the Islamic community from disintegration. According to mainstream Islamic historians, Abū Bakr's firm stand against the apostate tribes during the *ridda* wars prevented their secession from the burgeoning Islamic community. Ibn Ḥanbal's ability to withstand torture and defy the caliph and his chief judge captivated the imagination of the masses and led the Traditionists to victory over the deviating sects that controlled the caliphal court. In Islamic collective memory, Ibn Ḥanbal's defiance of his inquisitors catapulted him from the echelons of Traditionist leadership to the pantheon of historical heroes who are an inspiration to Muslims even today.

The study of Ibn Ḥanbal, an orphaned boy from an economically downgraded family who climbed to the heights of spiritual and political influence, highlights several aspects of Islamic society and religiosity. Firstly, Ibn Ḥanbal's rise to prominence demonstrates a common characteristic among Islamic societies: Religious prestige enabled the most humble man or woman to acquire social standing and political clout. Albert Hourani pointed out this particular feature: 'sanctity or religious learning served in Islamic society as a point around which social power crystallized.'[3] Many of the central figures of Islamic civilization, as well as countless individuals who gained the respect of their local communities, acquired their status by building a reputation for piety or learning.[4] From the founders of *madhāhib* (schools of law) and *ṭarīqāt* (ṣūfī fraternities) to mosque functionaries and ascetics, Muslims ascended the social ladder via religious rungs, and the case of Ibn Ḥanbal is a preeminent example of this phenomenon.[5]

Secondly, Ibn Ḥanbal's position as a religious authority and political leader places him at the heart of some of the cardinal events and processes of the formative period of Islam. His activities enable us to examine and reinterpret three central issues in regard to the newly developed Sunni milieu: The moral trends in Traditionist circles; the early stage of the Ḥanbali *madhhab*'s formation; and the *miḥna*, one of the decisive events of early Islam.

Finally, personal profiles from the world of medieval Islam are scarce. We know very little about the finances and relationships within specific families or the emotions and personalities of individuals. This portrayal of Ibn Ḥanbal is a rare opportunity for a glimpse at some of the mundane aspects of a medieval life.

Sources and Methodology

The foundations of Ibn Ḥanbal's biographic tradition were put in place by his contemporaries. The bulk of it were anecdotes that go back to his sons Ṣāliḥ (d. 265) and 'Abdallāh (d. 290), his cousin Ḥanbal b. Isḥāq (d. 273) and his concubine Ḥusn.[6] Together these informants constitute the 'family corpus.' Another group of contemporaries, who related anecdotes about him though these do not appear in the earliest biographies, is his classmates and his neighbors.[7] A third source are two contemporary scholars, Ibn Sa'd (d. 231) and Bukhārī (d. 256), who wrote very short notices about him in their biographical dictionaries.[8] The fourth contemporary source, and the only one that was antagonistic, was written by al-Jāḥiẓ (d. 255), whose interest in Ibn Ḥanbal was limited to his *miḥna* interrogation.[9]

The most copious source of anecdotes about Ibn Ḥanbal was his eldest son, Ṣāliḥ. Many of his stories have been collected into a book,

Sīrat al-imām Aḥmad b. Ḥanbal, whose contents are organized thematically: family and genealogy, scholarship, moral integrity, *miḥna*, and doxography.[10] The outstanding feature of this document is the light that it sheds on Ibn Ḥanbal's feelings, habits, and private life. It tells of his anger and of his relations with his sons and reveals such details as his eating habits. However, Ṣāliḥ's emotional involvement with his father had a price. At times the *Sīra* reads like an ideological manifesto. The vignettes about Ibn Ḥanbal's private life are imbued with moral undertones and the descriptions of the *miḥna* show him as a victorious defender of Traditionist theological sensibilities. In some instances Ṣāliḥ goes so far as to describe his own moral failures and his father's displeasure with him, presumably to enhance Ibn Ḥanbal's moral image.

Another relative who compiled anecdotes about Ibn Ḥanbal is Ḥanbal b. Isḥāq. His account of the *miḥna* drew upon Ibn Ḥanbal himself and on Isḥāq b. Ḥanbal (the author's father). This is probably the most detailed contemporary report of Ibn Ḥanbal's imprisonment, interrogation, views on other *miḥna* victims, and relations with the caliphs.[11] Together, Ṣāliḥ and Ḥanbal articulated the Ḥanbali narrative of the *miḥna.*[12]

The counter narrative to the Ḥanbali version appears in the essay *Khalq al-Qur'an* (creation of the Qur'an), which was written by al-Jāḥiẓ, a contemporary Mu'tazili (school of theologians) belletrist, who was the protege of several courtiers.[13] It was a polemic tract that furnished Abū al-Walīd (d. 239), the son of Ibn Abī Du'ād (d. 240) the *miḥna*'s chief interrogator, with arguments to justify the persecutions.[14] After a general presentation of the contested issue, i.e., whether or not the Qur'an was created, it records the exchange between Ibn Ḥanbal and Ibn Abī Du'ād. Al-Jāḥiẓ presents an anti-Ḥanbali account of events and observes that Ibn Ḥanbal was incapable of articulating his position, that he was stubborn and uncooperative, and most importantly, he capitulated even though he was not severely tortured.[15]

It is difficult to determine which of the accounts, the Ḥanbali or Mu'tazili, is the more accurate. Both al-Jāḥiẓ and Ibn Ḥanbal's relatives treated Ibn Ḥanbal's performance and its outcome as a piece of useful propaganda, so neither account can be considered to be completely reliable. Yet, their efforts to construct and disseminate an account of the event indicates how important it was to the struggle that was taking place between the Traditionists and Mu'tazilis.

Alongside the biographical material on Ibn Ḥanbal, his contemporaries began to collect the *ḥadīths* (Prophetic traditions) he transmitted, his opinions about other transmitters of *ḥadīth*, his legal judgements, and his theological views. The central figure in this effort was his second son, ʿAbdallāh, who compiled the *Musnad* [a compendium of *ḥadīth*s that were transmitted by Ibn Ḥanbal], collected his opinions about other scholars in the *ʿIlal* (weaknesses, i.e., criticism of *ḥadīth* transmitters), recorded Ibn Ḥanbal's polemic work, *al-Radd ʿalā Zanādiqa wa-'l-Jahmiyya* (Refutation of the *Zanādiqa* and *Jahmiyya*) and compiled his religio-political tract *Kitāb al-Sunna* (the Book of Tradition).[16] Whereas ʿAbdallāh compiled his father's *ḥadīth,* polemic writings, and criticism of Traditionists nearly single-handedly, Ibn Ḥanbal's *masāʾil* (*responsa*) were collected by many of his followers. The evidence in the *Ṭabaqāt al-Ḥanābila* (Generations of the *Ḥanābila*) suggests that dozens of Ibn Ḥanbal's disciples possessed and memorized his *masāʾil.*[17] Furthermore, we know of two more *masāʾil* collections that can be traced back to his disciples.[18]

The individuals who laid the foundations of Ibn Ḥanbal's biographic tradition and preserved his intellectual legacy were, for the most part, family members and close disciples. However, in subsequent generations an interesting development took place. Whereas Ibn Ḥanbal's thought was transmitted through the generations by Ḥanbalis, his biographic tradition was told and retold in much wider circles. One of the most interesting aspects of the transmission of Ibn Ḥanbal's biography in the ensuing generations is the relatively meager participation of Ḥanbalis. Among those who passed down Ṣāliḥ's *Sīra* were two scholars of traditions whose *madhhab* affiliation is not specified and a third who was a Shāfiʿī.[19] Similarly, not one of the transmitters of Ḥanbal b. Isḥāq's *Dhikr al-Miḥna* was a Ḥanbali, whereas two were identified as Shāfiʿīs.[20] In Abū Nuʿaym al-Iṣfahānī's (d. 430) *tarjama* (biographic entry) of Ibn Ḥanbal the chains of transmission begin with Ibn Ḥanbal's children and disciples, but after this first generation, few Ḥanbalis are included.[21] The collective profile of these transmitters indicates that stories about Ibn Ḥanbal circulated among Ḥanbalis, Shāfiʿīs, and unaffiliated Traditionists. The transmission of details about Ibn Ḥanbal's life by scholars of different affiliations suggests that wide circles among the Traditionists revered him.

The most important Ḥanbali contribution to the transmission of Ibn Ḥanbal's thought in later generations was made by Abū Bakr al-Khallāl (d. 311).[22] Though most of his work is not extant, it is reputed that he collected twenty volumes of Ibn Ḥanbal's *masāʾil* into a compendium called *Kitāb al-Jāmiʿ*.[23] Another of his important contributions was his history of the Ḥanbalis. Although this work is not extant, it was quoted by Ibn Abī Yaʿlā (d. 560), in his first volume of the *Ṭabaqāt al-Ḥanābila,* and is the basis for much of what we know about relations between Ibn Ḥanbal and his followers. Although Abū Bakr al-Khallāl did not contribute anything original to Ḥanbali legal thought, his diligence and fascination with Ibn Ḥanbal, his family and disciples has added crucial information to the study of Ḥanbalism.

Between the fourth and ninth centuries A.H., Ibn Ḥanbal's *tarjama* appeared in several biographic dictionaries, as well as in separate compilations dedicated to him alone.[24] The authors of these works shaped and reshaped his biographic tradition in accordance with their own polemical needs. In certain instances they went so far as to insert legendary elements. The individuals who are mentioned as the sources of these anecdotes are anonymous neighbors and classmates. One of them, al-Warkānī, was chastised by al-Dhahabī (d. 748), the author of *Ta'rīkh al-Islam*, for inventing a story about mass conversion of Jews and Christians on the day Ibn Ḥanbal died.[25] Another neighbor, Abū al-Munabbih tells about Ibn Ḥanbal's high moral standards as a youth.[26] Another story that depicts Ibn Ḥanbal's high moral standards when he was still a child is attributed to his classmate Abū 'Afīf.[27] The implausible story of the miracle of the trousers (which stayed on Ibn Ḥanbal while he was being whipped) goes back to two unknown contemporaries.[28]

The mainstay of Ibn Ḥanbal's biographic tradition, however, hinges upon the family corpus. Other anecdotes that appear in later biographies and were circulated by anonymous contemporaries were peripheral and were contested by such biographers as al-Dhahabī. It is interesting to note that later historians and biographers, even those who made use of dubious anecdotes such as his juvenile prefiguration of high morality or the miracle of the trousers, did not ascribe them to Ṣāliḥ, 'Abdallāh, and Ḥanbal, attributing them rather to anonymous contemporaries.[29]

Another important source for the present study was Ibn Abī Ya'lā's *Ṭabaqāt al-Ḥanābila* which covers 500 of Ibn Ḥanbal's followers and admirers in its first volume.[30] Although it was compiled two and a half centuries after Ibn Ḥanbal's death, it often relies on Abū Bakr al-Khallāl's work, who was a student of some of Ibn Ḥanbal's closest disciples. One of its most interesting features is its focus on the relations between Ibn Ḥanbal and his disciples, from which we get a glimpse at some social and even emotional aspects of the Ḥanbali circle. We thus learn who Ibn Ḥanbal befriended, who he admired, and with whom he discussed such controversial issues as theology and piety.

This survey of the sources raises a methodological question: Can we treat the evidence about Ibn Ḥanbal as reliable historical data from which we can reconstruct his life, or are these reports merely the result of textual manipulations, which reveal the ideological agenda of their writers?[31] This study argues that the two are not mutually exclusive and that the bulk of Ibn Ḥanbal's biographical tradition is made up of descriptions of concrete events that are at the same time ideologically constructed. Before describing the dual nature of this biographic tradition, we ought to distinguish between its two main components: The family corpus and the anonymous contemporaries. The descriptions in the family corpus are within the bounds of reason. We do not find unrealistic feats of healing, miracles, or even retroactive attribution of Ibn Ḥanbal's moral standards to his childhood or youth. There is nothing in these stories that is patently unbelievable. Although the image they wish to project is guided by ideological considerations, each specific anecdote seems reliable and will be used in the present survey of Ibn Ḥanbal's life. On the other hand, the anecdotes that have their source among Ibn Ḥanbal's anonymous contemporaries often appear to be exaggerations of his moral virtues and even relate fantastic, supranatural feats. Owing to the dubious elements found in the latter, they have to be analyzed carefully and used selectively.

The basic premise of my approach to Ibn Ḥanbal's biographic tradition is that all of its contributors and transmitters had an axe to grind. Each of them compiled Ibn Ḥanbal's biography so as to promote a particular religious worldview. However, I believe that it is important to distinguish between the construction of a moral image, on the one hand, and fabrication of anecdotes, on the other. Introduction of ideals and values into a biographic tradition does not necessarily involve fabrication of specific stories. It was possible to shape the image of Ibn Ḥanbal through an editorial policy that excluded events and deeds that were perceived as unsuitable to the image being conveyed. As a result of such omissions the ideological impact was made through the accumulation of one-sided anecdotes that revealed Ibn Ḥanbal in a favorable light. For example, admirers who wanted to convey a theologically 'clean' image of Ibn Ḥanbal merely omitted from his teachers' lists the names of scholars who were suspected or accused of theological deviation.[32] They did not have to fabricate new lists that would include teachers he never met. The same can be said about Ibn Ḥanbal's pious image.[33] Biographers who wished to present him as a paragon of morality, could compile true stories about his dietary habits and leave out instances in which he deviated from his 'moral' diet. Such an ideologically oriented editorial policy conveyed a misleading image of Ibn Ḥanbal. However in contrast to fabricated anecdotes, they were not necessarily invented. As a consequence, despite the fact that the overall image is warped, the specific actions that are described in these biographies may be true. Our ability to establish that his biographers had ideological biases is not a criterion to accept or reject an anecdote. Ibn Ḥanbal's more reliable biographers molded his biographic tradition by sifting through anecdotes and omitting whatever material was ideologically unsuitable. Censure, rather than invention, was the means they employed to shape his biographies.[34]

A second methodological question that comes up in regard to the present study is the extent to which a single life can shed light on wider historical contexts. In other words, to what extent can the study of Ibn Ḥanbal contribute to our understanding of the formative era of Islam? Can we, and if we can, how do we extrapolate from the idiosyncrasies of Ibn Ḥanbal's life broad observations or conclusions? This question has been raised recently by microhistorians, who have asked how can we profit from an intentional 'reduction of the scale of observation.'[35] According to G. Levi, who posed the question and answered it:

> Phenomena previously considered to be sufficiently described and understood assume completely new meanings by altering the scale of observation. It is then possible to use these results to draw far wider generalizations although the initial observations were made within relatively narrow dimensions and as experiments rather than examples.[36]

In this manner Levi highlights the potential of microhistory. However, the preoccupation with details has its risks. It can easily lead, and often has led, to the antiquarian accumulation of seemingly inconsequential minutiae. The trifle that served Sherlock Holmes as a revealing clue can remain a trivial and meaningless detail in the hands of historians.[37] The historian's preoccupation with details can be fruitful only if it goes beyond the mere collection of facts and improves the resolution of the subject such that differences and nuances are exposed in a phenomenon that was previously perceived as a unified mold.

The process of microanalysis is based on magnifying a circumscribed body of historical data in the hope of revealing new components, patterns, and connections. Several examples may illustrate how this approach works. The biographies of Ibn Ḥanbal recount stories about his daily activities such as eating and dressing. The antiquarian approach would do little more than compile this information in an inventory of Ibn Ḥanbal's actions and habits. However, it is possible to go beyond that and discern a pattern of 'mild asceticism' that runs through all of these anecdotes.[38] After identifying the shared characteristics of the descriptions of Ibn Ḥanbal's eating, dressing and home, it is possible to approach them as a behavioral model for wide audiences among the Traditionists, who told and retold these anecdotes. Furthermore, the etiquette can be used to expose the moral vision of its practitioners. Mild asceticism thus designates forms of behavior and their underlying moral justifications and comes into sharper focus when we compare it to norms of other social groups such as ṣūfīs and courtiers. What might have seemed to be a collection of unrelated stories about Ibn Ḥanbal's mundane activities turns out to be a literary expression of the etiquette and moral code of an important trend in the Traditionist milieu.

Another case in which magnifying a body of historical evidence led to new insights about broad developments, is the case of the Ḥanbali circle. On the face of it, the numerous descriptions of Ibn Ḥanbal's disciples in the *Ṭabaqāt al-Ḥanābila* can be viewed as unrelated personal details. However, if we bring them together and place them alongside the mildly ascetic image of Ibn Ḥanbal, we can gain important insights regarding the formative process of the Ḥanbali *madhhab*.[39] The ideological consistency in the descriptions of Ibn Ḥanbal and his disciples creates the impression that their shared values and codes of behavior helped in recruiting new adherents and forging a sense of group solidarity. By bringing together small bits of information about dozens of Ibn Ḥanbal's disciples we can elucidate the way in which moral values contributed to a social process the gathering of a group of adherents around Ibn Ḥanbal.

A third example of the potential of microanalysis is the case of Ibn Ḥanbal's interrogation protocols. In European contexts, Inquisition protocols have proven to be excellent material for microhistory.[40] However, the protocols of Ibn Ḥanbal's *miḥna* interrogation do not lead to such novel insights, simply because they cannot claim to unearth the lost voices of oppressed sects and individuals. After all, Ibn Ḥanbal and his supporters won the day, and there is no lack of evidence about their theological views. What they do reveal, however, is the Ḥanbali view of the *miḥna*, which will lead to the challenging of several important assumptions of modern historiography about the *miḥna*.

Microanalysis resembles the 'zooming-in' motion of a camera. It reveals many new details, allows the spectator to distinguish among elements of the subject being observed and at times to identify links and connections that were not noticed before. The most valuable contribution that it can offer through its magnifying process is to put forth new 'lines of inquiry and working hypotheses.'[41] In the subsections of this Introduction, I will use the life of Ibn Ḥanbal as a springboard for the presentation of three new interpretations of topics that were 'previously considered to be sufficiently described.'[42]

Piety

Some time around the turn of the third century A.H., there was an interesting shift in literary representations of renowned Muslims, and their biographies came to include information about their moral characteristics. The most important example of this new trend is the Prophet's biography. Whereas up to that period the Prophet's life was mainly a record of his military and diplomatic achievements, at the turn of the century his biographers began to include details of his moral merits.[43] These virtues were conveyed through accounts of his private life: eating habits, dress, relations with wives, possessions, etc. It is therefore hardly surprising to find that Traditionist scholars, who were compiling anecdotes about the Prophet and depicting him as a paragon of mild asceticism, would weave similar kinds of information into Ibn Ḥanbal's biographies.

Modern scholarship approached the issue of Islamic ethics from two perspectives. The first emphasized the doctrine of Traditionist ethics.[44] Its main thrust was to illustrate the importance that Traditionists placed on actual behavior, as opposed to *mutakallimūn* (particularly Mu'tazilis), who emphasized theoretical discussions of correct belief. Although these latter studies presented the underlying theoretical premises of Traditionist views regarding ethics, they did not delve into specific modes of conduct that were characteristic of the Traditionist milieu.

A second group of historians did pay attention to actual behavior, but focused on exceptional men and women such as Rābi'a al-'Adawiyya (d. 135 or 185), Ibrāhīm al-Adham (d. 165), Ḥasan al-Baṣrī (d. 110), and al-Tustarī (d. 282).[45] The characteristic that these figures have in common are their extraordinary feats of asceticism: Rābi'a al-'Adawiyya never married so as to keep her love of Allah undisturbed by earthly love;[46] Ibrāhīm al-Adham also chose celibacy, though he did not consider it more worthy than marriage;[47] Al-Tustarī is reputed to have fasted up to seventy days.[48] These, then, were extreme ascetics, whose notion of asceticism was one of harsh self-mortification and severance of social ties. Whereas these as well as other ascetics could boast of impressive feats of self-deprivation, their accomplishments were a very personal matter. Although they were respected by many believers and their achievements were told and retold, they were not representative of the modes of conduct that one found among pious Muslims.

Modern studies of Islamic ethics have paid little attention to Traditionist behavioral norms and their accompanying ethical outlook. They have also treated the sphere of asceticism as if it were the sole domain of religious virtuosos, and have not inquired into Traditionist notions of asceticism. In this study of Ibn Ḥanbal's private life, I will argue that he, too, was an ascetic, although he practiced an attenuated form of asceticism. Thus, the term 'mild asceticism,' was coined so as to distinguish between Ibn Ḥanbal's notions of asceticism and those of extreme ṣūfīs.[49] The behavioral norms of each of these modes of conduct are embedded in distinctly different ethical outlooks that touch upon the ascetics' views of their bodies, the society that surrounds them, and the appropriate relationship between the individual and society. Whereas the extreme ascetic will adopt a strenuous regimen of self-deprivation that will numb his bodily senses, the mild ascetic will impose upon himself a balanced discipline that takes into account the body's needs. While the extreme ascetic will aspire to suppress his bodily desires, the mild ascetic will seek to control yet sustain his appetites.

The difference between the attitudes of extreme and mild ascetics to their bodies correlates with their attitudes to emotions. Extreme ascetics will often search for ways to transcend their egos. They consider the ego to be man's worst enemy and seek ways to escape its allure. In contrast, mild ascetics will not spend much time on introspection. The self-criticism and psychomachia of extreme ṣūfīs are not common among mild ascetics. Where extreme ascetics practice harsh physical and spiritual self-mortification designed to unite them with Allah while their bodies and souls are still in this world, mild ascetics will obey the law and hope to unite with or be in the company of Allah in the next world.

A central issue in this study is the attitude of the mild ascetic to society. The rule of thumb is that a mild ascetic will participate in various social institutions, such as family and profession, while maintaining an independence of mind and a safe distance from corrupting forces such as patronage and the pursuit of riches. In a way that parallels his attitude toward his own body, the mild ascetic will do what he needs to do in order to sustain himself, but will avoid any unnecessary investment of time that will gain him riches. In contrast, extreme ascetics will sever their ties with society. They will often give up their properties, they will not practice their professions, and therefore will not have incomes. Some of them will leave their families while others will not establish families to begin with. Where the mild ascetic aims at a reserved collaboration with social institutions, the extreme ascetic wants to break away from any existing form of social cooperation.

Mild and extreme asceticism are two moral visions that inspired two separate codes of conduct. The two coexisted and the practitioners of both won the admiration of broad elements in Islamic society. Their notions of piety and practices of devotion were held in high esteem even by Muslims who did not imitate them. However, the mainstream of Islamic society adopted the moral sensibilities of mild asceticism and looked to Traditionist role models for guidance. Ibn Ḥanbal's behavior is an example of mild asceticism, and a study of his life and the manner in which biographers presented him furnishes insights into the basic elements of this evasive yet pervasive ethical posture. Part one of this study, 'Piety,' presents a detailed account of Ibn Ḥanbal's style of piety and how it constituted the foundations of his religious prestige in the Traditionist milieu. It ties in with the second part, which deals with the way in which this prestige contributed to the shaping of the Ḥanbali *madhhab*.

Pupils

In their earliest stages, the Ḥanbalis were a group of admirers that gathered around Ibn Ḥanbal. Gradually this group grew into the Ḥanbali *madhhab*, one of the four mass movements that are known as the Islamic *madhāhib*.[50] This development, by which groups of jurists came to have huge followings of lay, uneducated believers, is a singular Islamic phenomenon. In the ancient Middle East, jurists were not at the center of large social movements. By the fourth and fifth centuries A.H., Islamic society, whose structure was similar to that of ancient Middle Eastern societies, added a new form of social classification the school of law.[51] The *madhāhib* operated in a variety of ways: patronage systems that furnished their members with work in their religious and educational institutions; political interest groups that acted upon political and ideological views of their members; and an axis around which communities were formed.

The multifaceted nature of the *madhāhib* has influenced the historiography of the Ḥanbali *madhhab*. Modern historians of Ḥanbalism have touched on four central issues that contributed to its formation: Ḥanbali legal doctrine and jurisprudence, social background and politics, theological controversies, and moral outlook and social activism. The last three shed light on the transformation of Ḥanbalism into a mass movement. In what follows several important studies that touched on these themes will be surveyed and an assessment of their contributions and limitations will be presented.

Legal historians, such as J. Schacht and S.A. Spectorsky, view the Ḥanbali *madhhab* as a branch of the Traditionist movement that grew out of the Traditionists' dissatisfaction with al-Shāfiʿī's jurisprudential principles.[52] To quote Schacht: 'The legal doctrine as it had been elaborated by Shāfiʿī did not satisfy the uncompromising Traditionists.'[53] One of the 'uncompromising Traditionists' was Ibn Ḥanbal. Although it makes sense to discuss Ibn Ḥanbal's jurisprudence within the context of Traditionist discourse, I would argue that his disagreements with al-Shāfiʿī over jurisprudence hardly explain the formation of Ḥanbalism. The fact of the matter is that Ibn Ḥanbal and many of his early followers espoused al-Shāfiʿī's jurisprudence, including the controversial principle of *qiyās* (analogical inference).[54] Although Ibn Ḥanbal was dissatisfied with the frequency with which al-Shāfiʿī used *qiyās*, he did not disagree with him over the legitimacy of this juristic principle. Therefore, Schacht's allusion that jurisprudential disagreement between Ibn Ḥanbal and al-Shāfiʿī explains the rift in the Traditionist milieu is off the mark. It places too much weight on doctrinal differences that in fact did not cause a major controversy. The relatively minor disagreement regarding the extent to which *qiyās* should be used cannot stand as the critical cause for the formation of a separate *madhhab*, and we must search for additional factors.

Another approach that deals with the formation of early Ḥanbalism is found in I. Lapidus's works and emphasizes the political nature of this movement. According to Lapidus, Ḥanbali scholars articulated a vision that wrested spiritual authority from the hands of the rulers: 'The Hanbali view made scholars, not the caliphs, custodians of the truth.'[55] The effort to attain power prompted the Ḥanbalis to appeal to disgruntled soldiers: 'The Hanbalis were the first to convert informal, popular influence and sympathy into a sectarian movement … Preaching to their followers among former 'Abbasid soldiers and residents of the Harbiyya quarter of Baghdad, the scholars mobilized support.'[56] According to Lapidus, the Ḥanbalis played a crucial role in the dynamics of the separation of state and religion, and it is through these religio-political lenses that he views them.

The novelty of Lapidus's interpretation of the Ḥanbalis' formation is his departure from the commonly held views of doctrinal determinism and the inclusion of nonlegal factors such as political interests. Nonetheless, this linkage between Ḥanbali formation and caliphal politics is problematic.[57] To begin with, we have very little evidence of Ḥanbali involvement in any aspect of caliphal politics. Of the 500 disciples who appear in Ḥanbali sources, only one, Aḥmad b. Naṣr b. Mālik al-Khuzāʿī (d. 231), is said to have taken part in political activities.[58] If any of Ibn Ḥanbal's other disciples had a military background or were affiliated with a political faction involved in caliphal politics, the sources make no mention of it. This is not conclusive evidence that Ḥanbalis were not involved in caliphal politics, but it is a clear indication that this form of political activity (if it existed) was not an important factor in the Ḥanbalis' self-view.

Secondly, the nature of Ḥanbali political activity requires a clarification. Ibn Ḥanbal and his close followers kept away from caliphs and caliphal politics.[59] When frustrated Traditionists offered Ibn Ḥanbal the opportunity to participate in a rebellion against the executioners of the *miḥna*, he refused.[60] When al-Mutawakkil (d. 247), the caliph who put an end to the persecutions of the *miḥna*, invited Ibn Ḥanbal to his palace, the aged scholar made every effort to decline.[61] Ibn Ḥanbal's quietism and views on the corruptibility of rulers led him to avoid contact with them, whether friendly or confrontational. He believed that keeping a safe distance from the rulers was the best way to maintain moral and spiritual hygiene. Because of Ibn Ḥanbal's reluctance to associate with caliphs or confront them, I think that caliphal politics were out of the Ḥanbali purview and did not have a profound influence on the formation of Ḥanbalism.

A third approach examines Ḥanbalism in light of the theological confrontations of the third century. G. Makdisi argues that the Ḥanbali *madhhab* came into being as a consequence of Ibn Ḥanbal's theological beliefs: 'The Ḥanbali school came into existence *not* as the result of a legal stance taken by its leader, but rather as the result of a traditionalist theological stance taken by him against Muʿtazili rationalism on the question of the created character of the Koran.'[62]

The importance of Makdisi's remark is the fact that he links the formation of Ḥanbalism with the *miḥna*. However, although Ibn Ḥanbal played a central role in this clash and was the acknowledged leader of Traditionist resistance, the connection between the *miḥna* and the formation of the Ḥanbali *madhhab* is not obvious and the suggestion raises more questions than it answers. For example, how exactly was the confrontation between the Traditionists and the Muʿtazilis related to the formation of the Ḥanbali *madhhab*, which was a process that took place within the Traditionist milieu? We must keep in mind that the Ḥanbalis were part of that milieu so that when we attempt to explain why they set up a separate *madhhab*, we need to grapple with the reasons that moved them to break from the Shāfiʿīs and other Traditionist circles. Furthermore, if we take into consideration that all of the Traditionists were victims of the *miḥna*, i.e., that the *miḥna* was a shared experience of many Traditionists, then evoking the *miḥna* does not explain the internal divisions among them. On the contrary, we might even expect that the shared fate of the victims would bring the Ḥanbalis closer to other Traditionist trends and create a common front against their common enemies. Makdisi's remarks place scholarship on an important track, but we must ask how the *miḥna* influenced the internal relations among the Traditionists if we want to discern its connection with *madhhab* formation.

The fourth factor that scholars mention in regard to the Ḥanbali school involves its moral views and social activism. H. Laoust described the Ḥanbalis in the following manner: 'Ḥanābila ... denotes the followers of the school of theology, law and morality which grew up from the teaching of Aḥmad b. Ḥanbal (d. 241/855 [*q.v.*])'[63] This characterization brings together two of the three basic components that I have referred to above: theology and law. However, Laoust adds that the Ḥanbali school 'grew up from the teaching of' Ibn Ḥanbal. In other words, he approaches the formation of the Ḥanbali *madhhab* from the point of view of intellectual history. In another study that touches on the formation of the Ḥanbali school, Laoust contrasts Ḥanbali legalism with the rich interior life of ṣūfism.[64] However, he goes beyond this simplistic dichotomy and sketches a more nuanced picture of Ibn Ḥanbal's attitude toward the ṣūfīs and concludes by reiterating the shared moral values of Ḥanbalism and ṣūfism.

Another study that places special emphasis on Ḥanbali moral views is that of S. Sabari, whose discussion of Ḥanbali moralism is set within the framework of class struggle.[65] Her periodization places the origin of Ḥanbalism in the second half of the third century, when the caliphate began to decline. According to Sabari, this was a period of acute social tensions, and the Ḥanbalis expressed the views of the men and women on the streets of Baghdād. In contrast to other Sunni schools of law, the Ḥanbalis became a public movement that preached and practiced public activism. Their following was 'le petit peuple sunnite de Baghdad'[66] and their religious vision stressed loyalty to the past and socio-moral values. This moral outlook led them to criticize the caliphal way of life and the luxuries of the rich.

Sabari sets forth an accurate account of the tension between the Ḥanbalis' loyalty to the rulers and their reluctance to come into contact with them; of their efforts to shape public opinion and of their radical, communally oriented interpretation of *al-amr bi-'l-maʿrūf wa-'l-nahy ʿan al-munkar* (enjoining the good and prohibiting the evil). She also observes that the Ḥanbalis attracted ascetics, which is a particularly important point in this study.[67]

In light of revisionist works that argue that the schools of law were established as late as the mid-fourth century,[68] I would like to emphasize that all of the above mentioned studies share the assumption that the Ḥanbali school was founded during the lifetime of Ibn Ḥanbal or in the immediate decades after his death. The present study accepts the periodization of the studies that were reviewed above and it argues that the legal, theological and moral foundations of the Ḥanbalis were laid during Ibn Ḥanbal's life and a short while after his death. Furthermore, it assumes that a chain of transmission of knowledge begins with Ibn Ḥanbal and continues consecutively through the next centuries. Although later generations of Ḥanbalis did a great deal to change and reshape Ḥanbali ideas and doctrine, the foundations were first put in place during the life of Ibn Ḥanbal.

Despite my agreement with the periodization offered in these studies, it is important to point out that they suffer from two shortcomings. First, their treatment of Ḥanbalism is usually part of a more general discussion and, as a consequence, they deal with Ḥanbalism matter-of-factly, often dedicating no more than a page or two to its early stages.[69] Their focus is on the separation of state and religion (Lapidus), the development of Islamic law (Schacht), Islamic education (Makdisi) and social movements (Sabari). Thus, although all of them contain perceptive remarks about Ḥanbalism, none of them offers a thorough investigation of its formation

The second limitation is that each of these studies concentrates on one aspect of Ḥanbalism and ignores the others. While it makes sense to do so in studies that set out to deal with other topics, for a student of Ḥanbalism they all fall short of a comprehensive inquiry that brings together all the factors that shaped Ḥanbalism.

The present study addresses both of these shortcomings. Each of the topics that has been summarily touched upon in the works surveyed receives detailed attention in at least one chapter. Ḥanbali moral outlook and its social repercussions are examined in chapters 3 and 5; Ḥanbali jurisprudence is looked at in chapter 6; and the *miḥna* and its impact on the formation of Ḥanbalism is dealt with in chapters 7, 8, and 9.

At the heart of each of these investigations is an ideological or intellectual issue. Yet the inquiries in these chapters go beyond a description of Ḥanbali views and ask how these ideologies and ideas shaped the formation and dynamics of the Ḥanbali circle. The integration of ideas and social processes also comes up in chapter 4, which is a prosopography of Ibn Ḥanbal's followers. In this chapter, which concentrates on the social composition of the early Ḥanbali circle, we get a chance to see how friendship, admiration, trust, professional respect, and ideological congruence or lack thereof, come into play in the circle's internal dynamics. The amalgamation of social, emotional, and professional factors allows us to approach the Ḥanbali circle as a dynamic social entity and assess when and how each of the factors mentioned above influenced the formative process of the Ḥanbali circle *cum madhhab.*

When placed against this background it is possible to point to two stages in the formative process of the Ḥanbali *madhab*. The first is the formation of a Ḥanbali circle. In this early stage Ibn Ḥanbal's scholarly standing as transmitter of *ḥadīths* and articulator of legal decisions along with his reputation for piety attracted disciples and admirers who made up the core of the Ḥanbali circle. The second stage is the transformation of the circle into a *madhhab*. Such a process developed when a distinct Ḥanbali self-image, which set it apart from other Traditionist circles, came into being. This heightened sense of uniqueness and group solidarity evolved after the *miḥna* exposed the internal disagreements and tensions among the Traditionists. It is against the background of Traditionist controversies over the status of theology and the radical position of the Ḥanbalis in this controversy that the jurisprudential differences of opinion cracked open and transformed the Ḥanbalis into a separate *madhab.*

Power

Between 218–234 A.H., a group of *mutakallimūn* acquired the support of the caliphal court and attempted to impose the dogma that the Qur'an was created upon all Muslims. Under the policy that came to be known as the *miḥna*, believers who thought otherwise were threatened and persecuted. Some lost their jobs, others lost stipends, and a handful were put in jail, interrogated, and tortured. At its outset the *miḥna* was administered by the caliph al-Ma'mūn (d. 218) and his governor. However, four months after initiating these wide scale persecutions al-Ma'mūn died, and the administration of the *miḥna* was taken up by the chief judge (*qāḍī al-quḍāt*), Ibn Abī Du'ād, and a network of like-minded judges. The attempts of the caliph and chief judge to force an article of faith upon the population were met with passive, yet determined resistance. Fifteen years after the first wave of interrogations, al-Mutawakkil put an end to the persecutions.

Contemporaries who wrote about the *miḥna*, either as inquisitors or as victims, focused their attention on two episodes in the fifteen-years-long persecution. The first was the exchange of letters between al-Ma'mūn and his governor, who was an active inquisitor during the first four months of the *miḥna*. The second were accounts of Ibn Ḥanbal's interrogations, which were carried out during the reign of al-Mu'taṣim. Notwithstanding Patton's *Aḥmed b. Ḥanbal and the Miḥna*, most modern scholarship has concentrated on al-Ma'mūn's *miḥna* letters and ignored Ibn Ḥanbal's interrogations.[70] In the present study I will concentrate on Ibn Ḥanbal's interrogation and attempt to use these relatively untapped sources to reveal the Ḥanbali view of the event.

Modern scholarship concerning the *miḥna* has been guided by two important assumptions: First, the *miḥna* was a showdown between caliphs and *'ulamā'* (religious scholars) over spiritual authority. Second, the issue of contention was the createdness of the Qur'an.

The premise that the *miḥna* was a confrontation between the caliphs and the *'ulamā'* has been articulated in the seminal works of I. Lapidus. In one of them he described the developments leading up to the *miḥna* as follows:

> The emergence of two institutional structures with different elites and different ethos generated an intense struggle between the caliphate and the *'ulamā'* (religious scholars). From the very beginning, the caliphate had claimed to be the protector of both the religious and the political interests of the Muslims. To enforce these claims, the 'Abbāsid caliph al-Ma'mūn (813-833) initiated an inquisition that attempted to force the leading Muslim religious scholars to accept the doctrine of the createdness of the Qur'an and his authority to proclaim this doctrine.[71]

Lapidus's description conveys the impression that the *miḥna* is the culmination of a decades-long struggle between rulers and scholars. It also assumes that rulers and scholars were organized into distinguishable social bodies that were vying for power, had an articulated ideology, and strove to materialize collective interests.

For the most part, modern scholars embraced Lapidus's views. For example, M. Hind's understanding of the *miḥna*, as it appears in the

Encyclopaedia of Islam, is informed by this analysis.[72] It is reiterated in *God's Caliph*, where P. Crone and M. Hinds state that the *'ulamā's* perceptions of the Prophet's *sunna* jeopordized 'caliphal authority' and that 'an outright confrontation between caliph and *'ulamā'* had thus been on the cards long before al-Ma'mūn.'[73] It also comes up in an historiographic essay that focuses on the initiation of the *miḥna*, in which J.A. Nawas argues that al-Ma'mūn's motive for instigating the *miḥna* was part of an effort to halt the growing influence of the *'ulamā'*.[74]

In recent years, two studies have set out to revise our understanding of the background of the *miḥna*.[75] In one of these, M.Q. Zaman argues against the accepted wisdom of the field: 'that the early 'Abbāsid caliphs (except al-Ma'mūn) enjoyed or claimed any religious authority over and above the 'ulamā' is not as evident to this writer as it seems to be to the authors of *God's Caliph*;'[76] Zaman's convincing argument is that the overall 'pattern of state-'ulamā' relations' was relatively serene. The exception was al-Ma'mūn, who 'diverged from this pattern with his claims to religious authority over and above the 'ulamā'.'[77] Despite Zaman's important revision regarding the *miḥna*'s background, he is nevertheless in agreement with the historiographic trend that views the *miḥna* as a clash between caliph and *'ulamā'*. As he puts it, 'the *Miḥna* may be seen, in short, as a challenge calculated to undermine the authority as well as the social standing of the 'ulamā'.'[78]

The second premise of modern scholars is that the intellectual dimension of the *miḥna* was limited to the debate over the createdness of the Qur'an. M. Hinds, in *EI*[2] asks '... why should the issue have been the createdness of the Kur'an?'[79] He sets forth Watt's answer to this question that a created Qur'an would give more authority to politicians and scribes, while an uncreated Qur'an would place more authority in the hands of scholars – and discards this explanation. He also refers to Madelung's article on the controversy of the created Qur'an, in which the author points out that, originally, adherents of certain trends among the Traditionists were reluctant to participate in the debate about the createdness of the Qur'an because of their hostile views toward theology. Madelung's review of the history of the debate indicates that another question lurked in the background: Is it worthwhile and legitimate to carry out an investigation into this article of faith? However, barring Madelung's reference to the doubts of these Traditionists, most historians view the *miḥna* as the outcome of the debate over the createdness of the Qur'an.

One of the problems that has confounded modern scholars is the inability to find a link between the adversaries in the *miḥna* (whom they take to be the caliphs and the *'ulamā'*) and the issue that was contested (createdness of the Qur'an). Why should the caliph confront the *'ulamā'* regarding an article of faith? This led several historians to relegate theology to the sidelines and view it as a minor factor in the dynamics of the *miḥna*: 'The point at issue during the *miḥna* was therefore not a particular theological doctrine,...'[80] According to these historians we ought to substitute for theological controversy the political interests of the caliphs. However, I would argue that if we take the way contemporaries describe the events more seriously, it is possible to find a convincing connection between the antagonists and the contested issue.

The revision that is offered in the present study is based on a reinterpretation of the Ḥanbali accounts of the *miḥna*.[81] One of the most conspicuous features in these reports is the minor role that they attribute to the caliph, al-Mu'taṣim, in the debate. The main participants in this confrontation were Ibn Ḥanbal on the one hand and a group of Ḥanafi jurists joined by *mutakallimūn* on the other. The Ḥanbali account of the interrogation gives the impression that the struggle was not between the caliph and the amorphous entity '*'ulamā'*,' but rather between two groups of Islamic scholars.[82] Judging by these protocols, the Ḥanbali view of the *miḥna* was that it was a struggle between two camps, each of which articulated its own vision of Islam. Once we shift our attention from al-Ma'mūn and his *miḥna* letters (which will also be reinterpreted in this study) to Ḥanbali sources, the issue of caliphal authority fades away and the struggle over the orientation of Islam comes into relief.

The second observation that can be drawn from Ḥanbali sources is that the debate between Ibn Ḥanbal and his interrogators was carried out on two levels. The first and well-known level was the createdness of the Qur'an. However, the protocols indicate that in many of the exchanges the adversaries did not reach the point of discussing the Qur'an because they had to clarify another issue: the status of theology. When Ibn Ḥanbal demanded that his interrogators give him proof from the Qur'an or the *sunna*, he was raising a fundamental question: What constitutes proof in a theological investigation? When he continues and says that Ibn Abī Du'ād has simply given an interpretation about the createdness of the Qur'an, and that this opinion is not an article of faith, he is casting doubt on the status and value of theological speculations. In short, a great deal of the interrogation revolves around the preliminary and fundamental question: the standing of theological speculations in Islamic religiosity.

The present study will argue that the contestants were adherents of two trends of *'ulamā'*, the Traditionists and the *mutakallimūn,* and that the cause for this violent confrontation was the implicit problem of the status of theology. The explicit inquisitorial question, was the Qur'an created, was an offshoot of this disagreement over the standing of theology. Such an approach thereby better links the contested issue and the contestants: The Traditionists and *mutakallimūn* had a good reason to clash over the status of theology, as this was a crucial element in their decades long struggle to define Islam in accordance with their respective religious visions.

Interestingly enough it was not just the victims who viewed the *miḥna* as a confrontation between the Traditionists and the *mutakallimūn.* The inquisitors thought in similar terms. In his *miḥna* letter, al-Ma'mūn makes no mention of a confrontation between the caliph and the *'ulamā'*. On the contrary, he wrote that religious authority was shared by the *a'imma* (elite of scholars) and the caliphs. Al-Ma'mūn does assume, that caliphs are equal players in the spiritual arena. However, his reference to caliphal spiritual authority is no more than a means to justify his intrusion into a discourse that other caliphs avoided. Caliphal spiritual authority is neither the central cause of the *miḥna* nor the main argument in his letter. The main points of contention are the Qur'an and the status of theology. The enemy are not the *'ulamā'* as a whole but the Traditionists from among them. Al-Ma'mūn never challenges the *'ulamā'* as a whole. His main grievance is that a certain camp among the *'ulamā'*, with whom he disagrees sharply about the orientation of Islam, has gotten the upper hand and is threatening to become the sole intellectual and ideological force in the Islamic arena.

In a nutshell, although the *miḥna*'s perpetrators and its victims disagreed about the standing of theology, they did read the map of religious politics in a similar way. Each side identified the other as the enemy, and the controversial issue in their eyes was the status of the theological enterprise not the religious status of the caliph.

The historical record seems to corroborate this assessment of the *miḥna.* Our sources provide little evidence about tensions between the caliphs and the *'ulamā'*, yet they often refer to the friction and tension between the *mutakallimūn* and the Traditionists. Although the Ḥanbali narrative ignores this aspect, al-Ma'mūn and the *mutakallimūn* mention it. According to al-Ma'mūn, the Traditionists, or the 'self-styled sunnis' (lit. they relate themselves to the *sunna, wa-nasabū anfusahum ilā al-sunna*) as he refers to them, have persecuted the *mutakallimūn* and have tried to marginalize them and to gradually squeeze them out of the ranks of Islamic scholarship.[83]

This study assumes that the *miḥna* evolved in the following manner: During the century that preceded the *miḥna* the Traditionists persecuted the *mutakallimūn*. They did not rely on the state in their struggle against the *mutakallimūn* and therefore did not resort to brute force. However, they did have the ability to implement painful social sanctions against their adversaries, and this they did. On the whole, the caliphs avoided this struggle, making sure to stay out of the line of fire, often patronizing both sides. The sole exception was al-Ma'mūn, whose intellectual and ideological position placed him squarely in the *mutakallimūn* camp. Seeing that the *mutakallimūn* were being excluded from the legal and religious establishment he decided to change the traditional caliphal policy and to intervene in the internal politics of the *'ulamā'*. From this point of view, the *miḥna* was an act of retaliation to a long history of social sanctions. Al-Ma'mūn gave his support to the *mutakallimūn* and, being head of state, he could grant them the right to use violence. As a result, the *miḥna* introduced a level of violence hitherto unknown in these struggles between the *'ulamā'*.

Despite their victory, the Traditionists paid a high price during those fifteen years, for although most modern studies emphasize their success it is important to look at their anguish because it is there that we will find the key to the formation of a Ḥanbali *madhhab*.

This biography of Ibn Ḥanbal is not an exhaustive study of his life. Instead of focusing on biographic details, I have chosen to concentrate on three aspects of his career: the construction of his religious prestige; the formation of a circle of disciples and his resistance during the *miḥna*. Although these themes stand on their own, they do come together and complement each other. All three touch upon Ibn Ḥanbal's leadership and how it influenced the formation of Ḥanbalism. The nature of his leadership and the mark he left on Ḥanbalism will be discussed in the epilogue.

PART ONE

Private Life

Introduction

Ibn Ḥanbal was a man of ordinary background who led an extraordinary life. His exceptional achievements aroused the curiosity of his biographers, who added reports of mundane matters to stories of his outstanding accomplishments.[1] Many of these accounts were saturated with overt and concealed Ḥanbali values and the presence of this ideological agenda raises doubts about their reliability. I have approached this problem by subjecting the biographic information to source criticism and sifting between plausible and implausible components. I shall use those anecdotes that seem reliable, to depict certain aspects of Ibn Ḥanbal's life. At the same time I have attempted to decipher the moral code of Ibn Ḥanbal's biographic tradition and the manner in which it was used to construct an aura of religious prestige.

Chapter 1 presents Ibn Ḥanbal's ancestors, his wives and children, and their property. The information we have concerning his family history strikes me as reliable, and there seems to be little ideological embroidery in it. We learn that there were tensions among its members, that contrary to his wishes they cooperated with the authorities, and that they had some property that they rented out. These and other bits of information blemish Ibn Ḥanbal's pious image, yet they were incorporated into his biographies. It is precisely the awkwardness of these descriptions of Ibn Ḥanbal's family that lend them a sense of authenticity. Basing myself on this assumption I set out to sketch the ordinary dimensions of Ibn Ḥanbal's life.

Chapter 2 examines the forging of Ibn Ḥanbal's professional identity. Using lists of dozens of his teachers and reconstructing the periods in which he studied with them, I found that it is possible to trace his intellectual growth and ideological development. Whereas most of his biographers describe him as a committed Traditionist from the beginning of his studies, I suggest that at the outset of his career he was a curious youth who was not certain about his ideological commitments and that his ideological certitude and group affiliation crystallized only a decade later.

Chapter 3 moves from the ordinary man to the extraordinary role model. This shift, however, is not based on a new set of fantastic stories. The exceptional qualities of Ibn Ḥanbal are imparted through descriptions of his daily acts. The evidence of his piety is to be found in such mundane matters as the food he ate and the clothes he wore. The main problem here was to identify the moral message that was being conveyed in a seemingly haphazard collection of anecdotes. Once the moral code is deciphered, it is clear how Ibn Ḥanbal's pious image was constructed and how this image enhanced his religious prestige.

CHAPTER ONE

Forefathers and Family

Aḥmad b. Muḥammad b. Ḥanbal b. Hilāl b. Asad b. Idrīs b. 'Abdallāh b. Ḥayyān b. 'Abdallāh b. Anas b. 'Awf b. Qāsiṭ b. Māzin b. Shaybān b. Dhuhl b. Tha'laba b. 'Ukāba b. Ṣa'b b. 'Alī b. Bakr Wā'il b. Qāsiṭ b. Wahb b. Aqṣā b. Du'umī b. Jadīla b. Asad b. Rabī'a b. Nizār b. Ma'add b. 'Adnān b. Udd b. Udad b. al-Hamisa' b. al-Nabat b. Qaydhār b. Ismā'īl b. Ibrāhīm (PBUH).[2]

Nasab-Ibn Ḥanbal's lineage

What is in a pedigree besides a long list of names? For its bearer, it can be a source of pride. For the historian it may be an index of cultural transformation. Ibn Ḥanbal's lineage is an amalgamation of pre-Islamic form and Islamic meaning. The very idea that a list of individual and tribal names reveals something about the individual goes back to pre-Islamic conventions. What is more, most of the names that appear in the list are those of familiar figures and tribes from the pre-Islamic era. However, this list of names also includes figures drawn from the monotheistic tradition: Ibrāhīm and Ismā'īl. These new elements indicate that Ibn Ḥanbal's pedigree is a fusion of pagan ideals and monotheistic mythology.

Ibn Ḥanbal and his descendants, who wrote this pedigree and transmitted it to future generations, were conscious and proud of it. However, they were not the only ones who showed an interest in Ibn Ḥanbal's ancestral origins. Three centuries after Ibn Ḥanbal's death, the renown Ḥanbali, Ibn Abī Ya'lā (d. 560), discussed Ibn Ḥanbal's ancestral line in the *Ṭabaqāt al-Ḥanābila*, a Ḥanbali biographic dictionary.[3] Ibn Abī Ya'lā wrote of Ibn Ḥanbal's genealogy, 'this *nasab* has many perfect virtues and exalted status because of two reasons.'[4] The first is that Ibn Ḥanbal and Muḥammad are linked by a common ancestor: 'Because Nizār had two sons. One of them [was] Muḍar and our Prophet (PBUH) is of his offspring. And the other [son was] Rabī'a and our *imam* Aḥmad is of his offspring.'[5] The second reason is that Ibn Ḥanbal is of pure 'Arab stock.'[6] Ibn Abī Ya'lā, who lived into the sixth century A.H., did not shy away from using Arab descent in order to enhance his *imām*'s image. However, while taking pride in Ibn Ḥanbal's pure Arabic background, Ibn Abī Ya'lā Islamicized this component as well. He claimed that the importance and value of Arab descent stems from the connection between Arabism and Islam, and cites the Prophet who pointed out that the Arabs are to be admired because of three features – the Prophet is an Arab, the Qur'an is written in Arabic and Arabic is the language that is spoken in the Garden of Eden.[7]

Al-Khaṭīb al-Baghdādī (d. 463) was less enthusiastic with regard to Ibn Ḥanbal's genealogy. In contrast to Ibn Abī Ya'lā, al-Khaṭīb al-Baghdādī does not point to Ibn Ḥanbal's and Muḥammad's common ancestors. He opens his notice by referring to a number of opinions about the correct order of Ibn Ḥanbal's forefathers. Muslim scholars who dealt with Ibn Ḥanbal's genealogy could not agree about the descendent of Dhuhl b. Shaybān and Shaybān b. Dhuhl.[8] Yet al-Khaṭīb al-Baghdādī also subtly inserts Islamic values. In the course of these disagreements over the details of Ibn Ḥanbal's genealogy, the tribe of Dhuhl was praised because many of their offspring were 'scholars (*'ulamā'*), preachers (*khuṭabā'*), poets (*shu'arā'*) and genealogists (*nassābīn*).'[9] Of the four types of expertise mentioned here at least two, scholars and preachers, have an Islamic connotation. Thus the remarks are about the achievements of Ibn Ḥanbal's ancestors, but the criterion for pride is Islamic. At the same time these claims to fame are followed by more customary pre-Islamic concepts such as references to number of offspring, military prowess and tribal boasting.[10]

Despite the new Islamic values that were inserted into Arab society, being an Arab of pure lineage at the end of the second century A.H., conferred social and economic benefits. It is most likely that when Abū al-Nu'mān Muḥammad b. al-Faḍl (d. 223) made the remark, 'Oh Abū 'Abdallāh, I hear that you are from among the Arabs,'[11] he was expressing his surprise that Ibn Ḥanbal led such an austere existence when his family background was supposed to insure a comfortable pension.[12] Ibn Ḥanbal answered, 'we are a poor tribe (*qawm masākīn*).'[13] Poverty, however, did not detract from his affinity to his Arab family's background. In a conversation with the Traditionist 'Abdallāh b. Muḥammad b. al-Rūmī (d. 236)[14] who asked Ibn Ḥanbal why he visited the mosque of Banū Māzin so often, Ibn Ḥanbal answered that this was the mosque of his ancestors (*masjid abā'ī*).[15] Thus it is clear that Ibn Ḥanbal was aware of his family's background and expressed his respect to their memory by praying at the same site that they had.

Ibn Ḥanbal's awareness of his tribal background does not seem to have hindered his relations with colleagues of different ethnic backgrounds. Though information about this is scarce, we do know of one short comment, made by Yaḥyā b. Ma'īn (d. 233), who was not of Arab descent, which sheds light on Ibn Ḥanbal's attitude towards non-Arabs. Ibn Ma'īn notes '[Ibn Ḥanbal] did not ever brag (*mā iftakhara*) with regard to Arabism and did not mention it.'[16] These remarks indicate that if Ibn Ḥanbal took pride in his *nasab*, he kept it to himself and his family. Whether out of tact or simply because he did not think it was relevant, it seems that he did not bring up the fact that he was of pure Arab stock in front of colleagues. Ibn Ma'īn's comment may also hint that Ibn Ḥanbal's conduct was exceptional. We can get the impression that Ibn Ma'īn had come across people who were not as tactful as Ibn Ḥanbal.

Little is known about Ibn Ḥanbal's ancestors from the pre-Islamic and early Islamic periods. His paternal great-grandfather, Hilāl, and his father and grandfather, Asad and Idrīs, are no more than names in a long list that goes back to Ibrāhīm. We have no evidence that they distinguished themselves in any manner. Ibn Ḥanbal's remark that his tribe was a poor one suggests that if they participated in the conquering Arab armies, they were not of a high rank. Of his mother's side we know even less. She was called Ṣafiya bint Maymūna bint 'Abd al-Malik, and her maternal grandfather, 'Abd al-Malik b. Sawāda b. Hind, was said to have been from among the distinguished figures of the Banū Shaybān.[17]

Although little is known about Ibn Ḥanbal's ancestors, we have some information about their tribe, the Banū Māzin, who participated in the Islamic conquest of Iraq and Iran. They settled in Baṣra and later moved to Marw, perhaps in 51 A.H., when Ziyād b. Abīhi sent tens of thousands of Baṣrians and Kūfans to Khurāsān.[18] Other parts of the tribe participated in the conquest of Central Asia.

In Khurāsān Ibn Ḥanbal's grandfather, Hilāl, climbed out of his ancestors' anonymity. He was a relatively successful army officer and was appointed governor of Sarakhs.[19] Like many of his fellow Māzin tribesmen,[20] Ḥanbal b. Hilāl joined the 'Abbāsids in their revolution against the Umayyads.[21] He was probably killed in Bukhārā by al-Musayyab b. Zuhayr al-Ḍabbī, a senior 'Abbāsid military commander, as the result of dissension in the army.[22]

Ibn Ḥanbal's father, Muḥammad, resided in Marw. A little after 160 A.H., he immigrated to Baghdād, as did at least three of his brothers, Isḥāq, 'Umar and 'Abdallāh.[23] On his mother's side some relatives stayed behind in Khurāsān.[24]

In Baghdād the family maintained a unique relationship with the local authorities. Apparently they were part of an intelligence network that sent the governor reports. In an anecdote that seems to have some spurious elements, we come across a remark made by one Abū al-Munabbih, a neighbor of Ibn Ḥanbal's family, in which he states that a letter that one of Ibn Ḥanbal's uncles wrote to the authorities disappeared because Ibn Ḥanbal purposely hid it.[25] Though this description of Ibn Ḥanbal's behavior aims to present the future *imām* in exceptionally moral light and is therefore suspect, the part about the family's collaboration with the authorities rings true. The following anecdote, related by one Dāwūd b. Bisṭām, also gives the impression that Ibn Ḥanbal's uncle was in regular contact with the local authorities: 'The information from Baghdād did not reach me on time so I turned to Abī 'Abdallāh b. Ḥanbal's uncle, [and said] the information did not get to us today.'[26]

The authorities of Baghdād knew Ibn Ḥanbal's family. During Ibn Ḥanbal's investigation (which took place in the course of the *miḥna*), the caliph inquired about Ibn Ḥanbal's uncle.[27] 'Abd al-Raḥmān b. Isḥāq (d. 232), one of the important *qāḍī*s in Baghdād who had known the family for many years, answered: 'They are, O Amīr al-Mu'minīn, a respected family (*ahl bayt*) possessors of rank and standing.'[28] A similar assessment was made by another formidable *qāḍī*, Ibn Samā'a (d. 233), when the fate of Ibn Ḥanbal was discussed by al-Mu'taṣim's courtiers.[29] These exchanges indicate that Ibn Ḥanbal's family was recognized by some of the most important functionaries in the religious establishment.

Ibn Ḥanbal's ancestors were involved in the politics of their age. They participated in the conquests, were on the state payroll, and got involved in factional politics. In the two generations preceding Ibn Ḥanbal, the family made its living as soldiers, and his grandfather even served in a political post. Ibn Ḥanbal and his generation (primarily his cousin Ḥanbal b. Isḥāq) made a vocational shift. They broke away from the military circles and turned to the scholarly milieu. They sustained themselves through a variety of means, such as handicrafts, small commercial ventures and renting out family properties. In the case of Ibn Ḥanbal, the vocational shift was accompanied by an ideological break, since he refused to have any financial connections with the authorities.[30]

Wives, children and property

Ibn Ḥanbal's grandson, Zuhayr b. Ṣāliḥ b. Aḥmad b. Ḥanbal (d. 303), is said to have spoken twice about his grandfather's marriages. In both instances he took special care to mention the Arab descent of Ibn Ḥanbal's wives: 'My grandfather, Allah's mercy upon him, married the mother of my father 'Ā'isha bint al-Faḍl [who was] from the Arabs...'[31] In another comment that is ascribed to him he stated: 'When 'Ā'isha Umm Ṣāliḥ died, my grandfather married after her a woman from the Arabs...'[32]

Zuhayr b. Ṣāliḥ's remark on the Arab background of his grandfather's wives reveals the sensitivity that some members of the family had regarding their ethnic affiliation. Such an attitude dovetails Ibn Ḥanbal's legal views on suitability (*kafā'a*) of spouses.[33] Suitability, a legal principle whose contents and application were debated by Islamic jurists, was aimed at protecting women from marrying men of inferior social or economic status, an act that might lead to the detraction of their standing. The yardstick that determined the status of potential marriage partners were religion, lineage, financial means and freedom. However, although all jurists accepted the principle of suitability, they differed about what constitutes suitability. In contrast to jurists like Mālik b. Anas and al-Shāfi'ī, Ibn Ḥanbal was a firm believer in lineage as a means of determining the suitability of spouses. This meant that Ibn Ḥanbal insisted that Arab women marry Arab men.

Ibn Ḥanbal's views on lineage as a criterion for suitability are articulated in the following reply:

> I heard a man say to Aḥmad 'I have a paternal first cousin who is an Arab. Shall I give her in marriage to a *mawlā* (i.e., a non-Arab client)?'
> He said, 'No.'
> The man said, 'But she is sickly (*ḍa'īfa*).'
> Aḥmad said, 'Do not give her in marriage [to him].'[34]

Ibn Ḥanbal's opinion was straightforward and unbending. He was not willing to sanction a marriage between an Arab woman and a *mawlā* because of the man's inferior social status. His reluctance to compromise the principle of *kafā'a* is emphasized in light of his refusal to change this position even when his interlocutor seems to have pressed for some concession by raising the issue of the woman's poor health.

In his reply to another question regarding the marriage of an Arab woman and a *mawlā*, Ibn Ḥanbal took a firmer stand and argued for the separation of a husband and wife:

> I asked him about someone who marries off his daughter to a *mawlā*?
> He [Ibn Ḥanbal] replied: I would separate them. Then he [Ibn Ḥanbal] said: An Arab [married to] an Arab [is] suitable (*kafʾ*), and Quraysh [married to] Quraysh [is] suitable (*kafʾ*).
> Then he [presumably the interlocutor] asked: What would you think if a Zangī [Negro] married one of the offspring (*walad*) of Fāṭima? He [Ibn Ḥanbal] disapproved of it, and said: that is the doctrine of the *shuʿūbiyya*.[35]

This is a highly charged reply. To begin with, it does not limit the constraints of lineage to ethnic differences between Arabs and non-Arabs. Ibn Ḥanbal introduces another distinction, between the Quraysh and other Arabs, and places the Quraysh above the rest of the Arabs. The Quraysh's superiority stems from being Muḥammad's clan. Their social and political superiority manifested itself through such social barriers as prohibition of women to marry non-Qurayshi men and the sole right to serve as caliphs. Interestingly enough, the privileged position of Quraysh is another case in which pre-Islamic values, such as tribal standing and prerogative are enmeshed with Islamic values such as the superior standing of the Prophet.

The most volatile part of this opinion is Ibn Ḥanbal's final remark about marriage between the Zangī and an offspring of Fāṭima. Such a position is referred to as 'the doctrine of the *shuʿūbiyya*.' The *shuʿūbiyya* controversy was one of the expressions of ethnic strife in the early Islamic community.[36] The *shuʿūbis* were non-Arab Muslims who were opposed to the privileged position of Arabs within Islamic society. Their main grievance was that Islamic society did not live up to its egalitarian values. Ibn Ḥanbal's reference to the *shuʿūbiyya* in the context of a legal discussion is a fascinating case in which a legal position engages with a burning political problem.

Ibn Ḥanbal's disapproval of the *shuʿūbis* was not limited to legal problems. He also criticized their overall approach to Islamic society:

> He [Ibn Ḥanbal] acknowledged the Arabs' due, and their superiority (*faḍlaha*) and their priority (*sābiqataha*) and he loved them ... he [Ibn Ḥanbal] did not adhere to the doctrine of the *shuʿūbiyya* and the contemptible [among] the *mawālī* that disliked the Arabs and did not concede to them their [Arabs] superiority. He [ascribed to] them [*shuʿūbiyya*] innovation, hypocrisy and controversy.[37]

Ibn Ḥanbal's criticism of *mawālī*, who did not acknowledge the Arabs' superiority, is unmistakable. Furthermore, he did not shirk from making the connection between egalitarian demands (*shu'ūbiyya*) and ethnicity (*mawālī*). The range of meanings of terms such as *faḍl* and *sābiqa* make it difficult to sketch the exact contents of his racial outlook. If we use the milder meanings of these two words (such as merit and not superiority), then Laoust's assessment of Ibn Ḥanbal's views about the sensitive topic of equality in Islamic societies seems correct: 'he defended the Arabs, but without proclaiming their superiority.'[38] However, if we take them to mean superiority and precedence, Ibn Ḥanbal's views are of a more hierarchical nature. In either case, he was highly aware of the importance of the Arab contribution to the growth of Islam and thought that the uniqueness of the Arabs warranted a special social and political position.

Ibn Ḥanbal waited until the age of forty to start a family.[39] His first wife, 'Ā'isha bint al-Faḍl, was the mother of his eldest son, Ṣāliḥ.[40] It is not clear how long this marriage lasted, since Ibn Ḥanbal stated that he lived with her thirty years without getting into an argument (*wa-mā ikhtalaftu anā wa-hiya fī kalima*).[41] This number may be inaccurate,[42] and Ibn Ḥanbal's memory is probably a bit rosy. However, the remark itself is interesting because it demonstrates that Ibn Ḥanbal wanted his marriage to be perceived as a harmonious one.

When 'Ā'isha died, Ibn Ḥanbal approached one of the women of his family,[43] and asked her to propose on his behalf to one of his cousins. He married Rayḥāna bint 'Umar, the mother of his second son, 'Abdallāh, and lived with her at least seven years.[44] According to one of Ibn Ḥanbal's disciples, Khaṭāb b. Bishr (d. 264),[45] Ibn Ḥanbal pointed out to Rayḥāna that he did not approve of her shoes, on the pretext that such shoes were not worn at the time of the Prophet, and he wanted her to wear something that had the traditional stamp of approval.[46] Another comment Ibn Ḥanbal made about his relations with Rayḥāna was that they lived together twenty years without an argument.[47] Ibn Ḥanbal's observation about his domestic harmony may be accurate, but his arithmetic was not. This was pointed out by Ibn al-Jawzī (d. 597), who compiled these anecdotes, and noticed that their total was greater than Ibn Ḥanbal's seventy-seven years.[48]

Some interesting bits of information about Ibn Ḥanbal's intimate relationships with women can be gleaned from the anecdotes about his concubine (*jāriya*), Ḥusn.[49] After Rayḥāna died, Ibn Ḥanbal asked Abū Yūsuf b. Bukhtān to buy him a maid.[50] Before Ibn Bukhtān left together with Ibn Ḥanbal's close friend, Fūrān (d. 256), Ibn Ḥanbal instructed them that 'she is to have flesh.'[51] Though we are in the dark about Ḥusn's ethnic background, we do know something about her physical features and Ibn Ḥanbal's disposition towards them.

This intimate tenor runs through many of the anecdotes pertaining to Ḥusn. After listing all the children she bore – Zaynab, Ibn Ḥanbal's only daughter; al-Ḥasan and al-Ḥusayn, twins who died shortly after they were born; al-Ḥasan and Muḥammad, of whom we know next to nothing; and Saʿīd, who was born after Ibn Ḥanbal died[52] – we come across a series of unexpected stories. In the first, Ḥusn approaches her master and asks his permission to sell her anklet. Ibn Ḥanbal replied 'Will this please you?"[53] Compared to Ibn Ḥanbal's severe and solemn remarks about Rayḥāna's shoes, this agreeable answer is a bit surprising. Ibn Ḥanbal is depicted in this anecdote as a caring husband rather than a detached lawyer. The man who burdened his family because of his refusal to accept financial help, and pestered them because of unjustified expenditures, here goes along with his servant's whims.

The Ḥusn-related stories contribute a different quality to Ibn Ḥanbal's portrait. We read of Ibn Ḥanbal hiring a woman to help Ḥusn after she gave birth to Ḥusain.[54] In another instance, when Ibn Ḥanbal told Ḥusn that he had no money and would like to be treated by a cupper, she took out a piece of spun thread, sold it and paid a cupper. With the sum she received for the thread she also bought meat and perfume.[55]

Judging by the vignettes that describe his relations with ʿĀʾisha and Rayḥāna, Ibn Ḥanbal found it important to stress that he enjoyed marital harmony with his wives. However, we see no clue of intimacy, expressions of fondness or indication of any other emotion between him and his two wives. The only remark he makes about Rayḥāna's shoes is a typically moralizing statement. In contrast with the image of a severe and distant patriarch that emerges from these anecdotes, the relationship depicted between Ibn Ḥanbal and Ḥusn is of a more emotional nature. Through it we learn something about his taste in women, find him trying to please his concubine and going as far as compromising his ascetic practices.

Ibn Ḥanbal was depicted by his son Ṣāliḥ as a harsh and demanding father. Several of the anecdotes that Ṣāliḥ chose to include in Ibn Ḥanbal's biography tell of the son's failures to attain his father's moral standards. For example, it is told that Ṣāliḥ and his brother ʿAbdallāh bought some items and hid them because they expected their father would be upset if he found out about these acquisitions. On occasion, Ibn Ḥanbal did find out about this practice and scolded them.[56] In another instance, when Ṣāliḥ fixed the roof of his house, Ibn Ḥanbal made his disapproval known by mentioning a tradition about al-Aḥnaf b. Qays, who came home from a journey and refused to enter his house because the roof had been changed.[57]

Ibn Ḥanbal's harshest remarks were aimed at his eldest son. In the *Manāqib*, Ibn al-Jawzī informs his readers why Ṣāliḥ was in such trouble. He mentions that Ṣāliḥ 'was burdened (*ubtuliya*) with a family when he was young.'[58] Due to this, Ṣāliḥ was always in need of money and was more prone to accept gifts and donations than was his father. Ibn al-Jawzī hints that Ṣāliḥ aggravated his own difficult situation because he was 'a very generous man (*sakhiyyan*)'.[59] These observations are followed by anecdotes that tell of the tensions over finances between Ṣāliḥ and Ibn Ḥanbal, such as Ṣāliḥ's attempts to hide from his father various goods that he bought. In another story, Ibn Ḥanbal uses the visits of ascetics as opportunities to tell Ṣāliḥ he would like to see him in their condition. Ibn Ḥanbal had little success in influencing Ṣāliḥ's conduct, but he did manage to afflict him with pangs of guilt, which Ṣāliḥ recounts after he accepted the position of *qāḍī* in Iṣfahān.[60]

Even though Ṣāliḥ's conduct was a constant disappointment to his father in moral terms, his scholarship did not draw criticism from the demanding Ibn Ḥanbal.[61] However, the outstanding scholar from among Ibn Ḥanbal's children was 'Abdallāh, Ṣāliḥ's younger half-brother. 'Abdallāh's command of scholarship drew compliments from his father, and he had the reputation of being the most knowledgeable in his father's traditions.[62]

Two more children of Ibn Ḥanbal are mentioned, both from Ḥusn. The first, Zaynab, is Ibn Ḥanbal's only known daughter. In contrast to some of his contemporaries, Ibn Ḥanbal was apparently not disappointed about the birth of a girl in the family. When Ṣāliḥ had a daughter Ibn Ḥanbal consoled him by pointing out that 'the prophets were the fathers of girls.'[63] Another incident that reveals Ibn Ḥanbal's respect for women was his will, in which he bequeathed his granddaughters the same amount of money as he did his grandsons.[64] Another child of Ḥusn's of whom we know very little is Sa'īd (d. 303). He was born two months after Ibn Ḥanbal's death.[65] It is said that he served as *qāḍī* in Kūfa.[66]

Ṣāliḥ describes his father as an austere and highly disciplined individual and himself as a constant failure. This may be a rhetoric device to enhance his father's moral stature. However, it is interesting to note that two of Ibn Ḥanbal's children went against his moral principles and accepted the position of *qāḍī*, while another son, 'Abdallāh, chose to be buried in a different cemetery than his father. Apparently Ibn Ḥanbal's moral stature was a crucible they found hard to bear.

In the opening comment of the chapter that deals with Ibn Ḥanbal's money and livelihood, Ibn al-Jawzī mentions that Ibn Ḥanbal inherited a house and a chamber from his father and that he rented out the chamber. Ibn al-Jawzī observes that Ibn Ḥanbal 'was ashamed of (*yata'affaf*) the rent.'[67] This apologetic remark sets the tone for the anecdotes that follow, in which Ibn Ḥanbal is described as uncomfortable with owning property. In the first, Ibn Ḥanbal tells Muḥammad b. 'Ubaydallāh (d. 272),[68] that he paid *zakāt* for his house, and that he followed the regulations that 'Umar b. al-Khaṭṭāb used in the Sawād.[69] In another, an anonymous man asks Ibn Ḥanbal how living off real estate squares with his way of life, and Ibn Ḥanbal replies: 'I inherited this from my father, and if someone who could prove it is his would approach me I would move out and hand it to him.'[70] In yet another conversation that dealt with his property, Ibn Ḥanbal says: 'You know that this revenue (*al-ghalla*) does not maintain us, I take it only when compelled.'[71] We also learn that he drew a 'monthly revenue (*ghallatuhu*) of seventeen *dirham* from his property'[72] and that he rented out a shop (*ḥānūt*) for three *dirham* a month.[73] When we gather all the shreds of information found in Ibn Ḥanbal's biographies regarding his income from properties, we sense that he drew upon them more often than he would like to admit.

It is not clear if the revenue that these properties generated was sufficient to maintain Ibn Ḥanbal's family, but clearly they were not of the impoverished and dispossessed. Though he admired ascetics that gave up all their possessions and thought they should be role models for his sons, he had the means to receive a steady income without working and often used it.[74] Another indication of Ibn Ḥanbal's economic situation is that he did not work on a regular basis. We know that when he traveled in his search of knowledge he would, on occasion, work but this does not seem his usual conduct. We also know that when his family ran into financial problems, his wives would spin wool ("*taghzilu ghazlan*') and sell their wares.[75] Thus, the two most important sources of income in his family were property and handicrafts.

Family: Support and crisis

The evidence at our disposal portrays Ibn Ḥanbal's relations with his children and wives as rigid and strained. As in many other families, the cause of friction was money and the standard of living. The anecdotes that shed light on these relations are transmitted by the members of the family itself and usually depict Ibn Ḥanbal as the man of principle whose wife and children are incapable of living up to his moral standards. Thus it appears as if Ibn Ḥanbal and the other members of the family played specific roles. Ibn Ḥanbal's role was to set the moral standards for the family and scold its members when they did not live up to them, while his children broke the rules and received his moralizing in awe mixed with frustration. However, although the relationships were at times tense, it did not seem that they would break down.

The deterioration in these relations came in the wake of the *miḥna*. The pressure that was placed on the family, first when Ibn Ḥanbal was persecuted and later when the caliph courted him, altered the nature of their ties. Jail and victory sent shock waves through the family. At the outset of the *miḥna*, his uncle, Isḥāq b. Ḥanbal, supported Ibn Ḥanbal. But when the *miḥna* was over and al-Mutawakkil conceded, Isḥāq b. Ḥanbal and Ibn Ḥanbal's children pressed Ibn Ḥanbal to be more cooperative with the authorities. Their pressure and disobedience led to Ibn Ḥanbal's dissociation from his family. Interestingly enough, when the family was under duress, it united behind Ibn Ḥanbal. However, after their side won the fifteen-year-long struggle with the caliph, they fell apart.

During the cooperative phase when Ibn Ḥanbal was jailed, his uncle Isḥāq b. Ḥanbal's went to the officers and the possessors of power (*quwwād wa-aṣḥāb al-sulṭān*)[76] and requested that Ibn Ḥanbal be released. When these appeals remained unanswered he turned to the governor himself, Isḥāq b. Ibrāhīm.[77] When Isḥāq b. Ḥanbal approached the governor, he mentioned that their families had a long lasting alliance (*jiwār*) that went back to their grandfathers.[78]

The relationship between the two families lies at the heart of Isḥāq b. Ḥanbal's appeal. It is known that both grandfathers, Ḥanbal b. Hilāl and al-Ḥusayn b. Muṣʿab, resided in Khurāsān, and acquired relatively high military posts.[79] From Isḥāq b. Ḥanbal's petition we learn that there might have been an alliance between them and that they were members of the same social group. Thus, his appeal to Isḥāq b. Ibrāhīm follows the norms of familial and tribal alliances. It was clear from the governor's answer that he knew of these obligations, as he says: 'This has come to my attention.'[80] However, the governor did not release Ibn Ḥanbal, probably because he had new alliances and obligations to consider, such as his relations with the caliph. Yet, perhaps because of the families' alliances in the past, he did allow Isḥāq b. Ḥanbal to visit Ibn Ḥanbal.

The second argument that Isḥāq b. Ḥanbal raised was of a theological nature: 'Amīr, that which my brother's son [Ibn Ḥanbal] prefers does not reject the revelation (*tanzīl*), and that which they disagree about is only interpretation (*ta'wīl*).'[81] Here Isḥāq b. Ḥanbal emphasizes that his nephew and the governor agree about the status of the Qur'an. Hence, he is implying that whatever their disagreement, it is of little consequence since it is merely about interpretation. This remark encapsulates one of the basic arguments that Ibn Ḥanbal and his associates will make throughout the *miḥna* – opinions about the createdness of the Qur'an do not warrant persecution.

When Isḥāq b. Ḥanbal's visit to Ibn Ḥanbal was about to end, Isḥāq b. Ḥanbal tried to convince Ibn Ḥanbal to comply with the caliph's demands. He pointed out that all of Ibn Ḥanbal's friends had done the same and that Ibn Ḥanbal had spent enough time in jail. In so doing, Isḥāq b. Ḥanbal shows himself to be the head of a household, looking out for his nephew's well-being and willing to compromise in a theological confrontation. Ibn Ḥanbal replied to this: 'Oh uncle, if the knowledgeable reply [to the caliph's demand that the Qur'an was created] out of dissimulation (*taqiyya*) and those ignorant will remain unknowing, when will we make the truth clear?'[82]

Isḥāq b. Ḥanbal wanted Ibn Ḥanbal's quick release and suggested that the matter be settled in front of the *fuqahā'* and *'ulamā'*. He then made an interesting remark about his own suggestion: 'I did not mention to him [Isḥāq b. Ibrāhīm] the Traditionists (*ahl al-ḥadīth wa-'l-athar*).'[83] This comment suggests that by the year 219 A.H., the religio-cultural camps, *ahl al-ḥadīth* and *ahl al-ra'y*, were in place and were well aware of each other.

Victory and influence placed a heavier onus on Ibn Ḥanbal's family than did jail and persecution. During the years of economic hardships there were few opportunities to lure Ibn Ḥanbal out of his austere life style. As a result, even when his children annoyed him, the seams of the family were strained but did not tear. However, after al-Mutawakkil reversed the court's religious policy, he did all he could to gain the allegiance and approval of the Traditionist milieu.[84] It was only natural that he would turn to Ibn Ḥanbal and try to spread his net of patronage over the reputed leader of the Traditionist opposition. The new prospects of wealth placed Ibn Ḥanbal's family under a duress they could not withstand.

A few years after al-Mutawakkil adopted the Traditionist position regarding the Qur'an, he invited Ibn Ḥanbal to his court in Sāmarrā'.

Ibn Ḥanbal was reluctant to go but could not refuse the caliph's kindness. When he arrived he expressed his discomfort with the whole situation by refusing the luxuries that were given to him. The caliph did not understand Ibn Ḥanbal's subtle messages and it was up to the caliph's mother and his advisors to suggest that Ibn Ḥanbal should be sent home.[85]

To his dismay, while he was signaling to the caliph that he was unhappy to be his visitor, Ibn Ḥanbal's children enjoyed the luxuries placed at their disposal. Ibn Ḥanbal reproached them, saying that the luxuries, which he perceived as bait that was set before him to test his moral integrity, would not have been lavished upon them if it were not for him.[86] As a result of their behavior, Ibn Ḥanbal asked them to leave Sāmarrā'. Approximately two weeks after his arrival, Ibn Ḥanbal was sent home. But this was not the end of al-Mutawakkil's courting.

The caliph's generosity seemed to haunt Ibn Ḥanbal. After Ibn Ḥanbal returned to his home, al-Mutawakkil continued to send him money. Even though Ibn Ḥanbal refused to accept the caliph's financial support, al-Mutawakkil's messenger insisted that Ibn Ḥanbal take the money and give it to his family.[87] When Ibn Ḥanbal replied that they were well off and did not need it, the messenger simply handed the money directly to the members of Ibn Ḥanbal's family.[88] Afterwards he sent them 4,000 dirham every month. When Ibn Ḥanbal sent al-Mutawakkil a message protesting these actions, al-Mutawakkil replied: 'This is only for your children, why is it your business (lit. what is between you and it).'[89] This pension was sent to them until al-Mutawakkil's death.[90]

When Ibn Ḥanbal saw that the caliph could not be convinced to stop the outpouring of monies, Ibn Ḥanbal turned to his children and tried to dissuade them from accepting the caliph's money. However, in the course of this effort he was dealt an unprecedented blow. After telling Ṣāliḥ that he wanted him to give up the money that he was getting from the caliph, Ṣāliḥ committed an unheard-of act and refused. He reminded his father that he had a big family to look after, and that he had often complained about it to Ibn Ḥanbal, but was never given a practical answer. Ibn Ḥanbal confronted his son directly and asked him, 'By Allah, you will not do [as I ask you],' and Ṣāliḥ replied 'I will not.'[91] After this painful exchange, Ibn Ḥanbal had similar conversations with 'Abdallāh, his second son, and Isḥāq b. Ḥanbal, his uncle.

Ibn Ḥanbal's reaction to these acts of defiance was to dissociate himself from the rest of his family.[92] He blocked the door that connected his home with theirs and ceased praying in the mosque that they attended.[93] Ṣāliḥ writes in his biography of his father, 'In the past, before we accepted [money] from the authorities (*sulṭān*) he ate at our place, and sometimes we would send something to him and he ate from it.'[94] After this affair, and probably until his last days, Ibn Ḥanbal refused his sons food. His concubine, Ḥusn, tells the following story: 'One day I baked bread for my master when he was sick [with the malaise] from which he died. He said, 'Where did you bake it?' I answered 'in 'Abdallāh's house.' [He] said: Remove it and did not eat it.'[95]

CHAPTER TWO

Childhood and Learning

Childhood

Ibn Ḥanbal was born in 164 A.H., a few months after his mother, Ṣafiya bint Maymūna, arrived in Baghdād.[1] The new capital of the ʿAbbāsid empire, which was founded nineteen years before the pregnant Ṣafiya settled there, was in the midst of stunning growth. Its founder, al-Manṣūr, designated it a serene center of caliphal administration. Surrounded by bureaucrats and soldiers, al-Manṣūr hoped to steer and control his huge empire from Baghdād. But the economic success of the city served as a magnet for hundreds of thousands of immigrants, like Ibn Ḥanbal's parents, while its bustle and noise drove a number of ʿAbbāsid princes out of the city.[2]

Baghdād's commercial boom attracted merchants, craftsmen and artisans who gravitated to the new employment opportunities they found there. The ʿAbbāsid rulers brought with them their Persian administrators and scribes, the most famous being the Barmacids. At the same time many other Persians settled in Karkh, a quarter of Baghdād, and turned it into a dynamic commercial center. Jewish merchants passed through while Nestorian Christians made Baghdād the center of their community. The city soon became a colorful human mosaic that would inspire one of the great master pieces of literature, *The Thousand and One Nights.*[3]

The influx of Muslims, Jews, Christians and Persians, coupled with the city's economic boom, paved the way for the development of a unique intellectual climate. Eighth-century Baghdād was the home of a spectrum of ancient traditions and newly formed worldviews. In its salons and courts, Persian dualists, Christian Patriarchs, Muslim theologians and *ʿulamāʾ*, encountered and debated one another. The

Sunni worldview, which would grow into the predominant system of beliefs in the Islamic world, was being forged in its mosques and homes. As the city became the arena of vigorous intellectual activities, new tensions and clashes surfaced. In the days of al-Mahdī (d. 169), this religious and intellectual friction would lead to a concerted effort on the part of al-Mahdī and proto-Sunni *'ulamā'* to eradicate a group of religious deviants called *zindīqs*.[4] By 167 A.H., al-Mahdī would step up the 'hunt and search for zindīqs,'[5] and this policy would be followed by the renowned Hārūn al-Rashīd (d. 193). Walking the streets of Baghdād, Ibn Ḥanbal would not merely absorb the sights and sounds that inspired *The Thousand and One Nights*, he would also hear of the first widescale and systematic religious persecution in Islam.

In 167 A.H., when Ibn Ḥanbal was three years old, a 'severe plague' that 'spread death and coughing' in 'Baghdād and Baṣrah' may have caused the death of his father.[6] Muḥammad b. Ḥanbal was approximately thirty years old when he died. He left behind a wife and baby, and as can be expected, no impression on the baby's memory. The orphaned Aḥmad b. Muḥammad b. Ḥanbal was probably the only child of Ṣafiya bint Maymūna to whom he was strongly attached. A hint of Ṣafiya's place in her son's heart is found in a story that Ibn Ḥanbal told his son. During one of his journeys in search of knowledge, he ran a fever. In this moment of physical weakness, the image of his mother came back to him, either through a dream or a hallucination. After she appeared Ibn Ḥanbal would not let her go (*wa-lam akun ista'dhantuhā*).[7]

Another adult that figured in Ibn Ḥanbal's childhood is his uncle. Apparently this uncle was part of a network of informants that sent reports to the caliph's officials regarding the events in Baghdād.[8] In a dubious account about Ibn Ḥanbal and his uncle we learn that on one occassion the uncle asked Ibn Ḥanbal to hand a report to a messenger, but Ibn Ḥanbal decided to ignore his uncle's instructions and disposed of the report. The anecdote seems spurious because it presents Ibn Ḥanbal the youth as a fully committed *'ālim* who was willing to risk his family's livelihood and special relationship with the authorities because of moral considerations.[9]

Another report from his childhood, whose source was a schoolmate, depicts Ibn Ḥanbal in a similar fashion. Ibn Ḥanbal is once again described as a solemn, self-assured child in a world of morally weak adults:

> [Ibn Ḥanbal] was in the *kuttāb* with us. He was a youth (*ghulayyim*) whose merits we acknowledged. [At the time] the caliph was in

> Raqqa and the people (*al-nās*, i.e. soldiers) who were with him wrote to their homes.[10] Their wives sent [the following request] to the teacher: Send over Aḥmad b. Ḥanbal to write a reply to their [husbands'] letters. [The teacher] sent him and he arrived with his head bowed (*muṭa'ṭa' al-ra's*) and wrote replies to their letters. Sometimes they dictated objectionable things (*al-shay' min al-munkar*) and he did not write it for them.[11]

These vignettes ought to be taken with a grain of salt. They were told decades later by people who were probably not present at the events. However, they do shed light on how Ibn Ḥanbal's pupils and neighbors wanted to think about him. In their eyes, Ibn Ḥanbal was always true to his way. That is why they would be happy to believe that even as a child he resisted misguided patriarchal authority and followed his own convictions. From his youth he would not put up with collaboration with the state or indecent conduct between men and women. Such stories foreshadow his defiance of the caliph during and after the *miḥna*. It must have been satisfying for Ibn Ḥanbal's disciples to come across a story that confirms that even as a child, their master possessed the forceful personality and integrity that he demonstrated during his confrontation with the caliph. Furthermore, in light of the family's record of collaboration with the authorities it may even be that these stories were meant to set Ibn Ḥanbal apart from his relatives.

Search for identity

'I (started) to search for traditions (*ḥadīth*) when I was sixteen years old.'[12]At the outset (179 A.H.), Ibn Ḥanbal wandered between the teachers who lived and taught in Baghdād. These scholars satisfied his curiosity during the next three years, but in 182 A.H., Ibn Ḥanbal set out to other intellectual centers, such as Kūfa, Baṣra, Mecca and Yemen. Travel was expected from aspiring students because experts in religious knowledge settled down and taught in several of the big cities in the Islamic world. Many of these experts mastered particular prophetic traditions and the aspiring young scholars were required to make the rounds between them and acquaint themselves with the knowledge that circulated in those localities.

The expectation that novices would study with numerous teachers is reflected in the entries of *ḥadīth* scholars in biographical dictionaries, which open with long lists of teachers, colleagues and pupils.[13]

Unfortunately these lists teach us little about the dates that teachers and students met, the relative impact that specific teachers made on their students, the opinion these teachers had of their pupils, or the personal relationships that developed between teachers and pupils. If we want to trace the personal development and intellectual growth of a given Islamic scholar we cannot rely solely on these opaque documents,[14] we must find complementary sources of information.

The remarks scholars made about themselves and their colleagues serve as one such source of information. However, although biographical and autobiographical remarks can add interesting dimensions to the intellectual portrait of scholars, they too are laden with shortcomings.[15] For example, they rarely expose the ideological incertitude of young scholars in search of an intellectual and ideological identity, and gloss over the intellectual experiments that the respectable scholars had carried out in their youth. In general they mention the events and relationships that were conducive to forging the scholar's mature identity and leave out moments and acquaintances that diverged from this process. Notwithstanding major faults such as outspoken doctrinal deviations, the biographies conceal biographic nuances that are essential for sketching the intellectual growth of scholars.

In contrast to the average scholar, on whom there are few and short entries in biographical dictionaries, there is a fair amount of information about Ibn Ḥanbal and scholars of his standing. The method I propose for analyzing Ibn Ḥanbal's professional and ideological growth is based on an exposition and analysis of the teachers he chose. The underlying assumption of this approach is that if Ibn Ḥanbal was willing to study with a teacher who was known to have a specific jurisprudential or doctrinal outlook, he was tolerant of this outlook at that point of time. When the mosaic of Ibn Ḥanbal's teachers is pieced together, we can reconstruct in rough lines what fields of knowledge interested him and what sort of doctrinal and jurisprudential outlooks he was willing to tolerate.[16]

The teachers examined in this survey are those who taught him between 179 A.H.and 200 A.H. I shall begin with the Baghdādī teachers who tought Ibn Ḥanbal between 179 A.H. and 182 A.H. Ibn Ḥanbal's first teacher was Abū Yūsuf (d. 182). In 179 A.H., when Ibn Ḥanbal attended Abū Yūsuf's classes, the latter was one of the central figures in the 'Abbāsid Empire, serving as *qāḍī al-quḍāt*, tutor of high-ranking court officials and counselor to Hārūn al-Rashīd, the caliph who commissioned him to write the *Kitāb al-Kharāj*.[17] Abū Yūsuf's legal training was acquired in Abū Ḥanifa's circle, where he was considered one of the outstanding disciples. However, among certain Traditionists, Abū Yūsuf's involvement with the court and his Ḥanafi affiliation were not looked upon favorably.

Ibn Ḥanbal's discomfort with his own sojourn in Abū Yūsuf's classes is reflected in his attempts to downplay this episode.[18] His earliest biographies, such as the one written by his son Ṣāliḥ, do not even mention his studies with Abū Yūsuf. In later sources, Ibn Ḥanbal is said to refer to his studies with Abū Yūsuf, but these references reveal his ambivalence towards this powerful and influential figure: 'Abū Yūsuf is the first (teacher) on whose authority I wrote *ḥadīth*,' he wrote, but added, 'and I do not transmit on his authority.'[19] The statement acknowledges Abū Yūsuf's scholarship but also reflects Ibn Ḥanbal's posterior attempts to distance himself from his teacher. In another remark Ibn Ḥanbal explained why he set himself apart from his first teacher: 'Abū Yūsuf is truthful (*ṣadūq*) but it is inappropriate to transmit anything on the authority of the companions (*aṣḥāb*) of Abū Ḥanifa.'[20] These two remarks hint that in the course of time Ibn Ḥanbal changed his mind and became less tolerant of diverging views.

Ibn Ḥanbal's ambivalence touches upon the tension between the Traditionists and the *ahl al-ra'y*, who were usually affiliated with the Ḥanafis.[21] This was the most important division within the community of jurists in the first centuries of Islam, and Ibn Ḥanbal's attendance of Abū Yūsuf's classes suggests one of two possibilities. The first is that he was unaware of the tension among the *'ulamā'*. This would suggest that Ibn Ḥanbal did not have a defined professional and ideological identity at the time. The second is that even though he knew about the tensions, he chose to study with scholars of both orientations. Both of these alternatives indicate that at the age of sixteen, Ibn Ḥanbal was not a committed Traditionist.

Much like his jurisprudential pliability, at the age of sixteen Ibn Ḥanbal was tolerant of a variety of theological doctrines. An illustration of such flexibility was his decision to study with 'Alī b. Hāshim al-Burayd (d. 179) the year he began his search for knowledge. Al-Burayd was reputed to have Shī'ī sympathies, and some experts considered his Shī'ī tendencies extreme. Al-Jurjānī (d. 365) accused al-Burayd and his son of being extremists (*ghāliyan*) in the 'evil of their *madhhab*'[22], meaning that their Shī'ī tendencies went beyond the acceptably mild support for 'Alī. Being charged with extremism (*ghulūw*) jeopardized al-Burayd's credibility and threatened to keep him out of the ranks of acceptable transmitters. As a result of these accusations, his name appears in Ibn

Ḥibbān's (d. 354) *Kitāb al-Majrūḥīn*, a book that surveys problematic Traditionists and enumerates their faults. Like al-Jurjānī, Ibn Ḥibbān accused al-Burayd of going too far (*mufriṭ*) and of extremism (*ghulūw*) in his Shī'ī leanings.[23]

In 182 A.H., Ibn Ḥanbal was still an uncommitted Traditionist. This state of mind is exposed by his encounters with a number of unorthodox teachers, the most famous of them, was Ibn 'Ulayya (d. 193) whose classes Ibn Ḥanbal attended in the next ten years whenever he was in Baghdād.[24]

Ibn 'Ulayya's standing in the eyes of the Traditionists is fascinating because of its complexity. As a scholar he was hailed by all that knew him.[25] Most of the leading Traditionist figures of his time attended his classes. The lists of his pupils include Shu'ba b. Ḥajjāj (d. 160), Ḥammād ibn Zayd (d. 179), 'Abd al-Raḥmān ibn Mahdī (d. 198), Yaḥyā ibn Ma'īn (d. 233), 'Alī ibn al-Madīnī (d. 239), and al-Shāfi'ī (d. 204). At the turn of the second century one could hardly hope for a more distinguished group of students. In a somewhat flowery remark Ibn Ḥanbal said of Ibn 'Ulayya: 'I missed (*fātanī*) Mālik but Allah compensated me with Sufyān ibn 'Uyayna and I missed Ḥammād ibn Zayd but Allah compensated me with Ismā'īl ibn 'Ulayya.'[26] Three of the four scholars mentioned here were members of the Traditionist intellectual elite (*a'imma*). Professionally, Ibn 'Ulayya was on an equal footing with them. Even though he was compared to such outstanding Traditionists, Ibn 'Ulayya was not considered as one of the leaders of the Traditionist milieu. Something in his record was tainted. The blemish was Ibn 'Ulayya's support of theological inquiry. Ibn Ḥanbal remarks that Ibn 'Ulayya 'did not stop with his *kalām* until the day he died.'[27] *Kalām*, the study of theology, was a hotly debated issue that divided the Islamic community into two hostile camps.[28] However, it was not only a difference of opinion regarding theology that separated Ibn 'Ulayya from the Traditionists. Condescension and profound disrespect were intertwined with their differences regarding theology and strained their relations. Ibn 'Ulayya's animosity towards the Traditionists is demonstrated by his harsh reference to Ibn Ḥanbal when the student walked into his class: 'Who brought this [Ibn Ḥanbal] upon me?' Ibn Ḥanbal continued the anecdote by commenting: 'He [Ibn 'Ulayya] never ceased to hate (*mā zāla mubghidan*) the Traditionists.'[29]

These personal insults were an expression of the enmities between many of the *mutakallimūn* (theologians) and the Traditionists in the second and third centuries.[30] In an exposition of the insults that his contemporaries hurdled at each other, Ibn Ḥanbal refers to the names with which the *aṣḥāb al-ra'y* addressed the *aṣḥāb al-sunna*: Nabīta and Ḥashwiyya.[31] The second, Ḥashwiyya, denotes the scorn and disrespect that the *ahl al-ra'y* felt towards the *ahl al-sunna*. An example of this usage can be found in al-Ma'mūn's first *miḥna* letter, where he describes the masses that supported the Traditionists: 'The Commander of the Faithful has realized that [...] the base elements of the ordinary people [*ḥashw al-ra'iyya*] [...] have no farsightedness, or vision, or faculty of reasoning [...]. [These persons are] a people sunk in ignorance and in blindness about God[.]'[32] This condescending remark illustrates the tension between the *ahl al-ra'y* and *mutakallimūn* camp and that of the Traditionists. Ibn 'Ulayya's animosity towards the Traditionists clarifies why a widely respected scholar like himself was excluded from the ranks of the *a'imma* – the leaders of the Traditionists.

Another characteristic of Ibn Ḥanbal's early teachers was their low professional standing. One was 'Abd al-Mu'mīn ibn 'Abdallāh, whose main claim to fame was that Ibn Ḥanbal had studied with him.[33] Ibn Ḥajar mentions him in the *Lisān al-Mīzān*, and each reference to him has a negative connotation.[34] Another problematic teacher, 'Alī ibn Mujāhid al-Kābulī (d.c. 182), was somewhat more respected. His students included Jarīr ibn 'Abd al-Ḥamīd (d. 188) and Ibn Ḥanbal.[35] Though Ibn Ḥanbal studied with him and wrote on his authority, Ibn Ḥanbal's colleague Yaḥyā ibn Ma'īn preferred not to do so. Other Traditionists were even more critical of him, and even accused him of being a fabricator (*kadhdhāb*).[36]

The ideological and professional profile of the young Ibn Ḥanbal is further obfuscated by the fact that alongside these unorthodox and unprofessional teachers, he chose to study with some highly respected proto-Sunni Traditionists. One Hushaym b. Bashīr (d. 183) with whom Ibn Ḥanbal studied until the former's death, is at times mentioned as Ibn Ḥanbal's first teacher. This is inaccurate, but indicative of the way future biographers wanted to remember Ibn Ḥanbal.[37] Abu Zahra, Ibn Ḥanbal's modern biographer, has argued that Hushaym had a major influence in shaping Ibn Ḥanbal's intellectual orientation and steered him into the path of the Traditionists.[38]

Ibn Ḥanbal's references to Hushaym b. Bashīr in Ṣāliḥ's biography give the impression that he was happy to look back on his relationship with Hushaym. However, in other sources, Ibn Ḥanbal often charged Hushaym with being unreliable. One of his major accusations was that Hushaym practiced *tadlīs* (tampering with chains of transmission).[39] If we accept Abu Zahra's evaluation of Hushaym's impact on the sixteen-year-old Ibn Ḥanbal, and take into consideration the criticism that Ibn Ḥanbal made about Hushaym when he had matured, we can conclude that this change in attitude reflects the rise in Ibn Ḥanbal's professional standards.

The most respected Traditionist who taught Ibn Ḥanbal was 'Abd al-Raḥmān b. Mahdī (d. 198). He was the only early teacher from those years who belonged to the intellectual elite of the Traditionist milieu. Ibn Ḥanbal first met 'Abd al-Raḥman b. Mahdī in the Friday mosque (*al-masjid al-jāmi'*), and wrote six or seven hundred traditions on 'Abd al-Raḥmān's authority. They met again, in the course of Ibn Ḥanbal's travels, and he had the opportunity to write approximately 10,000 traditions on 'Abd al-Raḥmān b. Mahdī's authority. At that later stage, their studies were carried out on a very personal basis. At times, Ibn Ḥanbal studied with 'Abd al-Raḥmān alone,[40] while the teacher attended to his hair: 'I used to read to 'Abd al-Raḥmān, he and I alone, there being no one in his house except him, and at times I would read to him and he would dye his hair with *ḥinnā'*.'[41]

After four years of studying with Baghdādian teachers, Ibn Ḥanbal set out to study in Kūfa.[42] Although there is a dearth of information regarding Ibn Ḥanbal's stay in Kūfa, the little we do know of his choice of teachers in Kūfa reflects the same intellectual curiosity and lack of ideological commitment that had characterized the previous four years. A study of the jurisprudential and theological positions of Ibn Ḥanbal's Kūfan teachers makes it clear that at the age of twenty Ibn Ḥanbal was still exploring different intellectual trends of Islam. Most of his Kūfan teachers were of Ḥanafi leanings, suggesting their affiliation with the *ahl al-ra'y*. They included, for example, 'Umar b. 'Ubayd al-Ṭanāfisī (d. 185) and Yaḥyā b. Zakariyyā' (d. 182/183), who was one of the earliest students who wrote on Abū Ḥanifa's authority. Another somewhat perplexing choice was Abū Mu'āwiyya (d. 185/195), who was the vocal leader of the Murji'a in Kūfa in that period.

Between 186 A.H. and 191 A.H., Ibn Ḥanbal spent much time in Baṣra and Mecca. In contrast to his trip to Kūfa, which he passes over in silence, Ibn Ḥanbal mentions and specifies details from his visits to Baṣra and Mecca. In Ibn Ḥanbal's first visit to Baṣra, which took place in 186 A.H., he studied with Mu'tamar b. Sulaymān (d. 187), Bishr b. al-Mufaḍḍal (d. 186), Marḥūm b. 'Abd al-'Azīz (d. 187/90), and Ziyād b. al-Rabī'(d. 185/6). All died within four years of Ibn Ḥanbal's visit to Baṣra. The proximity of Ibn Ḥanbal's visit and the death of these scholars suggest that he chose the oldest transmitters he could meet in Baṣra. Interestingly enough, even though they were aged, none of the four was an exceptionally famous transmitter.

In 187 A.H. Ibn Ḥanbal went on his first *ḥajj*. In Mecca he studied with Sufyān b. 'Uyayna (d. 198), one of the most respected Traditionists of his era. He was the second of Ibn Ḥanbal's teachers who belonged to the *a'imma*, the Traditionists' intellectual elite,[43] and Ibn Ḥanbal made it a point to study with him every time he came to Mecca for the *ḥajj*.[44] However, even though he was one of the esteemed leaders of the Traditionist milieu, Ibn 'Uyayna was not above criticism. In several instances, Ibn Ḥanbal either accused Ibn 'Uyayna directly of *tadlīs* or alluded to such practice.[45] Ibn 'Uyayna's tendency to tamper with chains of transmission was common knowledge and was mentioned by Hushaym in his letter to Wakī'.[46] Along with this professional problem, Ibn 'Uyayna was linked to Shī'īsm and associated with Ḥanafism.[47]

In 191A.H., while performing the *ḥajj*, Ibn Ḥanbal met al-Walīd b. Muslim (d. 194) in Mecca. Al-Walīd was a Syrian Traditionist whom Ibn Ḥanbal considered to be one of the best scholars in Syria.[48] Though al-Walīd was highly respected, Ibn Ḥanbal pointed out that he made many mistakes and would even tamper with chains of transmission.[49] Al-Walīd was not the only Syrian with whom Ibn Ḥanbal studied. We know that Ibn Ḥanbal traveled to Syria and studied with at least one more famous Syrian scholar, 'Abd al-A'lā b. Mushir (d. 218), but we do not know when.[50] This lack of information makes it difficult to place the Syrian phase in the sequence of Ibn Ḥanbal's intellectual growth.

Three characteristics stand out in the profile of Ibn Ḥanbal's early teachers. First, as a group, these teachers lack doctrinal cohesion. They include an extreme Shī'īte, a *mutakallīm*, the chief of Murji'ite propaganda, an outstanding proto-Sunni Traditionist and a host of the *ahl al-ra'y*. Second, the reputed professional standards of this group were extremely varied. Some were outstanding scholars, while others were either anonymous or, even worse, known for their unreliability. Finally, nearly all of Ibn Ḥanbal's early teachers were extremely aged.

Consolidation of ideology

As Ibn Ḥanbal matured, his religious vision solidified and he lost much of his ideological flexibility. One of the clearest indications of this change was the parameters he used in choosing his teachers. In the 180's A.H. most of Ibn Ḥanbal's teachers were in their late sixties if not older, and their professional reputations ranged from unreliable liars to the most trustworthy transmitters of their generation. In the 190's A.H., this situation was reversed. The teachers' ages varied greatly while their professional reputation became uniform and reliable.

If we compare the age pattern of Ibn Ḥanbal's early Baghdādi teachers with that of the late Baghdādi teachers we can conclude that age ceased to be an important consideration. Whereas all of Ibn Ḥanbal's early teachers were in their late sixties to eighties when Ibn Ḥanbal came to study with them, four out of five of his late teachers were born between 134 A.H. and 140 H., i.e., all were in their fifties when they taught Ibn Ḥanbal.[51]

Ibn Ḥanbal's remarks about his late teachers suggest that professionalism was becoming the main concern in his choice of teachers. He often praised the professionalism of his late teachers, Abū Salama Manṣūr b. Salama (d. 207/9), Abū Kāmil Muẓaffar b. Mudrik (d. 207) and al-Haytham b. Jamīl (d. 213/4), and labeled them 'followers (*aṣḥāb*) of traditions (*ḥadīth*) in Baghdād.'[52] In one of the references Ibn Ḥanbal goes so far as to give the impression that they are the only Traditionists in Baghdād.[53] He also takes special care to explain why he held the three in such high esteem: 'They did not take [traditions] from everyone, and they did not write except on the authority of the trustworthy.'[54] Which means that the three were well informed about Traditionists and were adept in their criticism. The other two teachers from that period, Hāshim b. al-Qāsim (d. 205/7) and 'Affān b. Muslim (d. 219/20) were both relatively respected scholars of traditions and morally acceptable individuals.

The substitution of scholarly quality for age can be discerned when we examine the scholars that Ibn Ḥanbal met outside of Baghdād. In the 190's A.H. Ibn Ḥanbal studied with a growing number of highly respected transmitters of the Traditionist milieu. Yaḥyā b. Sa'īd al-Qaṭṭān (d. 198) was one. He was a prominent Baṣrian scholar, who was one of the foremost experts in the science of men (*'ilm al-rijāl*) had studied for twenty years with Shu'ba, one of the founders of this branch of knowledge,[55] as well as with Ibn 'Uyayna.[56] Nonetheless, Yaḥyā b. Sa'īd al-Qaṭṭān had his faults and idiosyncracies. He was, for instance, reluctant to write on the authority of young scholars.[57] At times he annoyed his colleagues by rejecting the legitimacy of widely accepted Traditionists, who took his criticism of transmitters with a grain of salt.[58]

While age and professionalism acquired inverse importance as criteria for choosing teachers, a somewhat less conspicuous change took place with regard to doctrine. We may call it an ideological clean-up. Among Ibn Ḥanbal's late teachers, none espoused such unacceptable positions as al-Burayd's extreme Shī'īsm, Abū Mu'āwiyya's Murji'i propaganda, and Ibn 'Ulayya's view on *kalām*. In the course of the years that he studied with Traditionists, Ibn Ḥanbal absorbed their values, integrated their theological outlooks and grew less tolerant of dissenters.

If this choice of relatively orthodox teachers reflects the crystallization of his doctrines, we ought to bear in mind that even these late teachers had some blemishes. For example, Yaḥyā b. Sa'īd al-Qaṭṭān and Wakī'b. Al-Jarrāḥ (d. 196) are referred to as Ḥanafis, while 'Abd al-Razzāq was reputed to be sympathetic to the Shī'ītes. There are indications that Ibn Ḥanbal knew about their doctrinal and jurisprudential dispositions. Wakī' b. al-Jarrāh's contemporaries were well aware of his leanings towards Ḥanafi jurisprudence.Yaḥyā b. Ma'īn, a leading Traditionist and a close colleague of Ibn Ḥanbal's, confirmed that Wakī''s jurisprudence was in line with Abū Ḥanifa's. He stated that Wakī' 'used to pass judgement *(yufti)* in accordance to Abū Ḥanifa's doctrine *(qawl)* and heard from him [Abū Ḥanifa] many things.'[59]

In contrast to Ibn Ma'īn, who spoke of Wakī''s Ḥanafi leanings in an explicit manner, Ibn Ḥanbal did not even refer to them. Though Ibn Ḥanbal made dozens of remarks about Wakī', he ignored his jurisprudential affiliation. Ibn Ḥanbal's subtle construction of jurisprudential history goes even further, when he describes Wakī' as one of the followers *(aṣḥāb)* of Sufyān al-Thawrī (d. 161), who was one of Abū Ḥanifa's chief opponents in Kūfa. It stands to reason that Ibn Ḥanbal made such a statement because he wanted to justify Wakī''s high professional status.

Another example is 'Abd al-Razzāq (d. 211), who was known in Traditionist circles as a Shī'ī sympathizer. Despite this, many Traditionists chose to study with him. Their way of coming to terms with his Shī'ī tendencies was to sift traditions, omitting anything that was meant to promote the Shī'ī cause.[60] Ibn Ḥanbal's reaction to 'Abd al-Razzāk was different from that of his colleagues. When asked about 'Abd al-Razzāk's leanings, he simply said 'as for me, I never heard anything of that sort from him.'[61] This answer is neither a denial of 'Abd al-Razzāk's pro-Shī'ī tendencies nor an acknowledgement or affirmation of 'Abd al-Razzāk's deviation. As in the case of Wakī' b. al-Jarrāḥ, while his colleagues admit and discuss various uncomfortable biographical facts, Ibn Ḥanbal does everything possible to ignore those matters.

The allegations of 'Abd al-Razzāk's and Wakī' b. al-Jarrāḥ's deviations could taint their records. But we must remember that the positions ascribed to them are minor ideological detours in comparison with those of Ibn Ḥanbal's early teachers. What is more, these scholars were first-rate Traditionists and few held professional credentials equal to theirs. It would be expected that Ibn Ḥanbal would study with them. What is particularly interesting is his refusal to admit to their weaknesses, which were discussed by many of his colleagues.

Despite the fact that Ibn Ḥanbal did not leave a comprehensive statement about the development of his intellectual and doctrinal worldview, his numerous remarks and our information regarding his teachers enables us to piece together a possible path of intellectual growth. Ibn Ḥanbal did not go through dramatic changes in outlook. He started out as an adventurous youth who was curious to learn, whose most distinctive feature was lack of affiliation to any camp. As he matured and gained knowledge he found himself growing closer to the Traditionist camp and developing a sense of commitment to the Traditionist milieu and its ideas. These new beliefs and outlooks are illustrated by his relationship with al-Shāfiʿī, one of the last scholars that he chose to study with in these years.

Al-Shāfiʿī

Ibn Ḥanbal met al-Shāfiʿī in Baghdād in 195 A.H. and 198 A.H. According to Shāfiʿī sources he was deeply impressed with him and tried to convince Isḥāq Ibn Rāhwayh (d. 238) his colleague and travel companion, to join al-Shāfiʿī's class.[62] The exchange between Ibn Ḥanbal and Ibn Rāhwayh offers insights into the concerns and status of all three scholars. When Ibn Ḥanbal suggested to Ibn Rāhwayh that he study with al-Shāfiʿī, Ibn Rāhwayh replied: 'What will I do with him, his age is close to our age. Have you left Ibn 'Uyayna al-Maqburiyya?'[63] Ibn Rāhwayh's reluctance reflects two interesting points. First, at the time al-Shāfiʿī did not enjoy a high standing among students of traditions. He was not an established teacher, and certainly not a member of the top echelon of Traditionists, who attracted students by the mere mention of their name. In Ibn Rāhwayh's view, it was surprising that Ibn Ḥanbal preferred to spend time with al-Shāfiʿī and not with the established Ibn 'Uyayna.

The second interesting aspect of Ibn Rāhwayh's answer is the age factor. Ibn Rāhwayh states explicitly that he refuses to consider entering al-Shāfiʿī's class because the age difference between the two was too small. In his bewilderment, he expressed one of the fundamental values of this milieu – studying with the elderly. In 195 A.H., al-Shāfiʿī was forty-five years old while Ibn Ḥanbal and Ibn Rāhwayh were approximately thirty. Ibn Rāhwayh considered a scholar fifteen years his senior as being too close to him in age, and was reluctant to enter a teacher-student relationship with such a person. Ibn Rāhwayh's remark demonstrates that many Traditionists, not just Ibn Ḥanbal, considered the scholar's age when choosing their teachers. Furthermore, it illustrates that Ibn Ḥanbal had matured and grown out of the need to have elderly teachers while at least one of his close colleagues had not. By the age of thirty, Ibn Ḥanbal had other concerns. In the case of al-Shāfiʿī, he was attracted to his articulate jurisprudential views.

The portrayal of Ibn Ḥanbal's and al-Shāfiʿī's relationship must be seen in the context of later Ḥanbali and Shāfiʿī competition over the eponymous founders' seniority in the Traditionist camp. The anecdotes that reveal the respect Ibn Ḥanbal felt for al-Shāfiʿī were put into circulation by later Shāfiʿīs and refer to al-Shāfiʿī's *raʾy*. They argue that although Ibn Ḥanbal was usually apprehensive about the use of *raʾy*, he is said to have preferred the use of al-Shāfiʿī's over that of Mālik b. Anas, Sufyān al-Thawrī or al-Awzāʿi.[64] His respect towards al-Shāfiʿī was probably the result of al-Shāfiʿī's ability to hold his own in arguments with the Ḥanafis. From Ibn Ḥanbal's point of view, the Ḥanafis attacked and undermined the legal foundations of the Traditionists and the Traditionists could not muster arguments in defense and this changed when al-Shāfiʿī appeared.[65] If Ibn Ḥanbal held al-Shāfiʿī in esteem, and it was not merely a retrospective attribution of future Shāfiʿīs, it was due to this ability to respond to the *ahl al-raʾy*'s challenge.

At the same time Shāfiʿī sources also write that Ibn Ḥanbal had reservations regarding al-Shāfiʿī's knowledge. For example, they ascribe to Ibn Ḥanbal the following remark: 'He gained from us what we did not gain from him.'[66] The relationship described in this quote is not that of teacher and pupil, but that of two scholars who cooperate. Furthermore, this observation hints to some sort of competition between the two of them. It is not clear whether Ibn Ḥanbal actually made this comment. It may very well be that the Ḥanbalis ascribed it to him in the course of later debates between members of both legal schools. Ibn Ḥanbal and al-Shāfiʿī were members of the same Traditionist camp and had similar jurisprudential views as well as common enemies. Their disciples, who belonged to different schools in this Traditionist camp vied for seniority over one other. This was very much a family feud: the two schools were aware that they belonged to the same camp, but tried to claim their superiority within it by ascribing seniority to their founders.

The relationship between Ibn Ḥanbal and al-Shāfiʿī is significant because of their contribution to Islamic law and because it sheds light on Ibn Ḥanbal's standing in Traditionist circles. Nearly all sources, Shāfiʿī and Ḥanbali, mention that al-Shāfiʿī relied on Ibn Ḥanbal for transmission of traditions. In al-Shāfiʿī's biography the evidence is presented as coming from Ibn Ḥanbal's son ʿAbdallāh, somewhat compromising its reliability.[67] Al-Subkī (d. 771), a Shāfiʿī who was often at odds with tradition-minded Shāfiʿīs and probably with the Ḥanbalis, did not rule out this possibility, though he did point to the limited number of times it could have happened.[68]

Al-Subkī's criticism stands alone. Most of al-Shāfiʿī's biographers do not doubt that Ibn Ḥanbal transmitted traditions to al-Shāfiʿī. Some, like Ibn Kathīr (d. 774), cite an explicit request by al-Shāfiʿī that Ibn Ḥanbal pass on to him any tradition he deemed to be true: 'If you consider a tradition to be true inform me of it and I will accept it (*adhhaba ilayhi*) whether it is from Ḥijaz, Syria, Iraq or Yemen.'[69] Ibn Kathīr emphasizes the latter part of the quote and interprets it as an attempt to combat the local chauvinism of certain lawyers (*fuqahāʾ*) who limited their use of traditions to those circulating in their own towns, ignoring others.[70] Ibn Kathīr considers the cooperation between al-Shāfiʿī and Ibn Ḥanbal as part of an effort to consolidate the status of Prophetic traditions.[71] Al-Shāfiʿī, the theoretician, and Ibn Ḥanbal, the compiler, are depicted as the champions of a trend that tried to give traditions a 'universalist' rather than a local validity.[72] Ibn Kathīr, however, is not oblivious to the personal implications of this statement. He concludes the discussion by pointing out that al-Shāfiʿī's remark enhanced Ibn Ḥanbal's reputation, spreading his name 'the world over in his youth.'[73]

Ibn Kathīr's final comment acknowledges Ibn Ḥanbal's early rise to fame and at the same time, draws attention to Ibn Ḥanbal's debt to al-Shāfiʿī. It presents al-Shāfiʿī as the mentor whose cooperation with Ibn Ḥanbal gave the younger (who was 'in his youth') the boost that won him widespread recognition. Other sources present this remark with a minor, yet crucial change. The very same request to receive transmissions from Ibn Ḥanbal is introduced with a very short confession 'you are [*antum*] more knowledgeable than me.'[74] This addition humbles al-Shāfiʿī, and to a certain extent turns their relationship around. The role reversal was completed in Ḥanbali sources, where al-Shāfiʿī is presented as Ibn Ḥanbal's student, due to the latter's greater expertise in traditions.[75]

The main difference between Ḥanbali and Shāfiʿī sources is that the Ḥanbalis emphasize the traditions that Ibn Ḥanbal transmitted to al-Shāfiʿī, while the Shāfiʿīs emphasize the *fiqh* that Ibn Ḥanbal learned from al-Shāfiʿī. It is difficult to assess the veracity of these descriptions. According to Shāfiʿī sources, al-Shāfiʿī was the senior partner and spokesman of the Traditionist camp who battled directly with their enemies Ibn Ḥanbal was willing to enter with al-Shāfiʿī into a teacher-student relationship. Perhaps to counter this the Ḥanbalis, and quite a few Shāfiʿīs, emphasized al-Shāfiʿī's debts to Ibn Ḥanbal regarding the transmission of traditions.

Rise in status

Once when Ibn Ḥanbal went to a class, he was asked: 'Ya Abū ʿAbdallāh, are you not embarrassed, until when will you run around with these youths? Ibn Ḥanbal replied: until death.'[76] If search for knowledge (*ṭalab al-ʿilm*) entails going to the classes of respected teachers, hearing, writing, and participating as a student, this alleged remark by Ibn Ḥanbal is inaccurate, since we have no evidence that Ibn Ḥanbal attended classes in his old age. If, however, it refers to a state of mind and the willingness to acquire new knowledge, it may serve as an interesting insight.

The question posed to Ibn Ḥanbal is no less interesting than his reply. It reflects a moment in which Ibn Ḥanbal had made a name for himself as a man of knowledge, but did not act the part. It was as if his behavior was one or two steps behind his fast-growing reputation. This gap between his self-view and his social standing in Traditionist circles probably appeared in the 190's A.H. It was in this decade that Ibn Ḥanbal became the discriminating pupil who developed high professional standards with regards to the teachers with whom he chose to study. Towards the end of the decade he would meet scholars like al-Shāfiʿī and consider them to be senior colleagues, rather than masters whose every word he would write down diligently.

A coincidental sequence of events that might have influenced Ibn Ḥanbal's self-view towards the end of the decade was the deaths of ʿAbd al-Raḥmān b. Mahdī (d. 198), Ibn ʿUyayna (d. 198), Yaḥyā b. Saʿīd al-Qaṭṭān (d. 198) and Wakīʿ b. al-Jarrāḥ (d. 198). This year, 198 A.H., was a difficult year in the Traditionist milieu, as four of its masters died. The four were considered by Ibn Ḥanbal and his generation to be the leading scholars of the Traditionist milieu. Their deaths must have created a vacuum of authority in Traditionist circles and this might have served as a catalyst in Ibn Ḥanbal's evolving self-view.

Before their deaths, these leading Traditionist scholars noted Ibn Ḥanbal's intellectual abilities and stated their opinions about him in public. For example, in a surprisingly frank exchange, we learn what Yaḥyā b. Sa'īd al-Qaṭṭān, thought of Ibn Ḥanbal. Ibn Ḥanbal told his son 'Abdallāh:

> I was staying with (*muqiman 'alā*) Yaḥyā b. Sa'īd al-Qaṭṭān, then I left for Wāsiṭ. Yaḥyā b. Sa'īd asked about me and they [presumably other students] said:[He] left for Wāsiṭ. He [Yaḥyā] said: What will he do in Wāsiṭ? They said: Stay with Yazīd b. Hārūn. [Yaḥyā] said: What will he do with Yazīd b. Hārūn? Abū 'Abd al-Raḥmān ['Abdallāh, Ibn Ḥanbal's son] said: Meaning, he [Ibn Ḥanbal] is more learned than him [Yazīd b. Hārūn].'[77]

Yazīd b. Hārūn was a respected authority and it is hardly surprising that Ibn Ḥanbal chose to study with him.[78] It is not clear why Yaḥyā b. Sa'īd made this uncomplimentary remark about the elderly Yazīd. Perhaps this was simply the reaction of an insulted teacher who was unhappy to learn that his prized student chose to spend some time with another teacher. Whatever his motivation, Yaḥyā b. Sa'īd chose to compare Ibn Ḥanbal to Yazīd b. Hārūn, and to depict the young Traditionist as the more learned of the two. Even if Yaḥyā b. Sa'īd's remarks exagerated Ibn Ḥanbal's abilities, the fact that he noticed Ibn Ḥanbal's departure, that it annoyed him, and that he compared a student with a teacher meant that Ibn Ḥanbal was much more than an anonymous student. Yaḥyā b. Sa'īd made his favorable opinion of Ibn Ḥanbal known in other circumstances and in a more acceptable manner when he stated that the outstanding pupils that came to him were Ibn Ḥanbal and Yaḥyā b. Ma'īn.[79]

Another indication of Ibn Ḥanbal's rise in stature was his relationship with 'Abd al-Raḥmān b. Mahdī, which evolved into an intimate apprenticeship. When they first met, in 180 A.H., Ibn Ḥanbal sat outside a mosque and wrote a few hundred of Ibn al-Mahdī's traditions. As time passed, Ibn Ḥanbal became a hand-picked pupil whose knowledge was bred in private by al-Mahdī, a leading transmitter of traditions. What is more, the relationship between master and pupil went beyond mere professional training. What started as an act of impersonal transmission of traditions evolved into a warm and supportive relationship, in which the elderly master admitted that his disciple is more knowledgeable than he in certain corpuses of traditions. He would say of Ibn Ḥanbal that he 'is the most knowledgeable in the traditions of Sufyān al-Thawrī.'[80]

The professional recognition that Ibn Ḥanbal got from teachers such as Yaḥyā b. Sa'īd al-Qaṭṭān and 'Abd al-Raḥmān b. Mahdī was complemented by the growing respect of his peers. Some time in the 190's A.H., many of the better students of traditions of Ibn Ḥanbal's generation heard of each other and gradually gravitated towards one another. They exchanged information about teachers and often set out in groups to far-away destinations in order to study with important transmitters. When Ibn Ḥanbal decided to perfom the *ḥajj* in 198 A.H., he traveled with Yaḥyā b. Ma'īn and Isḥāq b. Rāhwayh, two well-known scholars of his generation.[81] These young scholars formed a loose network whose members would become the future leadership of the Traditionist milieu. The praise and attention they received from the older generation along with their mutual acknowledgement created an informal elite of scholars.

When these young scholars won the recognition of their peers and teachers, they entered a transitional stage. A comical anecdote illustrates the difficulties they had in adapting themselves to their change in status. When Ibn Ḥanbal and Yaḥyā b. Ma'īn entered the class of the Kūfan Traditionist Abū Nu'aym al-Faḍl b. Dukayn (d. 219), the teacher showed his respect to the two promising students and invited them to sit next to him on the bench, Ibn Ḥanbal on his right-hand side, Yaḥyā b. Ma'īn on his left.[82] Their colleague, Aḥmad b. Manṣūr, sat on the ground. After the class began, Yaḥyā b. Ma'īn read a sequence of traditions that Abū Nu'aym had transmitted. In order to check Abū Nu'aym's integrity he slipped into this sequence of traditions, a tradition that Abū Nu'aym did not transmit. After each of the inserted traditions was recited to Abū Nu'aym, he denied having transmitted that specific tradition. Eventually Abū Nu'aym realized that Yaḥyā was testing him. He became furious and kicked him off of the bench.

This amusing incident indicates that when Ibn Ḥanbal and Yaḥyā b. Ma'īn were in their mid-thirties they were widely recognized authorities. At the same time, Yaḥyā b. Ma'īn's behavior suggests that he had not yet internalized the etiquette and self-view of a mature scholar. Though the tone and contents of this anecdote differ from the description of Ibn Ḥanbal running around to classes, the two stories do convey the same problem of two young and successful scholars who were going through a phase of adjustment.

This incident took place some time after Ibn Ḥanbal came back from Yemen, where he had studied with 'Abd al-Razzāq. In these years, the latter half of the 190's A.H., there were a number of indications that Ibn Ḥanbal's status was getting close to that of a teacher and legal authority.

Muhannā b. Yaḥyā al-Shāmī pointed to the trip to ʿAbd al-Razzāq as the period in which he met Ibn Ḥanbal and became his disciple.[83] Some time in the year 198 a group of Traditionists (*aṣḥāb al-ḥadīth*) approached Ibn Ḥanbal and asked him to instruct them in law (*fiqh*) and traditions and to pass judgements regarding the pilgrimage (*manāsik*).[84]

The biographic evidence at our disposal indicates that when he was in his mid-twenties Ibn Ḥanbal's professional and ideological profile took shape. Approximately a decade later, when he was in his mid-thirties, his standing in Traditionsit circles became solidified. Ten years later, his first students approached him.

CHAPTER THREE

Private Acts and Social Meaning

Most of the information in Ibn Ḥanbal's biographies is characterized by two seemingly contradictory qualities: veracity and a high level of manipulation. Chapters 1 and 2 were based on the assumption that the reports furnished by Ibn Ḥanbal's biographers were reliable. This chapter will expose the image that the authors of his biographies tried to construct. Seen from this perspective, the biographies reveal values and an ethical outlook rather than information that purports to be exact. Though the details it mentions may be true, it is not their truthfulness that matters, but the authors' moral perceptions and ideas about patterns of proper behavior.

The moral image that Ibn Ḥanbal's biographies convey is that of a mild ascetic. It was situated in the middle of a spectrum of ethical visions, between ṣūfism and court culture, and represented the predominant ethical vision of the Traditionist milieu. Like other ethical visions, this was an amalgamation of moral outlook and principles of etiquette. Mild asceticism was implemented in the most mundane matters of life. Three aspects of Ibn Ḥanbal's life – clothes, home and eating habits – illustrate the manifestations of mild asceticism.

Ibn Ḥanbal's wardrobe introduces us to the intricacies of mild asceticism. Unlike the ṣūfīs, Ibn Ḥanbal was not one prone to disciplining his body by exposing it to the elements. In the winter he kept himself adequately warm by covering himself with three layers of gowns (*qamīṣayn wa-jubba*).[1] At times he put on a thick fur and a gown. When the cold became more severe, he wore a fur over a gown, a turban (*'imāma*) over head gear (*qalansuwa*) and a thick dress (*kisā' thaqīlan*).[2] When he was asked '[what is with] all these clothes? he [Ibn Ḥanbal] laughed and replied: Oh Abū 'Imrān I am soft regarding the cold (*anā raqīq fī al-bard*).'[3] Ibn Ḥanbal seems quite at ease when discussing his habit of protecting himself from the cold, and apparently had no qualms about his dressing habits.

Unlike some ascetics who wore the same, usually uncomfortable, garments throughout the year, Ibn Ḥanbal adapted his clothing to the weather. As the seasons changed so did the number of layers that he wore. Whereas in winter he wore many layers and saw to it that he would be adequately warm, in the summer he would put on one or two layers, depending on the temperature. In general he wore a gown with pants and a loose outer garment. However, at times, probably when the climate became exceedingly hot, he did not wear more than the gown and the outer garment (*ridā'*).[4]

Ibn Ḥanbal's tendency to use regular garments and to avoid coarse and unpleasant ones, as well as his habit of adjusting his clothing to the weather, indicate that he did not abide by the codes and signs of the extreme ascetic milieu, whose members did all they could to afflict physical discomfort upon themselves.

On the other hand, he did not keep up with the fashion of genteel society. The textiles from which his garments were sewn were not the 'soft gowns (*al-ghalā'il al-riqaq*)' that *ẓurafā'* (possessors of elegance) etiquette demanded.[5] Ibn Ḥanbal's clothes were described by al-Maymūnī (d. 274), one of his closest disciples, as devoid of 'delicacy (*riqqa*)' or 'roughness (*ghilaẓ*).'[6] Al-Maymūnī's use of terms which evoke the well-known characteristics of both courtly garments and ṣūfī modes of dress, was probably intended to situate Ibn Ḥanbal between the ascetics and the courtiers.

Al-Maymūnī made a few more observations about Ibn Ḥanbal's wardrobe and possessions. He estimated the value of Ibn Ḥanbal's blankets (*milḥafathu*) at fifteen *dirhams* and the value of his clothes at one *dinar*.[7] He opened this assessment with the somewhat obscure observation that 'the clothing (*thiyāb*) of Aḥmad b. Ḥanbal are between clothing (*bayn al-thawbayn*).'[8] This probably meant that his clothing had an intermediate value. In other words they did not qualify as the expensive and delicate clothes of the *ẓurafā'*, nor the inexpensive and uncomfortable rags that the more extreme ascetics wore.

Much like his approach to clothing, Ibn Ḥanbal's attitude towards his house reflects a middle-of-the-road approach that is distinctly different from that of the ascetics and that of the *ẓurafā'*. To begin with, Ibn Ḥanbal owned a house. In and of itself, this places him outside the circles of extreme ascetics who were often, by choice or fate, dispossessed vagabonds. Being the inheritor of property, and having lived off its rent, Ibn Ḥanbal could not be considered as a practitioner of *tawakkul*, 'trust in God,' which meant giving up any source of livelihood and trusting that God would supply for one's needs.[9]

On the other hand, Ibn Ḥanbal's house was described as austere. Al-Maymūnī considered Ibn Ḥanbal's house as 'narrow and small (*ḍayyiqan saghīran*).'[10] 'Alī b. al-Madīnī likened Ibn Ḥanbal's home to that of Suwayd b. Ghafla, a Successor who was considered 'one of the ascetics in worldly matters.'[11]

These observations rely, primarily, on the run-down state of Ibn Ḥanbal's house. Ibn Ḥanbal's reluctance to invest in the maintenance of his house comes across in one of his remarks to Ṣāliḥ, in which he scolded him because he changed the roof of his home. In a typically Traditionist manner, he conveyed his discomfort by telling Ṣāliḥ a tradition about al-Aḥnaf b. Qays who refused to enter his own house after his family had changed its roof.[12] If this was Ibn Ḥanbal's attitude towards the maintenance of his own house, it should not surprise us that visitors were struck by its poor condition and the shabbiness of his mats and curtains.

Ibn Ḥanbal's eating habits are another personal issue that his biographers address. This is only natural, since food and its consumption are pivotal issues in all faiths. For the most part, ascetics of different religions considered nourishment of the body a potential threat to spiritual progress.[13] Tor Andrae, a student of Islamic and Christian asceticism, describes it in the following manner: 'To pamper and fatten the flesh is the death of the spirit. A spiritual human being (*pneumatikos*) ought ideally to renounce all earthly food.'[14] Both Islam and Judaism instituted ritual fasts. In Islam a believer is expected to fast during Ramaḍān, however, many believers add to that voluntary fasts called *taṭawwu'*.

Along with fasts, many ascetics maintained diets that were made up of little more than the bare minimum required to keep them alive. Andrae comments on this form of devotion: 'To eat only bread and salt was the strict discipline of fasting followed by the monks. On this diet many Muslim ascetics whom we know by name, lived for years ... Many Sufis were also in this respect faithful followers of their precursors among the ascetics of the early period. Fasting retained its place among the works of piety, but the motivation for it was subject to marked changes and showed strikingly personal variations.'[15]

Andrae's observation about 'personal variations' is a convenient springboard for the study of Ibn Ḥanbal's eating habits. Taking laws of purity and Ramaḍān as a point of departure, every pious Muslim could work out his own regimen and Ibn Ḥanbal was no exception. His habits of food consumption included at least one typically ascetic practice and the glaring omission of another, voluntary fasts. None of the chapters on his ascetic practices, piety and moral behavior, mentions any self-imposed fasting.[16] While many ṣūfīs 'developed fasting into a veritable art,'[17] Ibn Ḥanbal seems to have been satisfied with the obligatory injunctions of Islamic ritual.

On some occasions, however, Ibn Ḥanbal's diet took on the form of the self-deprivation that we would expect from an ascetic. 'At times' his son Ṣāliḥ commented, 'I saw my father take a slice [of bread] (*kisar*) and shake the dust of it and then he would place it in a plate, sprinkle on it water until it softened up, then he would eat it with salt.'[18] Bread, especially stale slices that need to be softened with water in order to become edible, and salt definitely deserve to be considered an ascetic diet. We should, however, bear in mind that Ibn Ḥanbal's diet was not always as minimal as bread and salt. Sometimes it included lentils, certain fruits and occasionally even meat.[19]

Ibn Ḥanbal's habits of food consumption reflect a very mild ascetic inclination. They do not add up to the hard-core asceticism of certain ṣūfīs that tormented their bodies. If we compare his regimen to that of 'Abdallāh al-Tustarī, who is said to have gone without food seventy days,[20] or other ṣūfīs of that ilk, we realize that his idea of asceticism was quite different. On the other hand, it is clear that Ibn Ḥanbal was even further away from courtly culture. He ate types of food that the courtiers looked down upon, such as watermelons (*baṭīkha*),[21] and seems to have adhered to a completely different etiquette of food consumption. His restrained food consumption, and his avoidance of excessive fasting, place him somewhere on the fringes of the ascetic milieu.

Although Ibn Ḥanbal's vision of piety brought him close to asceticism, he was not a full- fledged ascetic. While extreme ascetics tried to destroy their appetites by inflicting pain and discomfort on their bodies, Ibn Ḥanbal never went that far. He took no part in self-mortification, which served as a technique of spiritual ascent, as in Shaqīq al-Balkhī's (d. 194) 'alchemy of hunger.'[22] Thus, a fine line separated Ibn Ḥanbal from a whole group of more extreme ascetics. Ibn Ḥanbal conducted his worldly affairs in a manner aimed at controlling his appetites, but he did nothing to annihilate them. The extreme ascetics aspired to something different from mere control. They devised ways to destroy bodily appetites, to shatter their egos and achieve the ultimate spiritual goal: unity with Allah. Whereas Ibn Ḥanbal came to terms with his physical appetites and saw to it that they would be partly satisfied, the hard-core ascetics developed physical techniques that stunned and stifled their material needs. Where Ibn Ḥanbal sought control, they sought destruction.[23]

Ibn Ḥanbal had little use for the harsh physical and spiritual exercises that ascetics like Shaqīq al-Balkhī and al-Tustarī devised. His goals were different, and his techniques in line with them. His form of asceticism was aimed at abiding to the spirit of the law in the strictest manner; their goal was the quashing of bodily appetites, the annihilation of the ego and unity with Allah. For Ibn Ḥanbal asceticism was an ethical quest, for Shaqīq and al-Tustarī it was a spiritual journey.[24]

Faqr - The practice and ideology of poverty

'David (PBUH) did not eat except what his hands produced. I said to Abī 'Abdallāh: 'Can I transmit this on your authority?' He confirmed it.'[25] According to Ibn Ḥanbal, self-sustenance was the most appropriate form of acquiring money. In his reference to David, as well as in other anecdotes that open his *Kitāb al-Wara'* [Book of Piety], Ibn Ḥanbal makes his view quite clear that earning money by ones own work was at the top of the moral ladder.[26] One step below was revenue obtained from properties. 'Trade is preferred by me to the revenue of Baghdād,'[27] he said, meaning income obtained by work (trade) is morally superior to money obtained through rent.

Ibn al-Jawzī states that Ibn Ḥanbal inherited properties and was unhappy when he rented them out. However, he adds that Ibn Ḥanbal did so in order to avoid asking for financial help.[28] This was probably because he believed that it was better to rent out property than to rely on the presents and support offered by patrons and admirers. Though many believers accepted presents and support without pangs of guilt, Ibn Ḥanbal and like-minded mild ascetics opposed this practice. It is interesting to note that in contrast to the mild ascetics, the courtiers and some of the extreme ascetics were happy to accept other people's money. The courtiers were often pampered by patrons while some of the extreme ascetics lived off of charity.

Ibn Ḥanbal's views on the acquisition of livelihood are in line with his generally mild ascetic attitude. He did not reject efforts to obtain money. On the contrary, according to Ibn Ḥanbal it was essential to have sources of income. They ought to be modest, since work and earning money should not be used to enrich an individual, but merely to keep him and his family alive. What is more, to reject one's sources of income, a mode of behavior found among some of the extreme ascetics, meant to beg and be dependent on other individuals. This was something that Ibn Ḥanbal found reprehensible.

Long before he became a renowned scholar, courted by friends and political opportunists, Ibn Ḥanbal insisted on avoiding other people's money. The following anecdote illustrates this tendency: 'My father said: 'If I had fifty *dirhams* I would have gone to Jarīr b. 'Abd al-Ḥamīd to Rayy, [to whom] a group of our friends (*aṣḥābunā*) journeyed, but my leave was not possible bacause I did not have it [fifty *dirhams*].'[29] This report is exceptional because it does not mention an offer to help him. Most of the stories that relate something about Ibn Ḥanbal's financial difficulties include references to help that he was offered and refused. It should not surprise us that Ibn Ḥanbal was not offered any help, since the event took place long before he made a name for himself. The most important insight that can be gained from this episode is Ibn Ḥanbal's order of priorities – he preferred to miss a chance to meet an important Traditionist rather than compromise his integrity and ask for loans or presents.

The lowest one could stoop, according to this outlook, was to accept gifts. Starting with the days he searched for knowledge and was offered financial support by Traditionists, to the post-*miḥna* era when he was courted by the caliph, Ibn Ḥanbal constantly had to contend with the financial bait that was dangled before him. Friends and colleagues, anonymous admirers and manipulative politicians, all tried to help him in difficult moments or lure him into their networks of patronage. All were rejected.

One of the first indications of Ibn Ḥanbal's attempts to maintain his financial independence is from 198 A.H., the year he went to Yemen to study with 'Abd al-Razzāk. One of his colleagues, Isḥāq b. Rāhwayh, recounts: 'When Ibn Ḥanbal went to 'Abd al-Razzāk his revenue (*al-nafaqa*) ceased, and he rented himself out to some camel drivers until he came to Ṣanā'a, and his friends offered him help (*al-muwāsā*) but he did not accept anything from anyone.'[30] When he arrived in Yemen, he was told by 'Abd al-Razzāk that it was not a land conducive to trade,[31] which apparently referred to Ibn Ḥanbal's plans for making a living. He went on and offered to help him financially, but Ibn Ḥanbal replied that he was well off.

At that time, when Ibn Ḥanbal was thirty-four, he was a promising young scholar of traditions. Twenty years would pass before he would become a leading figure in the Traditionist milieu. Though the sums of money he was offered as a student were probably lower than the future donations, Ibn Ḥanbal demonstrated the same unbending refusal to improve his dire financial situation by accepting help.

In contrast to many ṣūfis, who entered upon endless spirals of self-criticism because of their fear of taking pride in their ascetic achievements, Ibn Ḥanbal did not shy away from discussing his moral achievements and comparing himself to other Traditionists.[32] For example, he pointed out to 'Abdallāh, his second son and most learned pupil, that Yaḥyā b. Ma'īn and Muslim al-Mustamlī took the money that Yazīd b. Hārūn (d. 206) offered them.[33] In light of Ibn Ḥanbal's conduct, it is clear that he was describing them as being morally deficient while he himself was not.

In the last decades of his life, particularly after what many considered his heroic resistance during the *miḥna*, Ibn Ḥanbal attracted the attention of believers from far and wide, especially from Khurāsān. Because of his fame and stature, people inquired into various aspects of his life, including his financial situation. Ṣāliḥ tells of one case that Ibn Ḥanbal's financial problems motivated someone to come to his help. This was a few years after Ibn Ḥanbal was released from jail, in the days of al-Wāthiq. A letter was sent to him, which he placed under a worn-out piece of wool (*labad*) on which he usually sat. While he was out of the house, his son Ṣāliḥ came in, found the letter and read it: 'I have heard O Abū 'Abdallāh that you are in [financial] distress (*al-ḍīq*), that you are in debt, and I sent you four thousand *dirham* by the hands of *fulān* to settle your debt, and bring comfort to your family, and this is not *ṣadaqa* nor *zakāt*, but only something I have inherited from my father.'[34] Ṣāliḥ laid down the letter, and when his father returned, asked him about it, making Ibn Ḥanbal blush. After he answered Ṣāliḥ's question, Ibn Ḥanbal dictated a reply to the sender, which Ṣāliḥ wrote: 'Your letter has arrived to me, and we are well off. As for the debt it is to a man who does not burden us [regarding its settlement], and as for our family they are in the grace of Allah, praise be to Allah.'[35] The story is followed by a number of similar anecdotes.[36]

The acceptance of unearned money was not solely Ibn Ḥanbal's problem. Traditionists in general had to contend with the moral implications of financial aid. Ibn Ḥanbal was highly suspicious of the systems of financial patronage and this suspicion was well placed because it was known that some of these funds came from the authorities. Isḥāq b. Mūsā al-Ansārī (d. 244) reports that 'al-Ma'mūn handed me money so as to distribute among the Traditionists.'[37] The Traditionist's willingness to go along with the authorities and to enjoy their material support is mentioned in the second part of al-Ansārī's report: 'There was not one from among them [Traditionists] who did not take it [al-Ma'mūn's financial support] except for Ibn Ḥanbal who declined.'[38]

Traditionist cooperation with the authorities is also revealed in one of al-Ma'mūn's *miḥna* letters.[39] As the caliph goes into a tirade, he threatens a number of scholars that he will stop giving them financial support, whether through donations or employment. This demonstrates that Ibn Ḥanbal's attempts to avoid financial aid were not typical of the Traditionist milieu.

Another example of Traditionist cooperation with the authorities is the acceptance of the position of *qāḍī*. As Ibn Ḥanbal won a name for himself as a scholar, he was approached by none other than al-Shāfiʿī, and offered the position of *qāḍī* in Yemen.[40] Perhaps al-Shāfiʿī was in the position to make such an offer because he had served there a few years earlier. Al-Shāfiʿī's offer reveals how the authorities cast their net of patronage over upcoming scholars. Judging by al-Shāfiʿī's case, the authorities did succeed in tempting some of the outstanding minds of the scholarly community. The offer outraged Ibn Ḥanbal, who rebuked his teacher and embarrassed him for raising such a possibility.

The seductive embrace of the authorities became unbearable during the reign of al-Mutawakkil. After he altered the Muʿtazili-oriented credo concerning the createdness of the Qur'an to that of the Traditionists, al-Mutawakkil did all he could to gain the support and legitimacy of the Traditionists. He courted Ibn Ḥanbal aggressively, sent him large sums of money, invited him to the court, and asked for his advice on various matters ranging from theology to the appointment of *qāḍīs*. Ibn Ḥanbal perceived these acts of generosity as moral challenges. He compared al-Mutawakkil's actions to al-Ma'mūn's, naming the former worldly inquisition and the latter an inquisition of faith.[41]

Ibn Ḥanbal's attitude towards money and properties resembled his attitude towards food and clothing, i.e. measured self-sustenance. He embraced a middle-of-the-road approach, which identified the deficiencies found in total denial of sources of income and at the same time, the moral problems that stem from incessant acquisition. The underlying assumption of Ibn Ḥanbal's mild asceticism was that material comfort jeopardized moral uprightness. This led him and many other Traditionists to limit their use of material goods, but not to the extent of assaulting their bodily senses, as the extreme ascetics did. Mild ascetics would not chase money; they would not, however, give up their sources of income.

Mild asceticism and social criticism

Ibn Ḥanbal was just one link in a chain of mild ascetics who served as the role models of the Traditionist milieu. He was preceded by well-known figures such as 'Abdallāh b. al-Mubārak (d. 181) and Fuḍayl b. 'Iyāḍ (d. 187).[42] It is only when we think of these two pious men in terms of role models that we can explain why Ibn Ḥanbal took pains to tell his son Ṣāliḥ that he had tried to study with them, but they had died before he could meet them. Ibn Ḥanbal could not claim to have gained knowledge from them, therefore his remarks about making an effort to meet these two renowned Traditionists had more to do with their reputation as pious role models than with their erudition. Ibn Ḥanbal's reference to 'Abdallāh b. al-Mubārak and Fuḍayl b. 'Iyāḍ indicates the sort of religious orientation and way of life that he wanted to adopt, and the moral milieu to which he wanted to belong. Who were Fuḍayl b. 'Iyāḍ and 'Abdallāh b. al-Mubārak, and what did Ibn Ḥanbal think he shared with them? Both were considered excellent scholars of traditions, both demonstrated a high level of involvement in communal matters, and both used their moral status as a platform from which to criticize their contemporaries.[43]

Ibn Ḥanbal's attempts to create an affinity between him and these revered Traditionists, was part of an effort to situate himself in a line of ascetics that constituted a particular ideological current within the Traditionist milieu. These scholars, who were highly admired for their learning, emphasized another aspect of Islamic religiosity, the believer's actions. They were respected for this combination of knowledge and upright conduct. Their moral reputations paved the way to positions of social power, and they were often asked to give the authorities advice, a demand which they found burdensome and even immoral.

Mild and extreme asceticism differed from each other on a number of issues. One was the social discourse that they generated and the modes of social criticism they articulated.[44] Though both forms of asceticism viewed worldly activities with suspicion, they expressed their apprehensions in different ways. Extreme asceticism completely rejected worldly appetites and institutions. The most extreme of them broke away from social institutions such as the family, made no effort to earn a living and exhausted themselves in the course of oppressing their appetites. The sort of social criticism that they elaborated was a sweeping rejection of physical appetites and society. By contrast, mild asceticism opted for measured cooperation with society and a disciplined *modus vivendi* with their appetites. As a result, their criticism was not a sweeping rejection but a more limited struggle with their appetites and a more specific attack on individuals who diverged from the sort of moral norms the mild ascetics espoused.

The austere practices of mild asceticism were not just personal efforts to adhere to the highest ethical standards. Such actions were also social statements. To begin with, these practices bolstered the prestige of the mild ascetic. The social standing of these ascetics within the Traditionist milieu derived from their ability to live up to ethical standards that most believers admired but could not achieve. A touching example of the gap between the behavioral ideals and the constraints of reality is the story about Ṣāliḥ's acceptance of the position of *qāḍī*. It is told that when Ṣāliḥ read the nomination letter from the caliph, which stated that he should serve as a *qāḍī*, he began to weep. After the sheikhs tried to calm him down, he asked: 'Do you know what brings me to tears? I remembered my father, if he would have seen me in this state he would have gone into mourning (*kāna 'alayhi al-sawād*).'[45]

It was difficult to uphold the kind of moral standards that Ibn Ḥanbal expected. His eldest son could not live up to them and was filled with shame and remorse when he failed to do so. In the course of his life, Ṣāliḥ had a number of arguments with his father. He was always on the defensive, justifying his behavior by turning to the heavy economic burden that he carried due to his large family. His apologetic tone indicated that he was aware that he had chosen the morally inferior path. It is also likely that Ṣāliḥ's reactions to Ibn Ḥanbal were intensified by their father-son relationship. However, Ṣāliḥ's reactions do reflect the sense of discomfort that many Muslims must have felt when they came across illustrious models of mild asceticism.

Ibn Ḥanbal was a pressing and constant presence in his circle of supporters and family. He did not hide in a secluded corner, divorcing himself from society. He used his moral stature to criticize the behavior of colleagues, family members and political figures, who did not conform to the etiquette and moral standards of mild asceticism. He often took aim at his sons, Ṣāliḥ and 'Abdallāh, making it clear that he was unhappy with their lifestyles. When attending a circumcision ceremony of a student of a colleague, he walked out, putting the host to shame, because he saw a silver vessel in the house.[46] He felt sure enough of himself to refuse al-Shāfi'ī's offer that he serve as *qāḍī* in Yemen, thus insulting al-Shāfi'ī.[47]

The unpleasant confrontations between Ibn Ḥanbal and his most intimate relatives, his sons and uncle, as well as his criticism of teachers and colleagues, indicate that he saw himself as a moral paragon who was in a position to criticize those in his immediate environment. This behavior began vis-a-vis his family and later characterized his general attitude towards the denizens of Baghdād and the rulers of the 'Abbāsid empire. It reappeared in Ibn Ḥanbal's discussions with his disciples about *al-amr bi-'l-ma'rūf wa al-nahy al-munkar* (embracing the good and prohibiting the evil), when he encouraged them to take a firm, at times physical, stand against such moral offenders as chess players, wine drinkers and musicians.[48] Such criticism reflects an exceptional level of self-righteousness and an intense involvement with the society that surrounded him.

At certain moments of his life, Ibn Ḥanbal lost the ability to convey his disapproval directly. When this happened he used self-denial to convey criticism. The following story illustrates how Ibn Ḥanbal's refusal to eat when he was hungry was actually another opportunity for him to criticize Ṣāliḥ. Sometime after the fight that Ibn Ḥanbal had with his children over the issue of accepting the caliph's presents he got into a difficult financial situation and he and his household went without food for three days. At that point he borrowed some flour from a friend. The flour was processed and baked, and when the bread was placed in Ibn Ḥanbal's hands he asked: "How did you do it? [How] did you bake it so quickly?' He was told: The oven in Ṣāliḥ's – his son – house was heated and we baked it with haste. He [Ibn Ḥanbal] said: 'Remove it', and he did not eat.'[49]

According to this anecdote, Ibn Ḥanbal did not ask that his son give him food. The flour was borrowed from a friend and the only help given by Ṣāliḥ's household was the use of his oven. The mere act of turning to an outsider, someone not part of the family, for material help is in itself an insult that signifies Ibn Ḥanbal's opinion of Ṣāliḥ's moral standards and conduct. By denying himself and his household food when his son next door had food in his house, implied that Ṣāliḥ's household did not meet Ibn Ḥanbal's moral demands. Going to a friend, who was not a member of the family, made Ibn Ḥanbal's criticism public. If it was not clear how unhappy Ibn Ḥanbal was with his son until this moment, now the whole of Ibn Ḥanbal's milieu would know that Ibn Ḥanbal was unwilling to touch his son's food even when he was famished. Ibn Ḥanbal's actions, however, went one step beyond this. Not only did he not agree to eat his son's food, supposedly because it was bought with money that belonged to the caliph, he refused any gesture of help. Ibn Ḥanbal's rejection of the bread that was baked in his son's oven was not merely an act of caution or of self-denial. It was an attempt to put his son to shame. After losing control over his children, Ibn Ḥanbal criticized them publicly by refusing their help.

The use of self-deprivation as a means of shaming and criticizing others has been identified in other eras and cultures. Social segments that were blocked off from ordinary channels of power often utilized it. In C. Bynum's discussion of 'food as control of circumstances,' she describes how women, who were deprived of power within the family, used 'food practices' as 'effective ways of shaping their lives, of rejecting roles they did not desire, of criticizing and redirecting the values of husbands and parents.'[50] Similarly, after being stripped of his power and authority within the family, Ibn Ḥanbal resorted to this type of self-denial, which symbolized the severing of domestic ties with his children, in order to convey to them his criticism. After being humiliated by their disobedience, all he could do was to shame them by insinuating that they were not even worthy of feeding him.

Another instance in which Ibn Ḥanbal expressed his displeasure and criticism through self-denial was during his visit to the caliph's palace. Norms of courtly hospitality prescribed luxurious lodgings, furniture and dining. Ibn Ḥanbal did not want to go to Sāmarrā' and meet the caliph, but he was not in the position to refuse the caliph's invitation. As a result, when he arrived at the palace, and refused the courtly luxuries that were put at his disposal, he sent the caliph a message that expressed criticism of the caliph's lifestyle and the purity of his money. This was an indirect and subtle form of criticism. As a matter of fact, Ibn Ḥanbal's messages were so subtle that the caliph did not understand them. It took the caliph's mother and advisors to suggest that perhaps Ibn Ḥanbal should be sent home. Notwithstanding al-Mutawakkil's lack of sensitivity, we can observe in Ibn Ḥanbal's sojourn in the court the same type of interaction as he had with his family. While being in an helpless situation and deprived of any leverage, Ibn Ḥanbal used himself, as a participant in a certain social exchange, to send a moral condemnation. In an act of self-denial he broke the norm of hospitality and in so doing expressed his criticism of his social superior.

PART II

The Formation of the Ḥanbali School

Introduction

One of the central theses of this study is that the Ḥanbalis were not merely a group of lawyers whose sole preoccupation was legal doctrine, but rather members of a social movement that maintained distinct moral and theological positions. Therefore, writing the history of Ḥanbalism entails taking into account a variety of factors, including social and moral ideals, theological articles of faith, social and political clashes and networks of personal relations. This section deals with some of the central factors, both social and intellectual, that influenced the formation of the Ḥanbali *madhhab*.

Chapter 4 examines the Ḥanbali network. Ḥanbali sources mention some 500 disciples of Ibn Ḥanbal during his lifetime, though the level of their commitment varied. Most of these students probably respected Ibn Ḥanbal and had some sort of interaction with him, but did not necessarily share all of his convictions and cannot be considered fully-fledged disciples. This study differentiates between two types of groups: On the one hand, the peripheral groups such as *qāḍīs*, *ṣūfīs*, and independent scholars, and, on the other, the committed disciples, who were close to Ibn Ḥanbal and did much to transmit his legacy to the next generation. One of the most interesting observations to come out of this investigation is the importance of emotions and ideological affinity as bonds that brought disciples to Ibn Ḥanbal and as criteria that determined their standing in the Ḥanbali circle.

Chapter 5 presents Ibn Ḥanbal's views on piety and asceticism in a broader historical context. It continues the investigation that begins in chapter 3, which looked at how Ibn Ḥanbal's biographers used his reputed asceticism to promote his religious prestige, and continues in chapter 4, which inquired into the impact of mild asceticism on relations between Ibn Ḥanbal and his disciples. According to Ibn Ḥanbal, piety and ascetic sensibilities were central axes of human history. They are important criteria that have differentiated among individuals throughout history. The Ḥanbalis identified with this historic moral elite and sought ways to confront the rest of society over moral issues. This chapter argues that the intermittent clashes over moral conduct with people surrounding them contributed to Ḥanbali group solidarity.

Chapter 6 looks into Ḥanbali legal thought and presents a detailed study of a number of legal issues that lead to the observation made by several historians of Islamic law: Ibn Ḥanbal did not reject the use of *qiyās*, but he did try to limit its use. This notion leads to an historiographic difficulty. How can we explain the foundation of a Ḥanbali *madhhab* if it did not differ from other Traditionists in its jurisprudential outlook? The answer offered in the present study is that we need to search in other intellectual spheres and to take account of historical circumstances.

In the Introduction I argued that *madhāhib* go through two stages of development. The first, formation of a circle and the second, its transformation into a *madhhab*. This section deals with the first stage from several angles. However, these factors, the Ḥanbali network, moral outlook and legal doctrine cannot explain the transformation of the circle into a *madhhab*. The conditions that led to the crystallization of a unique Ḥanbali self-view, and the creation of a separate *madhhab* must be sought, I believe, in the realm of the politics of theology.

CHAPTER FOUR

Bonds of Friendship and Learning

Uns, friends and early adherents

Ibn Ḥanbal was only thirty-four when Muhannā b. Yaḥyā al-Shāmī took to him as his teacher. They met in 198 A.H., when both journeyed across the Arabian desert to study with 'Abd al-Razzāq in Yemen. It was rare for an aspiring collector of traditions to consider one of his fellow students to be his teacher. Muhannā b. Yaḥyā al-Shāmī, a man of Syrian origin, would remain Ibn Ḥanbal's life-long adherent, and during the next forty-three years would become one of the foremost experts regarding Ibn Ḥanbal's legal decisions.[1]

Seven years would pass before another student of traditions and jurisprudence, the twenty-four-year-old 'Abd al-Malik b. 'Abd al-Ḥamīd al-Maymūnī, would testify that he considered himself to be Ibn Ḥanbal's pupil.[2] Like Muhannā al-Shāmī, al-Maymūnī was a Syrian. In comparison to the other early disciples, al-Maymūnī's standing was unique both among the Ḥanbalis and outside their circle. His superior status outside the Ḥanbali circle is indicated by the fact that he was the only one of Ibn Ḥanbal's early disciples to merit an entry in Ibn Ḥajar al-'Asqalānī's (d. 852) compendium of Traditionists, the *Tahdhīb*. His exceptional standing among the Ḥanbalis is described by Abū Bakr al-Khallāl, the earliest historian of the Ḥanbali school: 'He [Ibn Ḥanbal] did with him [al-Maymūnī] what he [Ibn Ḥanbal] did not do with anyone else.'[3] Their special activities were probably related to the answering of *masā'il*. This somewhat vague description gives the reader the sense that al-Maymūnī enjoyed a singular position within the Ḥanbali circle.

The intimacy of Ibn Ḥanbal and al-Maymūnī's relationship went beyond intellectual exchange. It was a warm and paternal one in which

Ibn Ḥanbal expressed great concern for the young man's livelihood, urging him to improve his living conditions (*wa-yaḥuththuhu 'alā iṣlāḥ ma'īshatihi*).[4] A comment of this sort, coming from a mild ascetic like Ibn Ḥanbal, makes one wonder what sort of life al-Maymūnī led.[5] In view of the nature and duration of their relationship, it is hardly surprising that Abū Bakr al-Khallāl referred to al-Maymūnī as 'the *imām* among the companions of Aḥmad' – bestowing upon him a position of leadership among the Ḥanbalis.

Muhannā and al-Maymūnī were privileged students who were allowed to question their teacher endlessly, even to the point of irritating him.[6] The intimacy that grew out of their relations with their teacher reveals a recurring feature among Ibn Ḥanbal's circle of disciples – a propensity to mix intellectual ties and admiration with friendship.

Nonetheless, Ibn Ḥanbal did not become a close friend with every early disciple who joined his circle. It does not seem that he had similar relations with three other early disciples, 'Abbās b. Muḥammad b. Mūsā, al-Faḍl b. Ziyād and Qāsim b. Muḥammad.[7] They probably won his respect, but there is no indication that Ibn Ḥanbal had special regard for any of the three. Of their geographical background we know that two were Baghdādis and the third was from Marw, the town from which Ibn Ḥanbal's father immigrated.

The two outstanding early disciples, al-Maymūnī and Muhannā al-Shāmī, were not Khurāsāni Baghdādis, while the three lesser-known ones shared some kind of geographic features with Ibn Ḥanbal. This suggests that geography cannot be considered the sole mobilizing force in the Ḥanbali circle, and in addition, that geographical background did not determine the status of Ibn Ḥanbal's adherents.[8]

Although Ibn Ḥanbal comes across as a harsh and demanding father as well as a detached and rigid husband, as a teacher he appears somewhat more relaxed. He is even described as smiling in the company of Abū Bakr al-Marwadhī (d. 275) and Ibrāhīm b. Isḥāq (d. 283).[9] Both were close friends of his, and the references to them in the *Ṭabaqāt al-Ḥanābila* provide a glimpse at Ibn Ḥanbal's emotions and habits of socializing. It was said of Abū Bakr al-Marwadhī that 'our *imām* [Ibn Ḥanbal] enjoyed his company (*ya'nas bihi*),'[10] and of Ibrāhīm b. Isḥāq, that Ibn Ḥanbal ate at his house.[11]

Another close friend of Ibn Ḥanbal was 'Abdallāh b. Muḥammad Fūzān (d. 256).[12] He is described as 'one of Ibn Ḥanbal's adherents whom he preferred and befriended (*yuqaddimuhum wa-ya'nasu bihim*) and with whom he would withdraw (*yakhlū ma'ahum*) into seclusion.'[13] It is interesting that this description uses the plural as it apparently refers to a number of individuals who had intimate relations with Ibn Ḥanbal – and suggests that there was a coterie of friends on close terms with him. Another figure who appears in Ibn Ḥanbal's everyday life, in a somewhat less dramatic light, was his neighbor Muḥammad b. Mūsā al-Mustamlī, who worked for Ibn Ḥanbal as a *Mustamlī* in his classes of traditions.[14] He too was among Ibn Ḥanbal's senior companions, although his biography seems to imply that his relations with his master were not marked by the same sense of closeness.

Demonstrations of trust are another facet of the intimacy between Ibn Ḥanbal and certain disciples. In moments of crisis, Ibn Ḥanbal turned to his close friends. The same 'Abdallāh b. Muḥammad Fūzān with whom Ibn Ḥanbal would spend time privately helped him in times of trouble. He is one of two individuals who loaned Ibn Ḥanbal money.[15] This can be understood as an exceptional compliment to Fūzān's integrity, considering Ibn Ḥanbal's constant refusal to accept financial aid from respected Traditionists. We also read about Fūzān visiting Ibn Ḥanbal in jail during the *miḥna*.[16]

Ibn Ḥanbal's tense relations with the court were not put to rest when he was released. During al-Wāthiq's reign the tension escalated. When the pressure and threats of the authorities became unbearable, Ibn Ḥanbal turned to another trusted disciple, Ibrāhīm b. Hāni' (d. 265) who was known as an exceptionally upright man (*rajul min al-abdāl*).[17] His son would go on to serve Ibn Ḥanbal, preserving the close ties between Ibn Ḥanbal and the family.[18]

Three characteristics emerge from the collective profile of Ibn Ḥanbal's early disciples. In contrast to observations that were made in modern works that ascribe a great deal of weight to the homogenous geographic background of Ibn Ḥanbal's followers, this study has found that Ibn Ḥanbal's early disciples come from a variety of regions. Whereas the majority had Arab Khurāsāni origins, some had Syrian roots, and little is known about the background of others.

Another somewhat elusive characteristic is their moral tenor. A collective moral outlook and behavioral code comes into relief from a variety of comments. Whether it is Muḥammad b. Mūsā al-Mustamlī's truthfulness,[19] Ibn Hāni''s poverty,[20] al-Marwadhī's[21] piety or Fūzān's honesty in financial affairs,[22] all can be characterized as possessors of exceptional integrity.[23] In contrast to the geographic division between early disciples and close friends, moral tenor is a feature shared by all of Ibn Ḥanbal's adherents.

Perhaps the most unexpected feature of this group of friends is their intellectual mediocrity. Almost all of Ibn Ḥanbal's confidants and early disciples were known for their loyalty to him and their moral uprightness, but none excelled as transmitter of traditions, and therefore nearly all were ignored by compilers of Traditionist biographical dictionaries.[24] Furthermore, none attempted any independent intellectual enterprise, such as compiling traditions or writing books. However, even though they did not figure highly in wide scholarly circles, they did play an important role in transmitting Ibn Ḥanbal's works. Both Ibn Hāni' and al-Marwadhī transmitted *masā'il* collections that are extant.[25] The two are mentioned as conveyors of Ibn Ḥanbal's *fiqh* and al-Marwadhī was the teacher of the most important Ḥanbali disciples of the next generation.

Prominent pupils

The friends mentioned above furnished Ibn Ḥanbal with ambiance and support in times of trouble. Yet friendship alone cannot account for the formation of a school of law. A wider group of pupils, many of whom were more talented than Ibn Ḥanbal's early companions, helped lay the school's intellectual foundations. Their professional interaction with Ibn Ḥanbal took place in two spheres. Like thousands of other students, they heard and transmitted traditions from their master. But unlike these throngs, Ibn Ḥanbal's close disciples collected his legal correspondence (*masā'il*) and learned the legal method by which he forged his decisions. They would also educate the next generation of Ḥanbalis.

The main collectors of Ibn Ḥanbal's *masā'il* can be divided into three groups: family; close friends who took an active part in Ibn Ḥanbal's intellectual activities (some of whom are mentioned above); and outstanding disciples who for a variety of reasons did not have close social relations with Ibn Ḥanbal.

When considering the role that Ibn Ḥanbal's family played in the foundation of the Ḥanbali school of law, it is interesting to note that the progeny of al-Shāfi'ī and Abū Ḥanifa also participated in the formation of the legal schools that were named after their fathers.[26] The participation of Ibn Ḥanbal's family in the process of school formation is therefore not unique. With the exception of 'Abdallāh b. Ḥanbal, Ibn Ḥanbal's children and relatives were not considered among the leading intellects of the emerging legal school. 'Abdallāh's primary contribution was in collecting and editing his father's compendium of traditions known as the *Musnad*, as well as a variety of *masā'il* covering theological and legal topics.[27] He was less than thirty years old when his father died, but he was considered Ibn Ḥanbal's most knowledgeable pupil.[28] Though there are no indications that he had his own circle, he did have a student with whom he edited the *Musnad*.[29] Whereas 'Abdallāh recorded Ibn Ḥanbal's knowledge, other members of the family contributed to the formation of the Ḥanbali school by enhancing the reputation of Ibn Ḥanbal. Ṣāliḥ's short biography describes his father's intellectual growth, moral behavior, some of his theological positions and the *miḥna*. Ṣāliḥ dedicated much attention to his father's moral virtues, most of which he failed to live up to. Ḥanbal b. Isḥāq, Ibn Ḥanbal's nephew, wrote a biography that dealt solely with the most widely known event in Ibn Ḥanbal's life, the *miḥna*. Neither of them wrote about topics such as traditions, transmitters of traditions, or theology.

When Ibn Ḥanbal's children began their studies, they joined an existing scholarly circle. The central figures of the group, al-Marwadhī, al-Maymūnī and Ibn Hāni', were introduced above primarily because of their social links to Ibn Ḥanbal. However, it is their intellectual activities, whether the collection of *masā'il* or the fostering of new disciples, that contributed to the formation of the Ḥanbali school. Al-Maymūnī was the only reputable scholar of the three but he was surpassed by al-Marwadhī in terms of grooming the next generation of Ḥanbalis.[30]

Al-Marwadhī trained the two most important Ḥanbalis of the next generation, Abū Bakr al-Khallāl and al-Barbahārī.[31] Neither met Ibn Ḥanbal, but through al-Marwadhī, they made major contributions to the consolidation of this school. Abū Bakr al-Khallāl was an assiduous compiler of Ibn Ḥanbal's *masā'il* and historian who left invaluable social and personal information about the first generation of Ḥanbalis.[32] Another interesting aspect of al-Marwadhī's contribution to the Ḥanbali school is the *masā'il* he chose to collect into a book. His interest in the behavioral code that Ibn Ḥanbal embraced led him to compile the *Kitāb al-wara'*, which focuses on expressions of mild asceticism and piety.[33] Al-Barbahārī, a fascinating figure, was both a high brow theologian who conversed with al-Ash'arī and Ibn Baṭṭa and a populist preacher who led an onslaught on the Shī'īs, Mu'tazilis and anyone else who did not live up to his moral and doctrinal expectations.[34] His activism was resented, and in 323 A.H. the caliph al-Rāḍī (d. 329) passed a decree expelling the Ḥanbalis from the Muslim community.[35] Both Abū Bakr al-Khallāl and al-Barbahārī instructed a third generation of important Ḥanbali scholars. Thus, their teacher, al-Marwadhī, initiated a chain of prominent Ḥanbali scholars.

It would be a misconception to assume that all of Ibn Ḥanbal's prominent disciples were close friends of his. Some had mutually respectful intellectual relationships with Ibn Ḥanbal, but probably did not socialize with him, and two, Abū Bakr al-Athram (d. 261) and Isḥāq b. Manṣūr al-Kawsaj (d. 251), even had strained relationships with their teacher. The two appear in the *Tahdhīb*, testimony to their fine reputations as Traditionists, though al-Kawsaj's standing was higher than al-Athram's.[36] Both had intellectual ties outside the Ḥanbali circle, although it seems that Abū Bakr al-Athram severed those ties when he joined Ibn Ḥanbal's circle.[37] Both were of Khurāsāni descent, and had reputations for being pious. Nonetheless, their professional reputation, similar background, and piety did not stop Ibn Ḥanbal from losing his temper with them.

Ibn Ḥanbal became angry with al-Athram and al-Kawsaj because of the manner in which they wrote *masā'il*.[38] In a conversation between Ibn Ḥanbal and his close friend and disciple, al-Marwadhī, Ibn Ḥanbal clarified that when he had said not to write on al-Athram's authority, he had not meant traditions, but rather *masā'il*. This indicates that some time before this conversation took place he had made an unfavorable remark about al-Athram's writings.[39] Al-Kawsaj went so far as to sell Ibn Ḥanbal's *masā'il*. When Ibn Ḥanbal heard of this he was livid and denied having given al-Kawsaj those answers. Later, when confronted by al-Kawsaj, Ibn Ḥanbal retreated from this position and confirmed (*aqarra*) their authenticity.[40]

The other distinguished disciples who did not have close social relations with Ibn Ḥanbal but did maintain good professional relations with him were Ibrāhīm b. Isḥāq al-Ḥarbī (b. 198; d.285)[41] and Sulaymān b. al-Ash'ath Abū Dāwūd al-Sijistānī (b. 202; d. 275).[42] Both were much younger than Ibn Ḥanbal and this probably accounts for the nature of his relations with them. Abū Dāwūd al-Sijistānī would go on to earn one of the most respected reputations in the Traditionist milieu.[43] His collection, the *Sunan*, is one of the six canonical compendia of traditions. Though he was a resident of Baṣra, he traveled to Baghdād to show Ibn Ḥanbal his collection.[44] His *masā'il* are structured according to the typical sequence of legal literature, but the last few chapters cover a variety of contested issues such as theology, legal method, social criticism and controversial traditions.[45] He also wrote a refutation against the Qadaris and a treatise on abrogation in the Qur'an.[46] Thus this relatively young adherent of Ibn Ḥanbal demonstrated more creativity and intellectual independence of mind than did Ibn Ḥanbal's older companions.

Ibn Ḥanbal's other young and independent-minded pupil was Ibrāhīm al-Ḥarbī. Interestingly enough, these younger students set their own course, both in their writings and with their pupils. Though Ibrāhīm al-Ḥarbī followed Ibn Ḥanbal zealously, a strain of individualism can be detected in his biographies: When his pupils referred to his superiority over his master, he reacted by scolding them.[47] Al-Ḥarbī's range of interests included such topics as traditions, proofs of Prophecy, politically oriented issues such as the renunciation of concealment (presumably against the Shīʿīs) and ceremonies during the pilgrimage.[48] His respect for his teacher was immense. He considered Ibn Ḥanbal an important model of behavior and followed his ways in asceticism, knowledge and piety.[49] Following Ibn Ḥanbal, he too boycotted Ibn al-Madīnī, who cooperated with the authorities during the *miḥna*.[50]

Alongside well-known disciples who collected Ibn Ḥanbal's *masāʾil*, Ḥanbali sources mention approximately 120 students who adopted and conveyed Ibn Ḥanbal's legal method (*naqalat al-fiqh*). Of all the names mentioned in these sources, forty-two have been identified.[51] The geographic origin of these forty-two adherents is similar to that of Ibn Ḥanbal's closer group of disciples. Although the majority was Khurāsāni, there was a clear presence of Syrians and a number of pupils from various cities in Iraq and southern Iran as well. The scant references to their intellectual credentials are a bit surprising. Most of these students were anonymous and probably unimportant transmitters of traditions. Of the forty-two Ḥanbalis, only fourteen achieved a reputation warranting a biographical entry in Ibn Ḥajar's *Tahdhīb*. This means that over half of the identifiable disciples of Ibn Ḥanbal were probably not very proficient in the science of traditions.[52] This is even lower than the ratio for Ibn Ḥanbal's close circle of disciples, which stands at half.

This survey of Ibn Ḥanbal's disciples corroborates Madelung's observation that the majority of Ibn Ḥanbal's followers were somehow related to Khurāsān.[53] What is the significance of this? The importance of their shared geographical background lies in its potential to facilitate the creation of a network. As scholars rightly pointed out, Ibn Ḥanbal's followers were Khurāsānis who relocated to Baghdād. Most settled in the Ḥarbiyya quarter; hence, it is safe to conclude that their original geographic background led to physical proximity in Baghdād. Living in the same quarter brought Ibn Ḥanbal into constant contact with other Khurāsāni Arabs. He prayed with them in the mosque, met them in the streets and did business with them in the *sūq*. We can assume that this is how he met the men who would comprise his circle of close friends and who would support him in rough times.

Another reason geographic background may have been instrumental in the creation of a network is cultural familiarity. Particular habits and mores often evolve among inhabitants of cities, regions, etc. Thus, coming from the same region (Khurāsān) may imply shared cultural norms. These create a sense of familiarity, which is an important factor for building a comfortable relationship with a teacher and colleagues. Knowing what is meant by a certain idiom; recognizing and appreciating dishes in a social gathering, and practicing the same idiosyncracies in acts of devotion are often related to one's region of origin and certainly assist in fostering social relationships.

Family ties might also have been conducive to the creation of a circle. Ibn Ḥanbal's uncle, children and nephew contributed to the transmission and the writing of his traditions, opinions of transmitters, theological positions and *masā'il.* They probably reinforced the Khurāsāni nature of the social network that would grow into the Ḥanbali *madhhab.* Ibn Ḥanbal socialized with his relatives, married his cousin Rayḥāna bint 'Umar, and attended his uncle's funeral. We can assume that he saw his family on other occasions as well, such as weddings, funerals and ceremonial events of this type.[54]

Nonetheless, geography in itself was no more than a facilitating circumstance. Physical proximity, family, and common culture helped individuals get close to Ibn Ḥanbal, but geographic background was not a decisive factor for acceptance into the Ḥanbali circle. Nor does the geographic factor in itself determine a disciple's standing among other students. Ibn Ḥanbal's followers joined his circle because they respected Ibn Ḥanbal and wanted to participate in the scholarly activities that he promoted. These events attracted quite a large number of Traditionists who were not of Khurāsāni descent, such as his first prominent disciples al-Maymūnī and Muhannā and his most accomplished pupil Abū Dāwūd al-Sijistānī.

Another element that played a central role in the molding of the Ḥanbali circle is the shared behavioral mores that I have labeled 'mild asceticism.'[55] This moral outlook and its accompanying code of conduct was a magnet that attracted disciples, and a crucial element when these individuals tried to enter the Ḥanbali circle and attain respect. Although this was an elusive factor, it played a major role in determining an individual's status among the Ḥanbalis. Propriety of conduct was probably the most important component in the inner dynamics of the Ḥanbali circle. Failure to abide to the mild ascetic code meant immediate, and at times harsh, sanctions from Ibn Ḥanbal, as the cases of al-Kawsaj and al-Athram testify.

Unaffiliated students of traditions

The first generation of Ḥanbalis – Muhannā al-Shāmī, al-Marwadhī and Ibn Hāni' – expressed their devotion to their master by studying exclusively with him. None of the three are known to have been affiliated with other masters or circles. This was exceptional in the Traditionist milieu because moving between masters was the most common way to study. The next generation of Ḥanbalis behaved differently. From the most pivotal members of Ibn Ḥanbal's coterie, such as Ibrāhīm al-Ḥarbī and Abū Dāwūd al-Sijistānī, to the passing student of traditions, almost all of Ibn Ḥanbal's pupils spent time with other teachers. On occasion this tendency led to joint membership in legal schools. The blurring of group identity is evidence of the doctrinal affinity between what would become the Ḥanbali school and the other Traditionist schools. On the whole it is rare to come by information that sheds light on this overlap. However, in the case of a few famous Traditionists these are sufficient sources and cross-references to clarify a few basic points about their school affiliation.

Among Ibn Ḥanbal's students of traditions were some of the outstanding Traditionists of Islamic civilization. Al-Bukhārī (d. 256), Muslim (d. 261) and Abū Dāwūd al-Sijistānī are three whose collections of traditions would go on to be canonized. Only six compendiums of traditions attained this standing and Ibn Ḥanbal's *Musnad* was not one of them. These three students appear in Ibn Abī Ya'lā's *Ṭabaqāt al-Ḥanābila* and al-Subkī's *Ṭabaqāt al-Shāf'iyya*, but only Abū Dāwūd al-Sijistānī was a full fledged Ḥanbali. Al-Bukhārī's theological position regarding the issue of *lafẓ al-Qur'an*, the creation of human enunciations of the Qur'an, placed him outside the Ḥanbali *madhhab*.[56] Muslim, who studied with Ibn Ḥanbal, seems to have been an independent jurist.

The school affiliations of these three scholars and that of Ibrāhīm al-Ḥarbī, another well-known Traditionist whose entry appears in Ḥanbali and Shāfi'ī biographical dictionaries, are revealing. As discussed above, all four are mentioned in both Ḥanbali and Shāfi'ī biographical dictionaries. However, two, Abū Dāwūd al-Sijistānī and Ibrāhīm al-Ḥarbī, appear in the Shāfi'ī compendium as Ḥanbalis. The compiler of Ibrāhīm al-Ḥarbī's biography concludes: 'And he [should be] mentioned among the Ḥanābila before being mentioned among the

Shāfi'iyya.'[57] A similar remark appears in the case of Abū Dāwūd al-Sijistānī whose entry in Subkī's compilation of Shāfi'īs includes the following observation: 'Abū Dāwūd utilized the jurisprudence (*tafaqqah ... bi*) of Aḥmad b. Ḥanbal and adhered to him for some time (*mudda*).'[58] Though it is usually difficult to identify the precise affiliation of a scholar who is appropriated by two different legal schools, the fact that al-Subkī, the compiler of a Shāfi'ī biographical compendium, referred to them as Ḥanbalis gives this observation a high degree of reliability. It also sets a standard: Those who make a joint appearance in Shāfi'ī and Ḥanbali sources but are not mentioned as Ḥanbalis in the Shāfi'ī compendium are less likely to be Ḥanbalis.

In the middle of the third century, membership in a school of law was not a given, as it would be a century or two later. The overlap between legal schools indicates that at that time affiliation in a school of law was not clearly defined. Ibn Abī Ya'lā, who wrote in the fifth century, makes an important distinction between transmitters of jurisprudence (*naqalat al-fiqh*) and transmitters of traditions (*naqalat al-ḥadīth*). Transmitters of jurisprudence were respected members of the Ḥanbali school of law that followed Ibn Ḥanbal's jurisprudential principles. Among them were all the close and prominent disciples mentioned above, including Abū Dāwūd al-Sijistānī and Ibrāhīm al-Ḥarbī. Transmitters of traditions were the countless students who came to hear a master in the field of traditions, as they did other masters of the field, without acquiring a jurisprudential identity or being considered members in any school of law. Studying traditions did not lead to membership in a legal school, and the surveys of the *qāḍī*s and *ṣūfī*s mentioned in the *Ṭabaqāt al-Ḥanābila* introduce students of traditions who remained on the fringes of the Ḥanbali circle.

Qāḍīs

In all three monotheistic faiths, pious believers are ill at ease with employment by the state.[59] 'Dignities of a worldly character,' writes Wensinck, were 'shunned by those who belong to the pious circles.'[60] Aversion from 'dignities of a worldly character' is a fine characterization of Ibn Ḥanbal's view of state employment. Ibn Ḥanbal's discussion of this ideologically charged topic, however, was not as clear as 'is presented above. For the most part, Ibn Ḥanbal refers to the problem in legal terms, and states that Islamic law does not prohibit this practice. In a statement about the '*sulṭān*'s money,' Ibn Ḥanbal admits that his position goes beyond the requirements of the law. 'I myself stay away from the *sulṭān*'s money, but it is not forbidden (*wa-laysa bi-ḥaram*).'[61] In another remark, though, he argues that part of the *sulṭān*'s money sometimes comes from unacceptable sources: 'The *sulṭān*'s money includes [lit. enters into it- *yadkhuluhu*] permissible (*al-ḥalāl*) money and forbidden (*al-ḥaram*).'[62]

Throughout his life, Ibn Ḥanbal refused to receive money from the state, whether through presents or position. The price he was willing to pay for this principle included a family crisis and a fallout with the much-admired al-Shāfi'ī. According to Ibn Kathīr, their harsh exchange began after al-Shāfi'ī and Hārūn al-Rashīd, the caliph, discussed the position open in Yemen. The Caliph asserted that al-Shāfi'ī should choose someone for the position. Al-Shāfi'ī offered the position to Ibn Ḥanbal, but the latter hurled at him sharp and insulting criticism: 'I visit you only on account of the little earthly knowledge (*al-'ilm al-muzhid fī al-dunyā*), and you bid me to take [the position] of *qāḍī*? If it were not for knowledge I would not speak to you after this incident [lit. after today].' Ibn Kathīr adds, 'and al-Shāfi'ī was embarrassed by him.'[63]

Besides demonstrating the strength of Ibn Ḥanbal's feelings on the issue, this affair tells us something about the scholarly community. Al-Shāfi'ī's connections with the court were not exceptional. Other jurists were in touch with the court, serving as *qāḍīs* and offering their advice on various matters. Among the top echelons of the Ḥanafis, for example, this was quite common practice.[64] Abū Yūsuf, Yaḥyā b. Zakariyyā' (d. 184), and Asad b. 'Amr (d. 188)[65], are three-well known Ḥanafi *qāḍīs* who were also Ibn Ḥanbal's teachers.[66] On the whole, the scholarly community was divided over the issue of state employment. The two extremes were the Ḥanbalis, who prided themselves on avoiding state employment, and the Ḥanafis, who generally accepted it. The Ḥanbali self-view is summed up by Ibn al-Jawzī, who distinguishes the Ḥanbalis from the Shāfi'īs and Ḥanafis by pointing out that only the Ḥanbalis stayed away from the authorities.[67] Despite Ibn Ḥanbal's adamant refusal to accept the position of *qāḍī* and the Ḥanbalis' pride in the fact that they refrained from serving as *qāḍīs*, Ibn Abī Ya'lā, the compiler of the *Ṭabaqāt al-Ḥanābila*, mentions ten *qāḍīs* among the first generation of Ibn Ḥanbal's disciples. How is it that these individuals, who were on the state payroll, were included in the *Ṭabaqāt al-Ḥanābila*? What was their standing in Ḥanbali circles, and most importantly, what were their relationships with Ibn Ḥanbal?

Judging by the *Ṭabaqāt al-Ḥanābila*, the most personal relationship Ibn Ḥanbal had with any of these *qāḍīs* was with Abū 'Ubayd, al-Qāsim

b. Sallām (d. 224), a polymath of Arabo-Islamic culture.[68] He was a scholar of Arabic grammar,[69] whose writings reflect expertise in jurisprudence (*fiqh*), traditions and Qur'anic interpretation. Ibn Ḥanbal commented on his compendiums of tradition quite favorably.[70] Abū 'Ubayd was the only *qāḍī* to visit Ibn Ḥanbal in his home, an encounter described vividly in the *Ṭabaqāt al-Ḥanābila*. When Abū 'Ubayd entered Ibn Ḥanbal's home, Ibn Ḥanbal embraced and seated him in the front row of the class, a gesture that expressed Ibn Ḥanbal's respect for him. Other Traditionists spoke highly of him as well. Ibn Rāhawayh gave Abū 'Ubayd a rare compliment by describing him as being more learned than he himself, Ibn Ḥanbal and al-Shāfi'ī. [71] It is clear that Abū 'Ubayd enjoyed good standing in the Traditionist milieu.

Two other *qāḍīs* who had some type of relationship with Ibn Ḥanbal were Duḥaym 'Abd al-Raḥmān b. Ibrāhīm (b.170; d. 245) and Yaḥyā b. Aktham (d. 243). Duḥaym, a Damascene, was affiliated with the Awzā'i school of law. Occasionally, he visited Baghdād and was treated with great respect by Ibn Ḥanbal and Yaḥyā b. Ma'īn, who 'sat in his presence as if they were youths.'[72] Among Duḥaym's students were respected Ḥanbalis such as Ibrāhīm al-Ḥarbī and Ḥanbal b. Isḥāq.[73] Though non-Ḥanbali sources imply that Duḥaym was Ibn Ḥanbal's teacher, Ibn Abī Ya'lā turns the relationship around and refers to Duḥaym as Ibn Ḥanbal's pupil.[74]

Another *qāḍī* who appears in the *Ṭabaqāt Ḥanābila* is Yaḥyā b. Aktham, who served as al-Ma'mūn's chief *qāḍī*. He was five years older than Ibn Ḥanbal[75] and of Marwadhī stock.[76] The biographical dictionaries refer to him as a Ḥanbali, Ḥanafi[77] and even a Shāfi'ī.[78] His standing with the Traditionists can be assessed by the fact that al-Bukhārī and al-Tirmidhi, two prominent compilers of traditions, studied with him.[79] There is no indication that he met Ibn Ḥanbal, though the latter helped clear the *qāḍī*'s name when he was accused of heresy.[80] In the eyes of Traditionists, Yaḥyā b. Aktham's greatest moment was his confrontation with al-Ma'mūn, when he refused to sanction *mut'a* marriage (temporary marriage).[81] Among his proteges was another *qāḍī* who appears in the *Ṭabaqāt al-Ḥanābila*, Aḥmad b. Muḥammad b. 'Īsā (d. 280), whose entry appears in Ḥanafi biographical dictionaries.[82]

Of the ten *qāḍīs* who appear in the *Ṭabaqāt al-Ḥanābila*, only two are described as affiliated with or known to be part of the Ḥanbali circle. The better-known of the two is Ṣāliḥ b. Aḥmad, Ibn Ḥanbal's first-born son, who took the position of *qāḍī* after his father's death. The second is Aḥmad b. Muḥammad b. Khālid, who was the only *qāḍī* that was labeled 'from the companions (*min al-aṣḥāb*)' of Ibn Ḥanbal, while presumably holding the position of *qāḍī*.[83] With the exception of Ṣāliḥ, there is no evidence that any of them endorsed Ibn Ḥanbal's jurisprudential views or used his *fiqh*. In terms of professional relations, there are indications that three of the ten *qāḍīs* studied traditions with Ibn Ḥanbal. As for the other five, it is not clear why they are mentioned in the *Ṭabaqāt al-Ḥanābila* at all. When treated as a group, the *qāḍīs* who appear in the *Ṭabaqāt al-Ḥanābila* are a body of students on the fringes of the Ḥanbali circle.

It is easy to ascribe the peripheral status of the *qāḍīs* to the incongruity of their moral code with that of the Ḥanbali milieu. At the same time, the evidence of Ibn Ḥanbal's relationship with a number of *qāḍīs* suggests that he was willing to overlook interactions with the authorities. Yaḥyā b. Aktham, whose integrity of faith Ibn Ḥanbal vouched for, was an influential figure in al-Ma'mūn's court, a patron of *qāḍīs*, and an advisor of al-Ma'mūn. Abū 'Ubayd, whom Ibn Ḥanbal took into his home, mingled freely with the wealthy and powerful, wrote his books at the request of 'Abdallāh b. Ṭāhir and was the protege of Thābit b. Naṣr b. Mālik. He taught Thābit b. Naṣr b. Mālik's son, and when Thābit was appointed to the position of governor of Tarsus, he assigned Abū 'Ubayd to the position of *qāḍī*. In contrast to 'Abdallāh b. al-Mubārak and Wakī' b. al-Jarrāḥ, Ibn Ḥanbal did not sever social ties with *qāḍīs*.

In light of Ibn Ḥanbal's warm and supportive relationship with such well-connected *qāḍīs*, it is clear that he did not shun them. It is difficult to explain the inconsistency between Ibn Ḥanbal's personal rejection of the position of *qāḍī* and his cordial, and at times admiring, attitude towards the *qāḍīs*. When compared to the ascetics of previous generations, whom he held in such esteem, Ibn Ḥanbal had a far warmer relationship with *qāḍīs*.

Ṣūfīs

At the beginning of the third century A.H., a number of ṣūfīs lived and taught in Baghdād. Ḥārith al-Muḥāsibī (d. 243), Sarī al-Saqaṭī and Bishr b. al-Ḥārith (d. 226) were some of the more renowned masters who founded their circles of disciples in the 'Abbāsid capital.[84] Some masters were in Ibn Ḥanbal's age group yet none are mentioned in the *Ṭabaqāt al-Ḥanābila*.[85] Six of their disciples, however, did attend Ibn Ḥanbal's classes of traditions. All of them were much younger than he.

The most famous ṣūfī in the *Ṭabaqāt al-Ḥanābila* is Junayd b. Muḥammad (d. 298) who was the leader of the Baghdādi school of mysticism.[86] He was a disciple of Ḥārith al-Muḥāsibī (d. 243) and Sarī al-Saqaṭī (d. 253). Another student who studied with Sarī al-Saqaṭī was Abū Ḥamza al-Ṣūfī (d. 269), who also attended Bishr b. al-Ḥārith's sessions.[87] Ismā'īl b. Isḥāq al-Sarraj (d. 286 or 293) was a disciple of al-Muḥāsibī[88] while Abū Ya'qūb al-Rāzī (d. 304) was a companion of the renowned Egyptian mystic, Dhū al-Nūn.[89] The interaction between these young men and Ibn Ḥanbal evolved primarily around the study of traditions. One, however, seems to have participated in forums that raised legal problems, and Ibn Ḥanbal even solicited his opinion.[90]

There was apparently very little personal interaction between these men and Ibn Ḥanbal, the sole exception being Ismā'īl b. Isḥāq al-Sarrāj. It is recorded in the *Ṭabaqāt al-Ḥanābila* that he had some special privileges (*ikhtiṣāṣ*) with Ibn Ḥanbal.[91] Other sources recount a famous story in which Ibn Ḥanbal asked al-Sarrāj for permission to come to his house when al-Muḥāsibī and his disciples held a meeting there[92]. In the course of the session Ibn Ḥanbal was moved to tears. However, after it was over and al-Muḥāsibī and his disciples left, he warned al-Sarrāj to stay away from them. Ibn Ḥanbal's special relationship with al-Sarrāj should probably be attributed to the fact that al-Sarrāj was the brother of Ibrāhīm b. Isḥāq, a Naysābūrī friend of Ibn Ḥanbal.[93] Thus, the special standing that he enjoyed was due to family connections and not any ideological or intellectual affinity.

The behavior of Ibn Ḥanbal and the Baghdādi ṣūfīs suggests respect and mutual suspicion. Their ambivalence is a complex problem that will not be treated fully in this work. The ṣūfīs' respect for Ibn Ḥanbal is indicated by their attendance of his classes; Ibn Ḥanbal's respect for the ṣūfīs can be assumed on the basis of his attendance of al-Muḥāsibī's session and his emotional reaction to it, if we take this story to be true. The suspicion, or mutual discomfort, can be detected in the lack of cooperation between Ibn Ḥanbal and the older generation of ṣūfīs and the peripheral roles that their disciples played in Ibn Ḥanbal's school.

Ibn Ḥanbal's cautious attitude towards the ṣūfīs derived from his disapproval of their ideas about the acquisition of knowledge. Concepts such as *ma'rifa* (gnosis), and the supposition that humans can reach direct communication with God probably made him uncomfortable. However, Ibn Ḥanbal and the ṣūfīs held similar attitudes towards worldliness, even if ṣūfī practices of worldly denial were at times more extreme than Ibn Ḥanbal's. The words of Junayd could easily find resonance in Ibn Ḥanbal's worldview: 'We do not acquire [the knowledge of] *al-taṣawwuf* from conversations (*ma akhadhnā al-taṣawwuf 'an al-qāl wa-'l-qīl*), but rather from hunger and world denial, and disruption of habits and pleasantries, for *al-taṣawwuf* is sincerity in practices of Allah, and its root is aversion from this world.'[94] The moral tenor of this statement, which emphasizes deeds over words, is a pivotal component in the Ḥanbali worldview. The ethical affinity between this trend of 'sober' ṣūfis[95] and the Ḥanbalis can explain why a certain level of mutual respect existed between the two groups.

A fascinating indication of this ethical affinity is the appropriation of Ma'rūf al-Karkhī (d. 200 or 204).[96] As his date of death (d. 204) reveals, Ma'rūf al-Karkhī died before Ibn Ḥanbal was surrounded by a large circle of students. It is not certain on what basis he is included in the *Ṭabaqāt al-Ḥanābila* but whatever the reason, his biography in the *Ṭabaqāt al-Ḥanābila* is one of the longest. The discrepancy between Ma'rūf's inclusion in the *Ṭabaqāt al-Ḥanābila* and the fact that he could not be considered Ibn Ḥanbal's pupil or disciple tells us more about the ascetic self-view of the Ḥanbalis and their aspiration to be integrated into a tradition of piety[97] than about Ma'rūf himself.

Ma'rūf attracted the attention of Ibn Ḥanbal and his followers and inspired some interesting exchanges between them. One of Ibn Ḥanbal's comments about this revered Muslim encapsulates the rudiments of Ibn Ḥanbal's view of knowledge and deeds. When pressed by 'Abdallāh, his son, to state his opinion on the breadth of Ma'rūf's knowledge, Ibn Ḥanbal replied by addressing the nature of knowledge: 'Son, he [Ma'rūf] had with him the peak (*ra's*) of knowledge: fear (*khashya*) of Allah.'[98] 'Abdallāh had asked about the scope of Ma'rūf's knowledge and presumably he meant knowledge of the law, traditions and other Islamic sciences. Ibn Ḥanbal did not consider this an important issue. His reply focused on the nature of Ma'rūf's knowledge, which can be discerned from Ma'rūf's pious behavior. In essence Ibn Ḥanbal was telling his son something that most ṣūfis would agree with. It was not the scope of one's knowledge, but one's behavior, that had the power to bring an individual to the peak of knowledge.

* * *

As can be expected, personal relations played a crucial role in the development of the Ḥanbali network. Ibn Ḥanbal maintained close relationships with friends, who as a result enjoyed a high standing in the Ḥanbali circle, even though some were not considered by Muslim scholars to be important transmitters of traditions. At the same time, there is no indication that Ibn Ḥanbal paid the slightest attention to some of the most important experts of traditions who sat in his classes, such as Bukhārī and Muslim. Friendship and personal ties even complicated ideological issues, as with Ibn Ḥanbal's close relationship with Abū 'Ubayd. It is therefore safe to conclude that even in the case of Ibn Ḥanbal, friendship could bend moral and professional principles.

Despite the above mentioned caveats, it is possible to sketch a coherent picture of the interactions in the Ḥanbali circle. The unifying feature of Ibn Ḥanbal's adherents was a common vision of piety, i.e., mild asceticism. This is what attracted Ibn Ḥanbal's disciples to him and what he sought and respected in others. As a result, this is what determined an individual's standing among the other followers. Alongside mild asceticism another factor emerged and attracted many students to Ibn Ḥanbal – expertise in traditions. Towards the last decades of Ibn Ḥanbal's life, a number of young experts in the field of traditions came to study with him and some even adopted his jurisprudential approach. These disciples, as well as a number of close friends, would collect Ibn Ḥanbal's judgements and cultivate the next generation of students. These two features – mild asceticism and jurisprudential outlook – will be examined in the next two chapters.

CHAPTER FIVE

Zuhd - Social Critique and Group Identity

Piety as a scheme of history

In Ibn Ḥanbal's eyes piety was not limited to a specific place, time or faith. It was a component of sacred history, practiced before and after the rise of Islam. In his *Kitāb al-zuhd* (Book of Asceticism), Ibn Ḥanbal presents a list of pious individuals that starts with Adam and includes a number of pre-Islamic prophets, Muḥammad, the four rightly guided caliphs (*Rashīdūn*), some of the Companions (*Ṣaḥāba*) and a group of Successors (*Tābi'ūn*).[1] This compilation is one of the first Islamic works dedicated to the lives of paragons of piety and devotion.[2] Although stories about the prophets circulated during the first centuries of Islam, Ibn Ḥanbal was the first to separate these Prophets from universal histories and place them in a chain of pious exemplars.[3] The novelty of the *Kitāb al-zuhd* lies in its structure and focus. Its organizing axis was the ascetics themselves rather than topics and its moral vision was conveyed through stories about their lives. This framework would be repeated in the future by Sulami and Abū Nu'aym al-Iṣfahānī in two classical biographical compendiums which recounted the history of piety and spirituality through its outstanding practitioners.

A cursory reading of the entries in the *Kitāb al-zuhd* illustrates that Ibn Ḥanbal's main intention was to tell the history of human piety. He blends the main events of humankind's sacred history, such as Adam's expulsion from the Garden of Eden,[4] Ibrāhīm's sacrifice of Isḥāq,[5] the miracles of Jesus,[6] and future events of the Resurrection,[7] with edifying anecdotes about these prophets' devotion or pious world-views. Criticism of the world and its material temptations can be found throughout the book: Adam's pain when he is driven out of Paradise and into a world in which he will toil and be confronted by material needs,[8] Ibrāhīm's description of death as the end of earthly trials,[9] and Jesus' instructions that human beings should prefer deeds of the next world to those of this.[10]

This criticism of worldly matters was carried into the Islamic period. 'Umar b. al-Khaṭṭāb (d. 23) is quoted as preaching against greed since it inevitably is transformed into poverty.[11] A vivid anecdote relates that as he passed by a pile of garbage he told those accompanying him 'This is your world (*dunyākum*) to which you aspire.'[12] Other Successors come out explicitly against specific worldly distractions that might steer them away from the path of piety. Ṭāwūs b. Kaysān (d. 106) begs Allah to deny him money and children.[13] He also refuses the Amīr al-Mu'minīn's financial support.[14] Once we enter upon the Islamic epoch, a new expression of piety appears – zealous performance of devotional acts. For example it is told of Sa'īd b. Jubayr (d. 95) that he recited the Qur'an every two nights and performed the *ḥajj* and *'umra* numerous times in his life.

The idea that there was a great chain of piety throughout history was particularly popular among the ṣūfīs.[15] In the fourth century A.H., a ṣūfī theory was elaborated which maintained that 'a fixed number of abdāl/awliā' are chosen by God and, by their presence, preserve universal equilibrium, especially during periods between prophets.'[16] This idea was articulated by al-Ḥakīm al-Tirmidhī (d. between 295-310).[17] According to Hujwīrī, al-Ḥakīm's followers believed that,

> God has saints (awliya) whom He has specially distinguished by His friendship and whom he has chosen to be the governors of His kingdom ... they have become entirely devoted to His business, and have ceased to follow their sensual affections. Through the blessing of their advent the rain fall from heaven, and through the purity of their lives the plants spring up from the earth, and through their spiritual influence the Moslems gain victories over the unbelievers.[18]

Ibn Ḥanbal also used the term *abdāl*, but it is not clear what he meant by it. He described his trusted friend Ibn Hāni' al-Nisabūri as one of the *abdāl*, and used this word to refer to an anonymous traveler who appeared at his doorstep.[19] While the usage of this term cannot prove that Ibn Ḥanbal espoused all the notions that were attached to it, it is interesting to note that later Ḥanbalis embraced this concept.[20] Information about the Ḥanbali understanding of this idea has come down to us through Ibn Abī Ya'lā, the author of the *Ṭabaqāt al-Ḥanābila*, whose father, Abū Ya'lā (d. 488) had been a strong upholder of belief in *awliyā'*.[21] That certain followers should develop these notions so explicitly suggests that these ideals had been circulating in the Ḥanbali milieu for some time, possibly as far back as the days of Ibn Ḥanbal. Despite the meaning that future generations of Ḥanbalis ascribed to the term *abdāl*, Ibn Ḥanbal's vision of sacred history differed from the ṣūfī interpretation. According to Ibn Ḥanbal, pious men and women played the central role throughout history. However, unlike al-Ḥakīm al-Tirmidhī's *abdāl*, Ibn Ḥanbal's pious heroes did not demonstrate supra-natural abilities. They are not described as setting the course of human history (Muslim victories) or influencing nature (rainfall or growth of plants).

On the other hand, Ibn Ḥanbal and the believers in the *abdāl* did share the idea that society has a moral elite. The fact that he made the effort to write about pious men and women indicates that Ibn Ḥanbal found such individuals worthy of being remembered, while consigning the more commonplace heroes of human history – kings and generals to oblivion. This historiographic choice indicates that according to Ibn Ḥanbal, moral incidents are the important stuff of which history is made and the true heroes are pious individuals. This historical vision of a moral elite will be echoed in Ibn Ḥanbal's attempts to recruit individuals who lived up to these high moral standards.

Recruitment and status in the Ḥanbali circle

The most conspicuous feature of the Ḥanbali circle was its large contingent of men and women who were renowned for their piety. The frequent references to the piety of Ibn Ḥanbal's adherents suggests the compilers of Ḥanbali biographic dictionaries felt it was important to highlight this aspect of the burgeoning circle of Ḥanbalis. As will be demonstrated in this section, Ibn Ḥanbal actively searched for and recruited like-minded ascetics. He turned to what he perceived to be members of the moral elite of his age and invited them to join his company. Mild asceticism, rather than scholarly credentials, was the crucial quality that Ibn Ḥanbal sought in his adherents. The evidence in the biographic dictionaries, which describe the members of the Ḥanbali circle, suggests that Ibn Ḥanbal was much more impressed by devotion than by intellectual ability. This Ḥanbali ethical posture permeated the social structure and internal relations of the Ḥanbali circle.

Around the core of his close disciples, who embraced the mild ascetic moral code, evolved a larger group of pupils who also shared Ibn

Ḥanbal's high standards of piety. A member of this circle, 'Abd al-Wahhāb b. 'Abd al-Ḥakam (d. 250 or 251), is depicted as one of Ibn Ḥanbal's most loyal and devoted adherents.[22] He considered Ibn Ḥanbal to be his role model and adopted his master's positions on a wide variety of matters including renunciation of the Shāfi'ī theologian Abū Thawr (d. 240).[23] 'Abd al-Ḥakam paid attention to devotional nuances such as the types of Qur'anic recitations that Ibn Ḥanbal preferred,[24] and like many of his generation, he was in awe of Ibn Ḥanbal due to the latter's ability to withstand his *miḥna* ordeal.[25]

His loyalty was reciprocated. Ibn Ḥanbal spoke very highly of his devoted adherent, and his trust in 'Abd al-Wahhāb was such that when he lay dying and was asked who should guide the Ḥanbalis about matters related to piety, he proposed 'Abd al-Wahhāb.[26] This choice puzzled some of his disciples, who argued that 'Abd al-Wahhāb 'did not possess the breadth of knowledge.'[27] When his suggestion was challenged, Ibn Ḥanbal replied: 'He is a righteous man, the likes of him will succeed in attaining what is proper.'[28] Here again, Ibn Ḥanbal demonstrates his priorities, which placed proper behavior and the ability to live up to high moral standards above scholarship.[29]

Another ascetic who adopted Ibn Ḥanbal as a role model was Aḥmad b. Ḥumayd (d. 244).[30] His relationship with Ibn Ḥanbal went back many years, and the two were very close. An indication of Ibn Ḥumayd's high standing among the Ḥanbalis was that Fūzān, Ibn Ḥanbal's trusted confidant, studied with him. Ibn Ḥumayd was described as 'persevering in poverty (*faqīran ṣabūran 'alā al-faqr*),'[31] an important compliment which added to his stature among the Ḥanbalis. His concern with asceticism is reflected in a conversation that he witnessed and transmitted in which Ibn Ḥanbal was asked to define asceticism.[32] Ibn Ḥumayd learned more than just intellectual and legalistic matters from Ibn Ḥanbal such as 'the way of modesty (*al-qanū'*) and of a trade (*wa-'l-iḥtirāf*).'[33]

Such interactions demonstrate that the master did not only pass legal knowledge on to his adherents. A disciple's way of life, conduct and material well-being, were considered worthy of notice and comment. Abū Bakr al-Khallāl, who visited Aḥmad b. Abī Badr (d. 282) in his home, remarked that his house and his abstinence (*qu'ūd*) were testimony to his 'perseverance in poverty.'[34] Ibn Abī Badr, a disciple of Ibn Ḥanbal, was in possession of traditions and *masā'il* and was considered one of the *awliyā'*. He, too, was recognized as one of the 'abstainers from this world (*al-'āzifīn 'an al-dunyā*),'[35] and was highly respected by Ibn Ḥanbal.

Numerous other ascetics are mentioned in the *Ṭabaqāt al-Ḥanābila*. Many of them, including those mentioned above, were close friends of Ibn Ḥanbal who earned his esteem. Some, like 'Alī b. Muwaffaq (d. 265)[36] and Ismā'īl b. Yūsuf[37] specialized in the study of traditions, while others, like Ja'far Abū Muḥammad (d. 279) heard many of his legal judgements.[38] All seemed to be drawn to Ibn Ḥanbal because of his exceptional moral stature which was manifested in his piety.

One of the most compelling figures from among Ibn Ḥanbal's ascetic disciples was Ja'far b. Muḥammad al-Nasā'ī. A close friend of Ibn Ḥanbal, he was mentioned by Abū Bakr al-Khallāl as a pious man. Al-Nasā'ī was also considered to be a truthful individual, and in fact this trait may have cost him his life, since he had a penchant for criticizing those around him (*'ammār bi-al-ma'rūf nahhā' 'an al-munkar*).[39] Apparently, this habit annoyed someone in Mecca to such an extent that rumor has it al-Nasā'ī was killed for it.[40]

One of the most striking features of the growing Ḥanbali circle was that Ibn Ḥanbal did not wait passively for students to come to him. He searched for and inquired about individuals who fit the mild ascetic mold and invited them to spend time with him and his followers. His close friend and disciple Abū Bakr al-Marwadhī reported that whenever Ibn Ḥanbal heard that an upright person or an ascetic asked about him, Ibn Ḥanbal would inquire about the ascetic's circumstances (*aḥwālahu*), and expressed his desire to meet him.[41] If the individual lived up to Ibn Ḥanbal's standards, the master would befriend him and express his admiration for him. If the new acquaintance disappointed him, Ibn Ḥanbal was known to lose his temper.[42] The behavior that al-Marwadhī described is particularly interesting when we bear in mind that Ibn Ḥanbal was not a sociable person. He had little patience for engaging in idle chat which he considered a waste of time, and did what he could to avoid social situations. 'Abdallāh, his second son, observed, 'My father was the most enduring of people [regarding] seclusion, no one saw him except in the mosque or at a funeral or visiting the sick, and he despised walking in the markets.'[43] In light of this attitude, his attempts to meet and talk with potential like-minded ascetics reflect his respect for these individuals and the importance he attached to drawing them to him.

Precisely because Ibn Ḥanbal does not come across as a man interested in company or in the habit of courting people, Marwadhī's description is striking. It is telling that the only stories about Ibn Ḥanbal befriending anyone were about individuals who had low social status and no material means. An important characteristic that distinguished the Ḥanbali circle from many other networks was Ibn Ḥanbal's refusal reap material benefits from the coterie of friends and admirers that surrounded him.[44]

Along with initiating contacts with individuals with pious reputations, Ibn Ḥanbal took pains to make paupers (*fuqarā'*) feel comfortable in his classes. Abū Bakr al-Marwadhī observed: 'He [Ibn Ḥanbal] was very modest [and] liked paupers ... he was inclined to them and neglected worldly people (*ahl al-dunyā*).'[45] This is quite surprising. We would expect that the talented pupils, those with good memories and a quick grasp of the topics studied, would be the ones to receive special attention in class. However, the students who excelled were not mentioned in any anecdote in either positive or negative terms. It was as if Ibn Ḥanbal was oblivious to this type of performance. His attention was given to devotion and lifestyle. Piety often went hand-in-hand with poverty and as a result Ibn Ḥanbal drew paupers close to him and drove the well-to-do into the periphery of the Ḥanbali circle.

Al-Marwadhī's descriptions of Ibn Ḥanbal's attitude towards pious individuals and indigent students are the most explicit formulations we have about the mechanics of the Ḥanbali group formation. The low social status and lack of material means that characterized the individuals that Ibn Ḥanbal courted underscores the fact that Ibn Ḥanbal could not reap material benefits or social clout from the coterie of friends that he collected. Thus, in contrast to, and perhaps in protest of, most circles and networks of the period, Ibn Ḥanbal avoided the accepted norms of patronage, particularly the one that called for the exchange of loyalty for material benefits. It may even be that the circle that evolved around Ibn Ḥanbal drew its identity and attracted its following due to what Laoust aptly characterized 'une maniere de protestation.'[46] Here, the protest was aimed at other networks and forms of patronage.

Ibn Ḥanbal's appeal was based on the subversion of the standard relations that developed in most circles. He refused to play the usual game of give and take that is typical of so many networks. When he was on the recieving end he declined any offer of help, whether from anonymous admirers, well meaning teachers or manipulative politicians. This drastically reduced his ability to give financial support to others and to act as the benefactor in his own circle, since he had no money to hand out. Ibn Ḥanbal's scrupulousness and refusal to play either role in the patron-client relationship when material benefits were involved comes across in the following anecdote:

> '[Ṣāliḥ] said: A son of mine was born and a friend gave me a present, afterwards he concluded [his affairs] (*atā 'alā*) in that month, and wanted to set out to Baṣra. He said to me: Speak to Aba 'Abdallāh [Ibn Ḥanbal] [so that] he will write [on my behalf] a letter [of introduction] to the *mashāyikh* of Baṣra. I [Ṣāliḥ] spoke to him. He [Ibn Ḥanbal] replied: Had he not given you a present I would have written in his sake, [as it stands] I will not write.'[47]

This story reveals that Ibn Ḥanbal was not opposed in principle to networking, and actively participated in some kind of network (presumably Traditionist) in which his word carried weight. The letter that Ṣāliḥ's friend requested was probably part of the mechanism used to mold reputations of scholars in the Traditionist world. Writing letters and exchanging opinions about scholars was a crucial part of the sub-field of knowledge named the science of men (*'ilm al-rijāl*). Ibn Ḥanbal was an important participant in these activities, and it can be assumed, a central figure in the Traditionists' network. Ṣāliḥ's friend's request and Ibn Ḥanbal's general willingness to cooperate, as revealed by his response, indicate that Ibn Ḥanbal played according to the rules of the Traditionist network.

Ibn Ḥanbal's refusal to write a letter of recommendation when it might have appeared to be a *quid pro quo* demonstrates the moral constraints that Ibn Ḥanbal set upon himself. Due to the importance he ascribed to the reputations of scholars, he was unwilling to state his opinion about any scholar when material gain was involved. Apparently, he felt that exchange of information about scholars was so vital that money or presents must not tarnish it. The unique nature of the Ḥanbali network becomes all the more apparent if we compare it with other networks in Islamic societies. In a penetrating study of social interactions in Buyid society (i.e., fourth century Baghdād), R. Mottahedeh set out an important trajectory of investigation: 'the way in which the individuals in this society formed commitments to each other.'[48] In Buyid society, it was argued, loyalty was traded for benefits. This form of behavior was prevalent among court bureaucrats[49] as well as other courtiers and companions who were loyal to their *amīrs* or caliphs.[50] It took a somewhat different form among the *'ayyārūn* who collected protection money[51] and the members of certain schools of law whose 'common belief was reinforced by patronage.'[52]

In light of the widespread practice of exchanging tangible benefits for loyalty, the pattern of behavior seen in Ibn Ḥanbal's circle was exceptional.[53] Ibn Ḥanbal's resistance to this practice – whether his refusal to accept the court's presents and distribute them to his followers or his anger with al-Kawsaj who taught for pay – suggests that the Ḥanbali circle operated in accordance with its own norms. An individual's knowledge or piety won him access to Ibn Ḥanbal and enhanced his standing among the other members of the group. In barring the normal patron/client relations, Ibn Ḥanbal and his disciples expressed their discomfort with the manner in which power was wielded in their society. This protest attracted a certain type of following. Ironically, it was Ibn Ḥanbal's stand in this matter that drew many of his disciples to him and transformed him into a strong, and at times feared political leader in Baghdād.

In light of the ways in which individuals were recruited into the Ḥanbali circle and the relations that Ibn Ḥanbal developed with his following, it stands to reason that Ibn Ḥanbal's disciples were attracted to his subversion of the types of relations that were characteristic of most circles. Ibn Ḥanbal had an elitist view of himself and his followers. To some extent, he probably saw himself as one more link in the chain of piety that went back through the Successors, Companions and the Prophets, all the way to Adam. Just as this historical elite did not play ordinary power games and offered an alternative to the political history of kings, Ibn Ḥanbal and his circle offered alternative rules of behavior and criteria of membership to the political networks of their day.

Social criticism and the Ḥanbali identity

Asceticism often entails criticism of the surrounding environment.[54] Ibn Ḥanbal's abstention from Ṣāliḥ's food, for example, was not merely an act of moral caution, but a means of criticizing his son. Taking this principle one step further, mild asceticism served as an ideological foundation for social criticism. The merger between mild asceticism and social criticism is most clearly demonstrated by the Ḥanbalis' understanding of *al-amr bi-'l-ma'rūf wa-'l-nahy 'an al-munkar.*

The meaning of *al-amr* has gone through a number of changes in Islamic thought. In a survey of the concept, it has been observed that the Khāriji, Mu'tazili and Zaydi interpretations of *al-amr* were attempts to legitimize rebellions against unjust rulers.[55] Other Muslims leaders, such as Abū Ḥanīfa, were more reserved regarding revolts against the Caliph than were these sects, which elaborated an ideology of political activism, but even so it seems that Abū Ḥanīfa also understood the concept as referring to relations with the rulers.[56] The same can be said of Ḥasan al-Baṣrī, who refused to revolt but understood the idiom as a means of legitimizing 'moral admonishment of the rulers.'[57] Ḥasan al-Baṣrī heralded Ibn Ḥanbal's interpretation because he was of the opinion that the admonishment should be aimed at 'members of the community' as well.[58]

Ibn Ḥanbal's understanding of the term is unique because the political nature of this concept disappears in his interpretation. As a modern historian of Islam observed 'one does not take the authorities as a target for the performance of the duty.'[59] Ibn Ḥanbal breaks from the political meaning that is associated with the concept when it is used to legitimize revolt or criticism of the rulers. He discards the widely held political contents of *al-amr* and emphasizes in its stead criticism of individuals who deviated from the *sharīʿa* or transgressed certain ascetic ideals of behavior.

Al-amr is part and parcel of the Ḥanbali outlook. It is interwoven into *masāʾil* collections, which are the repository of Ibn Ḥanbal's views of proper behavior. The act of incorporating Ibn Ḥanbal's positions on different matters related to *al-amr* within *masāʾil* collections indicates that the criticism of other people's behavior is considered to be part of Ibn Ḥanbal's legal and moral outlook.

This overlap in literary organization hints at a more meaningful connection between mild asceticism and *al-amr*. The contents of mild asceticism and *al-amr* indicate that they stem from similar ideological foundations. In a nutshell, both mild asceticism and *al-amr* lead a crusade against sensual pleasures. Music, games, and the physical pleasure of pleasant clothes, are interspersed in *al-amr* anecdotes as well as in the manual of devotion, *Kitāb al-waraʿ*. In this source, Ibn Ḥanbal prohibits the use of textiles and shoes and cautions his readers about children's toys. In the *al-amr* chapters of *masāʾil* literature, he forbids adults from playing games such as chess and engaging in activities that give sensual pleasure. Music is deemed the great enemy of moral uprightness because it 'cultivates hypocracy (*al-nifāq*) in the heart.'[60] As a result Ibn Ḥanbal allows his disciples to break musical instruments when they see them.[61]

Despite the literary congruence and common ideological foundations, mild asceticism and *al-amr* differ in their spheres of action. Mild asceticism focuses on the individual and the myriad deeds he is expected to take upon himself. First and foremost, it is a regimen of self-discipline composed of countless little decisions that a person makes in private: What to eat, how many times to pray each day, what to wear, and so on. By contrast, *al-amr* focuses on relationships. What kind of relationships ought a pious Muslim pursue with those guilty of different types of moral transgressions? Should he stop transgressors by use of physical force? Should he limit himself to issuing a warning? Should he take no action at all? These encounters took place in the public arena. The pious Muslim and the offenders met in the streets, markets or mosques.

Due to the dichotomy between the private and the public spheres, a series of questions appears in *al-amr* literature. These questions focus on where, when and how an individual should react to transgressions of the law. Ibn Ḥanbal's followers asked him about the legitimacy of using force when confronting someone in possession of intoxicants, of destroying musical instruments, and of breaking up a game of chess.[62] These 'how to' or 'is it legitimate' questions do not come up in discussions of mild asceticism because the implementation of self-discipline does not clash with any social norm. By contrast, intervention in other people's affairs and the invasion of privacy, even in the name of piety, pose problems.[63] This being the case, they give rise to discussion and constantly prompted Ibn Ḥanbal's followers to ask for his permission to take action.

The underlying premise of Ibn Ḥanbal's *masāʾil*, the *Kitāb al-waraʿ*, and *al-amr* treatise was to guide his disciples towards a moral way of life. All these works address the material and sensual pleasures that were deemed agents of moral corruption. They prescribe an etiquette that was expected to minimize exposure to corrupting forms of conduct. Their shared assumption that those pleasures lead to moral deterioration reveals their common ascetic point of departure. The solutions they offer also disclose their shared ascetic roots. The practice of self-denial and the act of preventing others from enjoying sensual pleasures indicate that mild asceticism and *al-amr* grew out of the same religious inclinations.

Moral chastisement had another function as well: To constantly remind the members of the Ḥanbali milieu that they were different from other believers and morally superior to many of their neighbors and acquaintances. The practice of criticizing others and interfering in the affairs of the people surrounding them created a sense of 'we' and 'they' among the Ḥanbalis.Thus, mild asceticism, through the agency of *al-amr*, helped to consolidate Ḥanbali group identity.[64] Although by no means the only, and perhaps even not the most important ingredient, of the Ḥanbali sense of group identity, mild asceticism and *al-amr* were two components of the socio-ideological composite called the Ḥanbali school of law.

Due to Ibn Ḥanbal's reinterpretation of *al-amr*, I would argue that this concept was an integral part of his ascetic and moral thought. The criticism that Ibn Ḥanbal and his followers hurled at the denizens of Baghdād was an expression of the ascetic values and codes of behavior that shaped their own practices of devotion.

CHAPTER SIX

Jurisprudence and *Madhhab* Formation

Qiyās – The use and limits of human reason

Throughout the second and third centuries A.H., an argument raged over the use and limits of human reason in Islamic sciences. One of the central arenas of this debate was jurisprudence. Islamic jurists ranged from those who felt free to offer their personal opinions when faced with a lacuna in the sanctified texts to jurists who rejected any use of personal opinion whatsoever. Between these extreme positions were a spectrum of approaches that adopted different ways to use human reason in legal decision-making. The most important contribution to this struggle over jurisprudential orientation was al-Shāfiʿī's articulation of the technique and constraints in using human reason.[1] Al-Shāfiʿī suggested that there was only one way to use human rational faculties in legal decision making – analogical reasoning (*qiyās*). He argued that when the sanctified sources, Qur'an and prophetic *sunna*, do not furnish a clear legal prescription, one can employ analogical reasoning, i.e., identify a similar case that appears in the sanctified sources and implement its prescription.

The greatest strength of al-Shāfiʿī's program lay in its fusion of two, seemingly antithetical elements: maintaining the primacy of the sanctified sources and enabling jurists to adapt the sources to the new and changing needs of Islamic society. However, certain Traditionist circles were unhappy with al-Shāfiʿī's jurisprudence. Some rejected any use of human reason.[2] Others were not comfortable with Shāfiʿī's tendency to rely on analogical reasoning all too often, and it is to this trend that Ibn Ḥanbal belonged.

Nineteenth and twentieth-century scholarship of Islamic law has dedicated relatively little attention to Ibn Ḥanbal's jurisprudential views and as a result there is no convincing exposition of his legal thought.[3]

Students of Islamic law have articulated three different, at times contradictory, assessments of Ibn Ḥanbal's jurisprudence. A middle-of-the-road group, which includes Goldziher, Schacht and Spectorsky, recognized that Ibn Ḥanbal's views differed from those espoused by al-Shāfiʿī, but does not specify how.[4] These scholars note that quite a few Traditionists were unhappy with al-Shāfiʿī's extensive use of human reason. Spectorsky, following Schacht, described their response as 'the traditionist reaction to al-Shāfiʿī.'[5] Their discussions of Ibn Ḥanbal's jurisprudential views, however, never deal directly with his attitude towards analogical reasoning. Instead, Schacht ascribes recognition of *qiyās* to 'later Ḥanbalis' such as Ibn Taymiyyah, and in so doing evades the question of Ibn Ḥanbal's attitude to the use of human reason in legal discourse.[6]

N.J. Coulson and a number of historians who wrote overviews of Islam maintain that Ibn Ḥanbal rejected the use of human reason altogether.[7] Coulson's assessment is as follows: 'From this latter group [extreme Traditionists] two more schools of law were formed [Ḥanbalis and Ẓāhiris], their common ground lying in their rejection of human reason in any form as a source of law...'[8] In contrast to Goldziher and his vein, who identify a difference between the Ẓāhiris and Ḥanbalis, Coulson and these historians discard such subtleties.[9] Coulson's view of Ḥanbali jurisprudence has one advantage: Because it focuses on what he takes to be a disagreement over the use of *qiyās*, it offers a neat explanation of the break between the Ḥanbalis and Shāfiʿīs. Coulson's assessment is patently wrong, as will be demonstrated below.

A third point of view is expressed by H. Laoust, who wrote the following: 'He [Ibn Ḥanbal] does not reject analogical reasoning (*kiyās*), but does not fully appreciate its value as an instrument of judicial systematization and discovery...'[10] I find that Laoust's judgement is the most accurate. As will be illustrated in this chapter, Ibn Ḥanbal utilized analogical reasoning, though silently and not in a polished manner. He did not state explicitly that he was doing so, and this question was never completely clarified even among his disciples.[11]

If Laoust's opinion is accepted, it is difficult to explain why the Ḥanbalis broke away from the Shāfiʿīs. Assuming the Ḥanbalis did not reject analogical reasoning, and even employed it on occasion, the difference between the two groups is not of principle but of emphasis. Such a distinction is not very helpful in explaining the formation of an independent school of law.

Despite the soundness of his description, Laoust did not examine in a systematic manner Ibn Ḥanbal's remarks or actual use of *qiyās*. I hope to begin such an analysis in this chapter. The main difficulty in such an enterprise is Ibn Ḥanbal's habit to keep silent about the matter. As a consequence, although he used *qiyās* he never stated it explicitly. However, on occasion he did make a remark that revealed his tolerance for personal opinions and interpretations. The following is an example.

> Abū Dāwūd said: I heard Aḥmad asked about the slave wife whose husband is a *mafqūd*.
> He said, 'On the basis of interpreting (*ta'wīl*) [this case in accordance with others], she waits two years [before starting an *'idda*]
> ... Another time Muḥammad said, to the same effect, 'they interpret, in this case (i.e., that of the slave woman), on the basis of one-half what the free woman waits.'[12]

In his answer Ibn Ḥanbal assumes that it is legitimate to interpret, in other words, to present a personal opinion based on an individual's rational faculties. Ibn Ḥanbal's willingness to express an opinion based on his own interpretation is the result of his sensitivity to the financial position of women. Though on other occasions he avoided passing a judgement and answered 'I do not know,' in the case of a husband who was *mafqūd* (missing), he would not agree to such a cautious position on the part of the jurist.

Due to the rarity of Ibn Ḥanbal's direct references to legal method, it is worthwhile to introduce another remark on juristic procedure:

> 'He [Ibn Ḥanbal] was told: 'There is a man in a village (*qarya*) who is asking about a matter of which there is disagreement (*ikhtilāf*)?
> He [Ibn Ḥanbal] said: He ought to deliver an opinion (*yuftā*) in accordance (*bi mā wāfaq*) with the Book and the Sunna, he ought to deliver an opinion on that basis (*yuftā bihi*), and as for that which is not in accordance to the Book and the Sunna he ought to keep away from it.'[13]

Writing an 'opinion' that is 'in accordance with the Book and Sunna' assumes that the sanctified sources do not make an explicit statement on the issue under discussion, because if they had, one would simply follow the clear prescription. Likewise if the sanctified sources had been clear on the matter, a disagreement (*ikhtilāf*) would not have arisen. The second implication of 'he ought to deliver an opinion in accordance to the Book and the Sunna' is that one can identify the common ground between the unresolved legal problem and a statement in 'the Book and the Sunna.' Identifying a shared element and implementing the solution of one case in another is the basis of analogical reasoning.

It should not surprise us that Ibn Ḥanbal permitted the use of personal opinion. It is quite clear that he was aware that some of his own judgements were based on his own views. His remark: 'I loathe that someone will write on my authority, opinions'[14] indicates that he himself did not shy from stating his opinion and making decisions that did not simply echo the sources. In principle, he did not find the elaboration of personal opinions to be improper. He did, however, set one limitation – a personal opinion should not obligate others. Personal opinions must remain personal and should not be transformed into legal precedents.

Case studies: Human reason in legal opinions

Ibn Ḥanbal's matter-of-fact comments on the legitimacy of personal opinions were one indication that he allowed the use of human reason. Nonetheless, these remarks do not reveal how and when Ibn Ḥanbal resorted to this technique. A number of case studies are examined below, offering a clearer picture of the use Ibn Ḥanbal made of analogical reasoning as well as its limits.

The mouse that fell into an oil container

> 'I asked my father [Ibn Ḥanbal] about a mouse that fell into oil and it [the container] was bigger than five *qurub*.
> He said: 'Oil in my opinion (*'indī*) is not of the same status as water. This is because water [can serve as a means of] purification of anything, and oil in my opinion does not have that status, and I would not venture to permit it, if the status of oil was the status of water then when cloth was hit by urine, washing it in oil would purify it; there is no purification by oil.'[15]

The problem raised in this question is part of a general discussion about states of purity. The issue of purity evolved around a number of central themes, two of them being what causes impurity and how impurity can be removed. The question of what happens when a mouse falls into a container of oil is part of the discussion pertaining to the removal of impurity. More specifically, the issue at hand is the purifying qualities of various materials and liquids. It is well known that Muslim jurists recognized the purifying attributes of water. The question arises with regard to other fluids and materials.[16] Islamic jurists disagreed whether the purifying attributes of water were unique. Some considered water as possessing 'an additional attribute that is not found in other things.'[17] Ibn Ḥanbal belongs to the group that assigns to water an innate purifying quality, and assumes that this quality distinguishes it from other fluids: 'Oil in my opinion (*'indī*) is not of the same status as water.'

Questions of purity and defilement merit thorough legal and anthropological investigations. However, the case of the mouse was presented in this study not because of the substantive legal issues that it raises, but because of Ibn Ḥanbal's legal reasoning. Although 'Abdallāh's question does not mention water, Ibn Ḥanbal directed his answer to the general topic of the purifying characteristics of water and other fluids.

Even though he did not have to add other justifications, Ibn Ḥanbal chose to present his position in a logical manner, and in the course of this effort, revealed his attitude towards the use of human reasoning. Ibn Ḥanbal starts out from what was apparently a well-known premise – oil cannot remove an impurity set in by urine. He then moves on to a crude and incomplete exercise in analogical reasoning: He argues that since oil cannot remove the impurity of urine, it cannot remove the impurity of a mouse. The shared element, which enables the employment of analogical reasoning, is oil. Ibn Ḥanbal argues that if we know that oil does not have a purifying effect in one circumstance, we can infer that it would not have one in others.

Ibn Ḥanbal was aware that there are no direct references to the purifying characteristics of oil when it comes into contact with contaminating animals, and therefore he uses the process of inference to settle this matter. He starts out with another case that refers to the purifying characteristics of oil, i.e., the inability of oil to purify cloth that came into contact with urine. Ibn Ḥanbal concludes from this second case that oil does not possess the purifying capacities of water. He returns from this general proposition to the specific case of the mouse in the oil container, and by way of deduction, concludes that oil cannot function as a purifying influence when a mouse falls into a large container, even though water would have done so. Though not stated explicitly, Ibn Ḥanbal uses analogical reasoning to move from the particular to the general and back to the particular.

Zakāt of a mad man

> 'Abū Dāwūd said: I heard Aḥmad questioned whether *zakāt* [ought to be extracted] from the money of the mad. He said: Yes, the minor (*ṣabiyy*), is he not like him [the mad] and he gives *zakāt* from his money?'[18]

Islamic jurists have not reached a consensus regarding the categories of individuals that are obliged to pay the *zakāt*. Abū Dāwūd al-Sijistānī, Ibn Ḥanbal's outstanding disciple, is aware of the disagreement and asks Ibn Ḥanbal for his opinion on the matter. The structure of Ibn Ḥanbal's reply is based on finding a resemblance between madmen and youths. The idea that he could extrapolate from the case of the youth to that of the madman indicates that Ibn Ḥanbal was willing to apply analogical reasoning. The common ground, which enabled Ibn Ḥanbal to move between the two cases was their shared status in the eyes of Islamic law. Neither youth nor madmen were considered to be *takalluf*, i.e., legally and religiously responsible for their deeds.[19]

Based on the position that the legal status of the mad and the minor were comparable, Ibn Ḥanbal felt he could articulate a legal decision regarding the *zakāt* of the mad. This move from a known case (youth) to an unknown case (mad) based on their similar legal standing is an example of *qiyās*. Despite the fact that Ibn Ḥanbal does not use this term or spell out what the two categories have in common, his inference takes advantage of analogical reasoning.

Purity and prayer

As was mentioned above, several historians of Islamic law correctly point out that Ibn Ḥanbal was reluctant to use analogical reasoning. The most important consequence of Ibn Ḥanbal's reluctance to use analogical reasoning was his search for alternatives, one being legal precedents of the Prophet's Companions (*ṣaḥāba*).[20] The inclusion of their decisions in the body of legal precedents enlarged the pool of authoritative sources and reduced the need for *qiyās* and personal interpretations. Ultimately, of course, this was Ibn Ḥanbal's objective. The following example is a rare instance in which Ibn Ḥanbal explicitly remarked on his jurisprudential priorities. Furthermore, a comparison between Ibn Ḥanbal's and al-Shāfi'ī's methods in this case demonstrates the differences in their approaches.

The requirement that believers be in a state of purity when praying is mentioned in the Qur'an: 'O ye who believe! When ye rise up for prayer, wash your faces and your hands up to the elbows, and lightly rub your heads and (wash) your feet up to the ankles.'[21] This verse specifies what the practitioners must do in order to purify themselves.[22] Should people pray while being in a state of impurity their prayers will not be received by Allah.[23] For the most part, the legal schools were in agreement that the four major causes for the loss of the state of purity were: contact with the skin of the other sex; relieving oneself; sleep or loss of consciousness; and contact with one's own sexual organ. Although adherents of the different schools agreed on the main points, they debated certain nuances. For example, Ibn Ḥanbal and al-Shāfiʿī disagreed about certain subtleties regarding contact with one's sexual organ. In the course of their discussions, each made use of a different technique of proof and argument.

While they agreed that contact with one's own sexual organ can annul the state of purity, Ibn Ḥanbal and al-Shāfiʿī differed about the definition of 'touch.'[24] Al-Shāfiʿī maintained that the only contact that annuls a state of purity, and thereby obligates the individual to perform the ritual of ablution (*wuḍūʾ*), is contact between the palm of the hand (*baṭn*) and the sexual organ. He did not consider contact between the back of the hand (*ẓahr*) or any other part of the arm with the sexual organ as nullifying the state of one's purity.[25] Ibn Ḥanbal's position was that contact with any part of the arm (*bisāʿidihi*) will bring about a state of impurity and obligate the person to perform ritual ablution.

Al-Shāfiʿī put forth a linguistic and logical exposition in support of his position. His point of departure was a Prophetic tradition which states that contact between the hand and one's sexual organ requires ablution. The tradition does not specify which part of the hand is meant, leaving this issue open for debate. When describing the movement of the hand, it does, however, use a specific word, 'if one of you reaches (*afḍā*) with his hand (*bi-yadihi*) . . .'.[26] Al-Shāfiʿī's argument hinges on the meaning of the word *afḍā*. He maintains that this word can only refer to the palm of the hand, and introduces a number of examples in which the term 'reaches out' *afḍā bi-yadihi* is known to mean only the palm of the hand.[27] Having established that there are two possible types of contact (the palm or the back of the hand) and that the term used in the Prophetic tradition implies the palm, he goes on to prove that contact with the back of the hand does not bring about a state of impurity.

Al-Shāfiʿī asserts that contact between a man's clothing and the blood of a menstruating woman does not impel the man to purify himself and states that blood is a stronger defiler of purity than is the male sexual organ. He then argues that if contact with blood does not require a man to perform ablution, then through the use of analogical reasoning (*qiyāsan 'alayhi*), we can presume that contact with a sexual organ does not either.[28] The sole exception to this rule is when we possess an explicit report (*al-khabr bi-'aynihi*) which instructs us to do otherwise.[29] Here al-Shāfi'ī means the tradition which uses the term 'reaches with his hand (*afḍā bi-yadihi*).'[30] Through the use of *qiyās*, al-Shāfi'ī demonstrated that in general, contact between one's hand and one's sexual organ does not necessarily lead to defilement and loss of purity.

In contrast, Ibn Ḥanbal held that any contact between the hand or arm and one's sexual organ causes nullification of purity and requires the individual involved to go through the ceremony of ablution. A difference of opinion between any two jurists is not surprising. What is exceptional here is Ibn Ḥanbal's rejection of the use of *qiyās*.

From Ibn Ḥanbal's point of view, the use of analogical reasoning reflects the inability to present a better argument: 'Those who say only a distinct part (*inamā huwa 'udw minhu*) [those who limit the defiling contact to one part of the human body] say this on the sole [basis] of analogy and do not say this [on the basis] of something they heard [a transmission from the Prophet, Companions and Successors] on the matter.'[31] According to Ibn Ḥanbal, reliance on analogy when there are precedents of Companions and Successors at one's disposal reflects a mistaken hierarchy of legal sources.[32]

In their treatment of the problem, the two scholars supported their respective positions in a manner that exemplified their general views on jurisprudence. Al-Shāfi'ī turned to reason and Ibn Ḥanbal to precedent.

The breakup of the Traditionist milieu

Despite Ibn Ḥanbal's prediliction to avoid analogical reasoning where al-Shāfi'ī tended to use it, their legal outlooks did not contradict. Both of them recognized the legitimacy of using *qiyās* and both considered the Qur'an and the *sunna* as the basis upon which the whole jurisprudential system is built. The resemblance of their views steers us away from a jurisprudential explanation of the breakup between the two circles and the formation of a separate Ḥanbali school of law and prompts us to search for other factors that can explain this process. What were the forces that shook the Traditionist camp so vigorously that the existing jurisprudential cracks widened into an unbridgeable gap?

It is difficult to unravel the tangled relations of the Shāfiʿīs and Ḥanbalis. Beginning with al-Shāfiʿī and Ibn Ḥanbal themselves the relationship between the two camps had its ups and downs. In its better moments, mutual respect and cooperation characterized it. For example, when Ibn Ḥanbal studied with al-Shāfiʿī in Baghdad and tried to bring other students to study with the young teacher. At times it deteriorated into acrimony, as when al-Shāfiʿī offered Ibn Ḥanbal the position of *qāḍī* in Yemen and was humiliated by Ibn Ḥanbal's response.[33] The tense intimacy between Shāfiʿīs and Ḥanbalis continued for generations. There were frequent debates between Shāfiʿīs and Ḥanbalis about which of the two masters benefited most from their relationship.

The question of the relationship between the Shāfiʿīs and Ḥanbalis becomes all the more puzzling if we take into account the overlapping intellectual networks. Ibn Ḥanbal himself and some of his outstanding disciples, such as Abū Dāwūd al-Sijistānī and Ibrāhīm al-Ḥarbī are considered disciples of al-Shāfiʿī. The dual affiliation is hardly a coincidence. Shāfiʿīs and Ḥanbalis went through similar career paths, studied the same topics (primarily Traditions) with the same teachers, and ascribed to very similar jurisprudential views. The centrality of Ibn Ḥanbal and al-Shāfiʿī in this milieu motivated their adherents, as well as independent scholars like al-Bukhārī, Muslim and Ibn Rāhwayh, to study with both of them or with their students. This web of intellectual connections could be expected to further consolidate the cohesion of the Traditionist milieu and the Shāfiʿī circle, which was its earliest institutional expression.

Al-Shāfiʿī, Ibn Ḥanbal and their Traditionist colleagues shared more than a jurisprudential outlook and a similar pool of students, they also had a common ideological enemy, the *ahl al-ra'y*. During the second and third centuries A.H., the *ahl al-ra'y* led a forceful intellectual attack on the Traditionists, creating a sense of unity among the Traditionists that went beyond having a common jurisprudential method. They now shared a cultural threat. The *ahl al-ra'y*, their ideological enemies, were doing their utmost to marginalize the Traditionists. As one traditionist put it: 'The adherents of *ra'y* mocked (*yahaza'ūn*) the adherents of traditions, until al-Shāfiʿī taught them [a lesson] and presented them with proof (*wa-aqām al-ḥujja ʿalayhum*).'[34] Ibn Ḥanbal described a similar situation: 'We intended to refute the exponents of *ra'y*, but we did not succeed; then al-Shāfiʿī came and led us to victory.'[35]

According to the Traditionsits, during the second and third centuries A.H., their own side had difficulties and was losing the battle to the *ahl al-ra'y*. It is not clear if this meant that growing numbers of scholars were deserting their ranks or that they did not have the intellectual tools to compete with the *ahl al-ra'y*'s jurisprudential views. Traditionists, Ibn Ḥanbal included, considered al-Shāfi'ī's articulation of a jurisprudential theory to be the turning point in this struggle.[36] In his *Risāla*, al-Shāfi'ī elaborated the principles of a jurisprudential approach that would later be embraced by most Traditionists. This jurisprudential framework enabled the Traditionists to place enormous weight on Traditions, primarily Prophetic ones, as legal precedents. As a result of al-Shāfi'ī's *Risāla*, the growing importance of traditions was finalized and their status as sources of Islamic law was firmly established.

PART III

Miḥna

Introduction

In the Introduction, it was pointed out that the *miḥna* was described from at least two points of view, the Mu'tazili and the Ḥanbali. This chapter leans heavily (though not solely) on the Ḥanbali perspective, but it does not describe the sequence of events in Ibn Ḥanbal's interrogation. It does not concern itself with the insoluble question: Did Ibn Ḥanbal break down under torture or not?[1] Rather, it analyzes the arguments that were raised during the course of the debate and attempts to discern what the Ḥanbalis thought about the *miḥna*. It also deals with how the Ḥanbalis felt after the *miḥna* was over. It may seem surprising, but the victorious Traditionists went through a crisis after the *miḥna* came to an end. I attempt to show that this crisis was probably the most important factor in shaping the Ḥanbali *madhhab*.

Chapter 7 begins with the well-studied topic of al-Ma'mūn and his motives for initiating the *miḥna*.[2] Its opening premise is that al-Ma'mūn was part of the *mutakallimūn* milieu. This is a crucial, well-known, yet often neglected fact. Its implication is that al-Ma'mūn need not be pigeonholed as a Shī'ī, Mu'tazili, or Murji'i. He supported all *mutakallimūn* and their belief that faith ought to be approached with theological tools. It is only when we take into account that al-Ma'mūn supported the efforts of all *mutakallimūn* to define faith through theological discourse and did not attempt to advance the interests of a single camp within the *mutakallimūn* milieu that we can reconstruct his views on the *miḥna*. Such an approach is the best way to understand his political interests. Al-Ma'mūn's political target, as it appears in his letters, was to block the Traditionists, who were marginalizing all the streams of the *mutakallimūn*, and enable the latter to shape Islamic religiosity.

Perhaps the best way to uncover al-Ma'mūn's political agenda is to look at who executed the religious policy after his death. The chief inquisitor from that time on was Ibn Abī Du'ād, and his accomplices were a group of *qāḍī*s and *mutakallimūn*. The rest of the chapter examines how he, together with these *qāḍīs*, who constituted the inquisitorial network, ran the *miḥna.*

Chapter 8 is the heart of the interpretation presented in this study. It is a close reading of Ibn Ḥanbal's interrogations, which reveals the Ḥanbali view of the event. Much like al-Ma'mūn's letter, Ḥanbali accounts of the Inquisition do not mention the tension between the caliphs and the *'ulamā'*. The clash is rather between the adherents of two intellectual trends who are battling over the nature of Islam. Each of these scholarly networks is a discursive community that has its own principles of proof, ideals of knowledge, and norms of intellectual interaction. The protocols of Ibn Ḥanbal's interrogation reveal that the gap between the two is so wide that most of the exchanges between Ibn Ḥanbal and his inquisitors deal with how to go about the interrogation and not about the Qur'an itself.

Chapter 9 exposes the darker side of the Traditionist milieu after its victory over the courtiers and *mutakallimūn*. The generation of Traditionists that saw some of its leaders sent to prison and die there was not very forgiving to those scholars that cooperated with the inquisitors. Ibn Ḥanbal voiced some of the harshest criticism against them. Along with Ibn Ḥanbal several Traditionists waged an internal battle against other Traditionists over an unsettled theological question: *lafẓ al-Qur'an* (the utterance of the Qur'an). Below the surface was, again, the question of the status of theology, and this controversy, in which the Ḥanbalis were very active, is the background for the transformation of the Ḥanbalis from just another circle in the Traditionist milieu to a *madhhab*.

CHAPTER SEVEN

The Inquisitors

Al-Ma'mūn

When al-Ma'mūn entered Baghdād in 204 A.H., he asked Yaḥyā b. Aktham, a young Baṣrian *qāḍī* with many friends who excelled in knowledge and *murū'a* (chivalry and honor), to send some of these people to him. 'Choose from among your friends a group that will keep me company and visit me often, and [Yaḥyā b. Aktham] chose twenty among which was Ibn Abī Du'ād...'[3]

Al-Ma'mūn's request does not reveal a preference to any particular intellectual trend. This anecdote and others, which refer to the intellectuals that al-Ma'mūn gathered around him, create the impression that he did not discriminate between theologians of different trends. On the contrary, al-Ma'mūn sought thinkers of various persuasions who could debate one other and address theological and cultural topics from different angles. In a long citation that discusses al-Ma'mūn, al-Mas'ūdī describes him in the following manner: 'He [al-Ma'mūn] held sessions with theologians and admitted to his company scholars who had distinguished themselves in dialectic disputation and debate, people like Abū-'l-Hudhayl and an-Naẓẓām as well as their partisans and adversaries.'[4] Al-Ma'mūn's tendency to surround himself with intellectuals of varying, even contrasting, views is made clear in the observation that 'he held sessions with' partisans of one trend and their adversaries.

There was, however, one condition that scholars whom al-Ma'mūn invited had to fulfill. It was expected of them to accept the assumption that human beings could and should discuss the essence and attributes of Allah, and to excel in these debates. Once this condition was met, it did not matter what specific position was espoused. It seems that al-Ma'mūn was interested in theological investigation and not in a particular dogma. It did not disturb him if the *mutakallimūn* did not agree with one another or with him on such theological queries as free will, the createdness of the Qur'an, or the status of 'Alī. What mattered to al-Ma'mūn was that the members of his intellectual entourage would embrace similar attitudes towards theological inquiry and agree upon the principles of discussion.

A dramatic chapter from al-Ṭabarī's *Ta'rīkh*, where al-Ma'mūn is described as being brought to tears because of an exchange with Ṭāhir b. al-Ḥusayn, who killed his brother during the civil war, contains a long and fascinating digression that reveals some of the names, topics, rules of etiquette and forms of discourse that al-Ma'mūn endorsed. Bishr b. Ghiyāth al-Marīsī (d. 218), a well-known Murji'i, relates: 'I together with Thumāmah (b. Ashras al-Numayrī) and Muḥammad b. 'Alī al-'Abbās (al-Ṭūsī) and 'Alī b. al-Haytham, was present at 'Abdallāh al-Ma'mūn's court. They were engaged in a disputation about Shī'īsm.'[5] This short list of participants includes a Murji'i (Bishr al-Marīsī), a Mu'tazili (Thumāma b. Ashras) (d. 213), a Zaydi theologian ('Alī b. al-Haytham) and a commander from al-Ma'mūn's army (Muḥammad b. al-'Abbās) and illustrates the openness typical of al-Ma'mūn's court. Despite the fact that each of the participants belonged to a different trend, they were capable of maintaining a dialogue, precisely because they all ascribed to the principles of *kalām* (theology).

The debate grew hot and insults were exchanged. Al-Ma'mūn interrupted the participants and scolded them in a monologue that revealed how he viewed religious disputations:

> 'Al-Ma'mūn, who was at first reclining on a cushion, then sat up and spoke out, 'Hurling insults is unseemly, and unpleasant language is reprehensible. We have allowed theological disputation to take place and have staged the open presentation of [religious] view-points [*aẓharnā al-maqālāt*]. Now upon whoever speaks the truth, we provide instruction; and in regard to whoever is ignorant of both ways [of disputation], we make a decision as to what is appropriate for him. So, you two, come to an agreement on basic principles [*aṣl*], for *kalām* is concerned with secondary, derivative matters [*furū'*], and if you pursue a topic into all its secondary aspects, you nevertheless come back in the end to the basics...
> The two of them discussed the topic of the divinely-ordained prescriptions and laws (*farā'iḍ wa-al-sharā'i'*) in Islam, and argued together after that.'[6]

Al-Ma'mūn's remarks clarified his expectations of disputations and *kalām*. Theological disputation is meant to arrive at and convey truths.

The technique leads the participants through 'basic principles' and 'derivative matters.' This technique could be employed in a discussion about Shī'īsm or 'divinely ordained prescriptions and laws.' Yet, what is particularly instructive is the expectation that theological discussions should have rules, and that if these rules are observed, one can expect to arrive at the most basic truths of the universe. This is the underlying assumption of all *mutakallimūn*, and because they shared this basic position, they were capable of disputing members of other *mutakallimūn* trends. Al-Ma'mūn's terse remarks touches upon the manner that the *mutakallimūn* communicated, regardless of their partisan affiliation.

Al-Ma'mūn's patronage of the *mutakallimūn* and the support he extended to projects that advanced their intellectual endeavors, is well known.[7] The foundation of the Bayt al-Ḥikma, the expeditions to Byzantium to find and purchase books of ancient Greek wisdom, and the search for like-minded intellectuals who would converse with him about philosophy, theology, the sciences, poetry and other subjects, are familiar themes in the history of Islamic civilization. Al-Ma'mūn's ambitions of cultural control, however, were not limited to the *mutakallimūn*, but included the Traditionists as well. We are told by Isḥāq b. Mūsā al-Anṣārī (d. 244), a reputable transmitter of traditions who also served as a *qāḍī*: 'Al-Ma'mūn gave me money to divide among the Traditionists if any of them is weak [financially], not one of them [Traditionists] refused [the handout] except Aḥmad b. Ḥanbal, he declined.'[8]

From the little that we know about Isḥāq b. Mūsā al-Anṣārī, he was the ideal mediator between the court and the Traditionists.[9] His reputation as a fine scholar of traditions enabled him to approach other Traditionists; hand-in-hand with this he was willing to work for the court, as his position of *qāḍī* indicates. Though this anecdote does not specify how often al-Ma'mūn distributed money among the Traditionists, it does demonstrate that al-Ma'mūn was interested in gaining influence in this circle.

Isḥāq b. Mūsā al-Anṣārī was not the sole Traditionist to receive money from al-Ma'mūn's court. In a conversation among a number of *miḥna* victims, 'Affān Abū 'Uthmān (d. 220) told his friends that Isḥāq b. Ibrāhīm, al-Ma'mūn's governor in Baghdād, was instructed to threaten 'Affān in the course of the interrogation that he would 'cut that which we usually give him.'[10] According to Ḥanbal b. Isḥāq, 'Affān received 500 dirham monthly from al-Ma'mūn.[11] 'Affān was not shaken by this threat and was willing to give up the subsidy.

These two stories do not furnish enough information for a comprehensive assessment of al-Ma'mūn's activities among the

Traditionists, but, they do indicate that the range of al-Ma'mūn's philantropic activities covered the full spectrum of Islamic intellectual currents. Al-Ma'mūn's threats of withdrawing his support from the interogees suggests that his patronage was widespread and manipulative.

Two features of al-Ma'mūn's religio-political policy deserve emphasis. First, al-Ma'mūn did not display political favoritism towards any of the trends that made up the *mutakallimūn* milieu. He helped all the members of this milieu by placing them in positions of intellectual influence and supporting them financially. Whatever his personal beliefs may be, he chose counselors from different theological currents. If we want to reconstruct how al-Ma'mūn envisioned the religio-political map, we ought to ignore the theological nuances that distinguished one *mutakallimūn* trend from another, because in political terms al-Ma'mūn did not have any preferences.

Second, the significant religio-cultural divide during al-Ma'mūn's reign was between the Traditionists and the *mutakallimūn*. At the outset, al-Ma'mūn's policy towards the Traditionists followed the lines of previous caliphs, as he like them distributed financial aid to the Traditionists. However, when al-Ma'mūn realized that the Traditionists accepted his financial support but not his intellectual directives, he changed his policy. The fact of the matter is that long before the *miḥna*, al-Ma'mūn failed to attain control of the Traditionists and he was probably aware of their independence and their success in winning the support and admiration of the masses.

In light of al-Ma'mūn's failure to control the Traditionists through patronage and to advance the *mutakallimūn*, he resorted to a new and more aggressive policy. In his letter that initiates the *miḥna* he depicts them as the enemies of *kalām* that must be eradicated from the community of believers. Although he does not use the term *muḥaddithūn* – i.e., Traditionists, he uses terms that hint to them. For example, he writes of his ideological opponents: 'They consider themselves adherents of the *sunnah*…'[12] Al-Ma'mūn was not willing to confer upon his enemies the status of the 'adherents of the *sunnah*,' as it would be giving them much religious credit. However, he was aware that that is how they viewed themselves and so he describes them as those that 'consider themselves' as such. Since the term *sunnah* meant the habits and norms of the Prophet, 'adherents of the *sunnah*' referred to those scholars who studied and transmitted anecdotes about the behavior of the Prophet. Gradually this term, which initially connoted an intellectual preoccupation with the Prophet's life, came to describe a particular group of scholars characterized by a number of specific ideological features. Al-Ma'mūn noticed the growing influence of these self-ascribed 'adherents of the *sunnah*' or Traditionists, and instigated the *miḥna* so as to stop them.

Al-Ma'mūn's descriptions of his adversaries do not utilize the term *'ulamā'*, which refers to all scholars, nor does he challenge their spiritual authority. Rather, al-Ma'mūn employs more limited and specific phrases, such as self-styled 'adherents of the *sunnah*' or 'people of ... and unity (*ahl...wa-'l-jamā'a*),' terms used to describe the proto-Sunni Traditionists. This indicates that al-Ma'mūn struck at a circumscribed segment of the *'ulamā'*, the Traditionists, that resisted his theological views and not at the *'ulamā'* as a whole.

Al-Ma'mūn referred to the resistance, or as he would put it, the inability of the Traditionists to carry out a theological inquiry.

> 'The Commander of the Faithful has realized that the broad mass and the overwhelming concentration of the base elements of the ordinary people ... have no farsightedness, or vision, or faculty of reasoning by means of such evidential proofs as God approves along the right way which He provides, or faculty of seeking illumination by means of the light of knowledge and God's decisive proofs.'[13]

Here again, the letter does not give an indication that al-Ma'mūn perceived the *miḥna* in terms of caliph versus *'ulamā'*. His references to the caliph's responsibilities and intellectual gifts were probably intended to bring the caliph back into the intellectual and religious arenas, after his 'Abbāsid predecessors left these spheres in the hands of the *'ulamā'*. He emphasized the caliph's responsibility to guard the faith, not his ability to define it. There is no indication in al-Ma'mūn's letters that he as caliph has intellectual capacities or sources of knowledge that the *'ulamā'* do not possess. Proclamations about the caliph's importance and religious responsibility never came at the expense of the *'ulamā'*. He did not point to the inherent religious or intellectual superiority of the caliphs over the *'ulamā'*, but rather mentioned the training and intellectual abilities that an individual must have in order to comprehend religious matters. These intellectual tools, which al-Ma'mūn shared with the *mutakallimūn* who surrounded him, evolved around human intelligence and the skill to use rational faculties. According to al-Ma'mūn, the caliph is not the sole spiritual guide of the community. He has partners, intellectuals trained in the appropriate techniques and religious sciences.

The *miḥna* letters reveal another aspect of al-Ma'mūn's views about Islamic society. According to al-Ma'mūn the religio-intellectual enemies who rejected the implementation of human rational faculties to theological dogma, the self-styled 'adherents of the *sunnah*,' were gaining the upper hand in their struggle with the *mutakallimūn*. He remarks that the Traditionists had attained 'for themselves glory in their [ignorant masses] eyes and securing for themselves leadership and a reputation for probity amongst them [ignorant people].'[14] The *mutakallimūn*'s enemies, he says, were winning the struggle over the spiritual leadership of the Islamic community. They were gaining the support of the masses despite the caliph's continuous efforts to advance the *mutakallimūn*. Al-Ma'mūn discusses their achievement quite candidly: 'Thus their testimony had been accepted because they [the ignorant ones or the people of the false way] have declared them [those who claim to be the people of truth] to be veracious witnesses, and the prescriptions of the Book have been put into effect through them [those who claim to be the people of truth] . . .'[15]

What is more, al-Ma'mūn was keenly aware of the weapons that the Traditionists wielded in this struggle. In one of the most telling sentences of al-Ma'mūn's letters, he accuses the Traditionists of asserting that 'all others are people of false beliefs, infidelity and schism.'[16] This charge sums up decades of grass-roots persecution in which the Traditionists used the auxiliary science of traditions, *'ilm al-rijāl* (knowledge of men), to accuse the *mutakallimūn* of embracing 'false beliefs,' thereby ruining many of their careers. Such activities prompted al-Ma'mūn to depict the Traditionists as the companions of Iblis, who uses the Traditionists to strike 'terror into the heart of his adversaries [the *mutakallimūn*] . . .'[17]

The *miḥna* reversed the direction of the accusations, but kept their content. It was now the *mutakallimūn* who accused, interrogated and tortured the Traditionists who did not accept their views on theology. Interestingly, many of al-Ma'mūn's accusations of the Traditionists bear a close resemblance to the accusations that the Traditionist *'ilm al-rijāl* experts hurled at the *mutakallimūn*. Victims and persecutors changed roles, but the accusations remained the same.

In other words, just as the Traditionists had accused the *mutakallimūn* (Qadaris, Murji'is, Shī'īs and Kharijis) of theological deviation, al-Ma'mūn used the theological question of the Qur'an as a means to argue that the Traditionists were deviants from Islam. Just as the Traditionists stopped transmitting on the authority of the *mutakallimūn* and gradually pushed them out of the legal establishment, al-Ma'mūn's argument provided grounds for not allowing the Traditionists to participate in the activities of the legal establishment.

In another accusation al-Ma'mūn argues that anyone who rejects his theological truth deserves 'to be branded as liar in his utterances and as a forger of false testimony...'[18] This touches upon one of the burning issues of the period, the fabrication of traditions. During the second and third centuries A.H., scholars of different ideological camps invented traditions because they wanted to confer prophetic legitimacy to their views. *'Ilm al-rijāl* was supposed to curb these fabrications. Often, *mutakallimūn* lost their credibility as transmitters of traditions because they embraced controversial theological positions. Thus, when al-Ma'mūn refers to 'the person who most properly deserves to be branded as a liar...' he is using the very techniques that the Traditionists employed to delegitimize the *mutakallimūn*. The charge is almost identical, except this time the *mutakallimūn* are making the accusation rather than being accused themselves.

Al-Ma'mūn's remarks about the antagonism of the self-styled 'adherents of the *sunnah*' towards the use of rational faculties and their inability to use such tools, as well as his implied references to their scare tactics and the delegitimization of their adversaries, indicate that the *miḥna* should to be perceived as an alliance between an exceptional caliph and the *mutakallimūn*. The historical context in which al-Ma'mūn operated was the protracted struggle between the Traditionists and the *mutakallimūn*. The achievements of the Traditionists drove him to initiate an unprecedented policy of persecution, and the tactics he chose were similar in many ways to the grass-root persecutions of the Traditionists. One of the clues that this was not a battle between the caliph and the *'ulamā'* is the fact that after al-Ma'mūn's death, only four months into the *miḥna*, it was administered by a handful of *qāḍīs*, most of whom were known to be of the *mutakallimūn* or the *ahl al-ra'y*, rather than by the caliphs who succeeded al-Ma'mūn.

Ibn Abī Du'ād

Rise to power

After the death of al-Ma'mūn, the caliphs and their governors moved to the sidelines as another group of officials took the administration of the *miḥna* into their hands. At the center of this group was Ibn Abī Du'ād, whose stature in the 'Abbāsid court has been compared to that of the

Barmacides in their heyday.[19] He was introduced to the court during the reign of al-Ma'mūn, and it was due to al-Ma'mūn's admiration of Ibn Abī Du'ād that the latter became the chief *qāḍī* during the reign of al-Mu'taṣim. In al-Ma'mūn's testament to al-Mu'taṣim, his brother and future caliph, he recommended that al-Mu'taṣim will 'make sure that he [Ibn Abī Du'ād] does not abandon your [al-Mu'taṣim] side, and associate with him as an adviser in all your affairs, for he is indeed a repository of good advice for you.'[20]

Taking his brother's advice, al-Mu'taṣim dismissed the chief *qāḍī* Yaḥyā b. Aktham, and appointed Ibn Abī Du'ād in his stead. From his new position, Ibn Abī Du'ād wielded enormous political and economic power. Two years after his appointment he felt comfortable enough to approach al-Faḍl b. Marwān (d. 250),[21] another key figure in al-Mu'taṣim's entourage, whose rise to power was as swift as his own had been, to counsel him on how to improve his behavior at the court. Al-Ṭabarī, who recounts this conversation, observes that Ibn Abī Du'ād was a man of astute political acumen who was an uncanny judge of human nature. Thus, when al-Faḍl, sounding like a novice at court, asked Ibn Abī Du'ād:

> 'But what, then, am I to do when he [the caliph] demands from me what I don't have [large sums of money]?' I [Ibn Abī Du'ād] said, be prepared to say, 'O Commander of the Faithful, we will devise some means or other for getting that, and you will secure for yourself a delay of a few days until he is prepared, and then you will take to him part of what he seeks and put him off in regard to the remainder.'[22]

This answer reveals Ibn Abī Du'ād's style of manipulating people with whom he worked. He obviously did not shy away from telling his superiors what they wanted to hear, even when he knew that what he was saying was not true or impossible to achieve. In addition, he was not in awe when addressing the caliph. Quite the contrary, he seems to have been relaxed and to have kept his wits about him. Despite his concession that Ibn Abī Du'ād was right, al-Faḍl b. Marwān could not change his habits of behavior, and fell back on his old style of straightforward and unpleasant replies. According to al-Ṭabarī, al-Faḍl's inability to adapt himself to the requirements of courtly politics cost him his job.[23]

Ibn Abī Du'ād's presence was broadly felt in court and outside of it. He facilitated the release of 'Alī b. Isḥāq 'who was in charge of police duties (*al-ma'ūnah*) at Damascus' and was involved in the killing of a tax collector.[24] His staff supervised the division of booty after the renowned conquest of Amorium.[25] Occasionally he was involved in decisions regarding the expenditure of large sums of money, such as the digging of an irrigation canal in Khurāsān,[26] and the distribution of five million *dirhams* to the merchants of Karkh, the southern quarter of Baghdād, after it was devastated by a fire.[27] The accounts of Ibn Abī Du'ād's involvement in this event demonstrate his outstanding skills in pulling strings at court and getting his own way. He convinced al-Mu'taṣim to spend a huge sum of money by arguing that news of such generosity would reach his enemies, who would dread him on account of his wealth.[28] After the caliph agreed to the expenditure, Ibn Abī Du'ād persuaded him that the money must be handed out by him (i.e., Ibn Abī Du'ād): 'O Amīr al-Mu'minīn, I fear that if anyone else will hand out [the money] it will not be divided equally.'[29] This transparently self-serving statement portrayed Ibn Abī Du'ād as indispensable to al-Mu'taṣim and belittled the other courtiers. It achieved its goals: Ibn Abī Du'ād was given the responsibility and prestige of distributing the money. To this list of achievements we ought to add what was perhaps his greatest political achievement, that would also be his undoing, the nomination of al-Mutawakkil to the throne.[30]

The inquisitorial network

Ibn Abī Du'ād's savvy ways and his familiarity with the ins and outs of al-Mu'taṣim's and al-Wāthiq's courts helped him implement the interrogations. As chief *qāḍī*, he was in charge of advising the caliph with regards to nominating *qāḍīs*. He used this prerogative to appoint like-minded men to positions where they could help him execute his policies. Gradually, Ibn Abī Du'ād put in place a network of *qāḍīs* who administered the *miḥna*.

One of the first appointments made during Ibn Abī Du'ād's tenure was that of Shu'ayb b. Sahl to the position of *qāḍī* of Ruṣāfa, the eastern part of Baghdād. Shu'ayb was reputed to be an advocate of Jahmī doctrine, which meant that he believed the Qur'an was created.[31] He had a reputation for hating the Traditionists whom he annoyed so much that several of them burnt down his house.[32] A group of people met two Jahmīs and ganged up on them. They then went to a mosque to erase an inscription Shu'ayb had made, which said that the Qur'an was created. After being confronted by Shu'ayb's servant, they headed to Shu'ayb's home and set it ablase.

Shu'ayb's fiasco occured in 227A.H., the year al-Mu'taṣim fell sick and died. It may be that as al-Mu'taṣim's health deteriorated and he became less involved in politics, Ibn Abī Du'ād intensified the *miḥna* interrogations. One of the steps Ibn Abī Du'ād took was to require that *miḥna* interogees would be sent to Baghdād. Egypt's *qāḍī* did not follow these instructions and Ibn Abī Du'ād replaced him with the more cooperative Muḥammad b. Abī 'l-Layth al-Aṣamm. Ibn Abī 'l-Layth did not disappoint his mentor. He sent people to Baghdād where they were imprisoned. Some, like the renown Shāfi'ī, Yūsuf b. Yaḥyā al-Buwayṭī, died in jail (d. 232).

When al-Mu'taṣim died and his son al-Wāthiq became caliph, he ordered Ibn Abī 'l-Layth to step up the persecutions. At this point it became apparent that Ibn Abī Du'ād's decision to appoint Ibn Abī 'l-Layth *qāḍī* had proved itself. Historians testify that Ibn Abī 'l-Layth interrogated all of the scholars that he could lay his hands on. Many were put in jail and others fled. He specifically directed his harassment at Shāfi'īs and Mālikis, hinting that the *miḥna* was aimed at helping Ḥanafi lawyers and curtailing the success and popularity of Traditionists of different schools. His policy was lauded by the poet al-Jamal al-Akbar as 'having 'protected' the *kawl* of Abū Ḥanīfa and having 'smashed' the *kawl* of the Shāfi'īs and Mālikis.'[33] This provides another indication that the *miḥna* was perceived as a legal as well as a theological matter. It also illustrates that the dividing line was between the Traditionists (who were often Shāfi'īs and Mālikis) and the *ahl al-ra'y* (who were usually Ḥanafis).

Another *qāḍī* nominated by Ibn Abī Du'ād was 'Abdallāh b. Muḥammad al-Khalanjī. Al-Khalanjī belonged to the *ahl al-ra'y*, i.e., the jurisprudential environment of the Ḥanafi school of law, and was a staunch believer in the creation of the Qur'an.[34] He was also part of a network known 'the companions of Ibn Abī Du'ād.'[35] Its not clear what this characterization refers to, yet we can assume that it implied a high level of legal and theological congruity, and perhaps social connections as well. Al-Khalanjī was appointed *qāḍī* in the days of al-Mu'taṣim. After Ibn Abī Du'ād spoke with the caliph, al-Khalanjī was placed in Hamdhān. At the outset of al-Wāthiq's reign, in 228 A.H., Ibn Abī Du'ād appointed in Baghdād a number of *qāḍīs* who were strident supporters of the *miḥna*. One, al-Ḥasan b. 'Alī b. al-Jad, was a Ḥanafi and was labeled Jahmī.[36]

The *miḥna* was carried out in a number of locations: Baghdād, Egypt, Mecca Kūfa, Hamadhān, and the frontier towns (*thughūr*).[37] Many of the interrogators were part of Ibn Abī Du'ād's circle or members of the ideological milieu to which he belonged. The main ideological features of this cadre were a Ḥanafi affiliation and a predisposition to the theological investigations that were commonplace among the *mutakallimūn*. Al-Ma'mūn, his advisors Bishr al-Marīsī and Ibn Abī Du'ād, and the dozen or so *qāḍīs* who administered the *miḥna* were in one way or another Ḥanafis and participants in theological discourse. Up until the initiation of the *miḥna*, they were the victims. After the new religio-political policy was put into motion, they were the persecutors.

The interrogators

One of the most dramatic events of the *miḥna*, which captured the imagination of those living at the time as well as later generations, was the clash between Ibn Ḥanbal and the Mu'tazili chief *qāḍī*, Ibn Abī Du'ād. Both the Ḥanbalis and the Mu'tazilis left accounts of this episode.[38] Although several of the chronicles mention the argument that occurred between Ibn Ḥanbal and Ibn Abī Du'ād, only one, that of Ḥanbal b. Isḥāq, mentions the names of Ibn Ḥanbal's interrogators.[39] The key figure in the interrogation was Ibn Abī Du'ād, who was assisted by a number of *qāḍīs* and at least one *mutakallim*.

Ibn Abī Du'ād was apparently aware that he would have difficulties convincing al-Mu'taṣim of his position during his show down with Ibn Ḥanbal. He was also cognizant of the fact that al-Mu'taṣim was unhappy with the interrogation itself and would have preferred to avoid putting Ibn Ḥanbal on trial.[40] Al-Mu'taṣim's lack of commitment to the *miḥna* may have been the reason that Ibn Abī Du'ād invited other judges and *mutakallimūn* to attend. In the course of the investigation, when he and Ibn Ḥanbal reached a deadlock, Ibn Abī Du'ād made use of this entourage of jurists and *mutakallimūn*. He turned to the caliph and said: 'These are your judges and lawyers ask them [if Ibn Ḥanbal was misleading his listeners].'[41]

During the first day of Ibn Ḥanbal's interrogation, he was questioned by Ibn Abī Du'ād and 'Abd al-Raḥman b. Isḥāq.[42] A Ḥanafi, 'Abd al-Raḥman began his career as a judge in Raqqa, and was brought to the capital by al-Ma'mūn. He served as *qāḍī* in Baghdād until the later years of al-Mu'taṣim's reign. 'Abd al-Raḥmān posed a number of questions to Ibn Ḥanbal, but according to Ḥanbal's account, had no answer to Ibn Ḥanbal's retort.[43] He reappears in Ḥanbal's account when he discusses with the caliph what should be done with Ibn Ḥanbal and he speaks of Ibn Ḥanbal's loyalty to the caliph and the faith.[44] Both 'Abd al-Raḥmān and Ibn Samā'a, another Baghdādian judge who was one of the *ahl al-ra'y*,[45] took issue with Ibn Ḥanbal about the Qur'an, but defended him in front of the caliph. Though they disagreed with Ibn Ḥanbal about the createdness of the Qur'an, they constantly emphasized Ibn Ḥanbal's respected family and his devotedness.[46]

Ibn Samā'a and 'Abd al-Raḥmān were part of the *ahl al-ra'y* milieu, but they were not members of Ibn Abī Du'ād's circle of friends. Thus, they disagreed with Ibn Ḥanbal and disputed his positions, but did not wish to hurt or execute him. The verdicts of two other interrogators, Shu'ayb b. Sahl and Muḥammad b. 'Īsā Burgūth were much harsher. 'Burgūth said: Oh Amīr al-Mu'minīn, [he is an] apostate [whose] blood is permitted, behead him and his blood is my responsibility (*wa-damuhu fī 'unuqī*). And Shu'ayb said the same.'[47] This is the Shu'ayb b. Sahl that was mentioned above, whose antagonism towards the *ahl al-sunna* was well known and moved some of them to burn down his house.[48]

The most interesting figure in this group was Muḥammad b. 'Īsā Burgūth. He was neither a *qāḍī* nor a Baghdādi but a Baṣri *mutakallim* who had been invited to participate in Ibn Ḥanbal's interrogation. Burgūth was not a very popular thinker and it is hard to find anyone who wrote a good word about him. It is hardly surprising that Sunnis like al-Dhahabī described him as 'the head of the innovation (*bid'a*) Abū 'Abdallāh Muḥammad b. 'Īsā the Jahmī.'[49] It is somewhat more unexpected to find that other theologians, such as Abū 'Affān al-Raqqī, wrote treatises entitled 'Against Burgūth, about the resemblance (*al-Musāwāh*) between him and the heretics (*al-mulḥidūn*);'[50] Despite the treatises written against him, Burgūth attracted a following and founded a sect called the Burgūthiyya. Al-Baghdādi's *al-Farq Bain al-Firaq* classifies the Burgūthiyya as part of the Najjāriyya sect, a current within the Murji'i movement.[51] The Najjāriyya are described by al-Baghdādi in the following manner: 'They agree with us in some fundamental dogmas and with the Kadarites in others.'[52] According to al-Baghdādi, al-Burgūth was an adherent of 'most of al-Najjār's doctrines,'[53] and agreed with the Qadaris on a number of issues, one being 'that the word of God was created.'[54]

The intellectual profile of Burgūth is somewhat blurred. His intellectual genealogy is composed of Murji'is and Mu'tazilis. He was probably part of a Murji'i network that was close to the Mu'tazilis. The obfuscated nature of Burgūth's intellectual make-up is significant. When Burgūth is placed alongside the gallery of advisors and inquisitors that administered the *miḥna* and belonged to several trends of the *mutakallimūn*, it becomes clear that the *miḥna* was not meant to advance the views or interests of any specific trend of *mutakallimūn*. Thus, the *miḥna* was not designed to promote the ideas or interests of a specific current of *mutakallimūn*, but the whole *mutakallimūn* milieu. Its administrators sought to advance their collective interest. The *miḥna* was not about divisive theological polemics. It was about the ability to carry out theological inquiry.

Ibn Ḥanbal on his enemies

To understand the interests, tactics, alliances and enmities that generated the *miḥna*, we must rid ourselves of the notion that an examination of a particular theological view of the *mutakallimūn* can explain this religio-political policy. Theological dogmas, which were incessantly debated among the *mutakallimūn*, cannot account for the cooperation between them. However, to discard the politics of theology, as many modern historians do, simply because the *miḥna*'s administrators were members of different theological sects, is to miss a crucial element of the *miḥna* – the shared political interests of these different sects.

The political cooperation between Mu'tazilis, Murji'is and other *mutakallimūn* did not come about because of questions of dogma. On the contrary, the members of these sects united during the *miḥna* despite their theological disagreements. The irrelevance of hairsplitting theological polemics to the dynamics of the *miḥna* comes across when we assess how their opponents described the *mutakallimūn*. When Ibn Ḥanbal and his companions referred to the inquisitors of the *miḥna* they did not search for precise names that distinguished between the different currents of *mutakallimūn*. They did not bother to discern a particular theological dogma, ascribe it to a specific group, and identify a unique political interest that went hand in hand with the belief. The names they used reveal that they did not identify one specific sect that could be blamed with the instigation and administration of the *miḥna*.

Ibn Ḥanbal was not interested in the finer points of theology that preoccupied the theologians. When he described his interrogators, he referred to them as 'those Baṣrian Mu'tazilis such as Burgūth and his companions.'[55] Heresiographers and modern historians consider Burgūth to be a Murji'i and not a Mu'tazili. Ibn Ḥanbal may or may not have known what these heresiographers and scholars knew when they labeled Burgūth a Murji'i, but this did not determine how he refered to him. From Ibn Ḥanbal's perspective, the theological subtleties that distinguished between the sects of the *mutakallimūn* were unimportant. What mattered was that in the battle over the politics of theology, all of them were one front, with one interest.

The same attitude is revealed in Traditionist references to Bishr al-Marīsī, whom heresiographs and historians label a Murji'i, and who was considered a major influence that caused al-Ma'mūn to instigate the *miḥna*. For the most part, Traditionists refered to al-Marīsī as a *kāfir* (apostate), but when he was linked to a group or sect, it was to vague entities such as Jahmī or Zindīq. Thus, Ibn Ḥanbal did not bother to use the seemingly precise heretic nomenclature. He preferred Jahmīyya and Zanādiqa, vague names rather than precise descriptions of theological camps.

It is not a coincidence that the most prevalent labels used to describe the *miḥna*'s administrators, Jahmīyya and Zanādiqa, went back to amorphous groups of free-thinkers that were persecuted throughout the 'Abbāsid reign. The names Ibn Ḥanbal used to describe his opponents indicate that he did not view the *miḥna* as an attempt to advance the political interests of any single existing sect from the *mutakallimūn* milieu and suggests that he did not identify one specific sect that should be blamed with this political move. The point that he conveyed with these amorphous names was that it would make no sense to differentiate between the sects with specific names that designate particular intellectual trends, because they all shared an underlying assumption about the legitimacy of theology.

CHAPTER EIGHT

The Interrogation

Discursive communities

One of the most telling characteristics of the interrogation were its impasses, which were interpreted by both sides as an indication that they could not conduct a dialogue with the other, not even one of a polemic nature. These dead ends were the outcome of a profound disagreement over the rules of the argument, as each of the sides perceived evidence and proof in a different manner. In effect, we find that the two sides could not relate to each other's arguments.

The differing perceptions of discourse were the product of different approaches to theology. These contrasting visions of the theological enterprise will come into sharper focus once we distinguish between two levels of theological discussion. The first is that of concrete theological problems; for example the createdness or uncreatedness of the Qur'an, divine omnipotence and divine justice. These issues can be discussed and elaborated upon in many ways, generating a number of answers. The *mutakallimūn*'s efforts to come to grip with these concrete problems resulted in a variety of answers. The differences of opinion among the *mutakallimūn* led to their splintering off into countless streams and sub-streams of thought. When we survey the intellectual map from this point of view, we can identify a number of central streams – Mu'tazila, Murji'a, Khawārij and Shī'īs – all of which were, again divided into numerous sub-streams.

However, despite the differences of opinions that caused the *mutakallimūn* to incessantly debate one other, they all shared a basic attitude towards theology. This brings us to the second perspective from which theological discussion can be examined: The underlying attitude towards the theological enterprise? When discussing this issue the gamut of *mutakallimūn* sub-streams come together into one unified trend of thought. All sub-streams agree that theological problems should be raised, that such problems should be analyzed rationally, and that the outcome of such analysis constitutes articles of faith.

The *mutakallimūn*'s consensus regarding theological enterprise and their parting of the ways regarding specific theological problems made them a discursive community. If two theologians took issue with one other, they would have been able to maintain an argument. Each would have presented his proofs and criticized his opponent's line of reasoning. They may not have agreed on any particular issue, but they would have been able to talk to one another. This was not the case when a theologian argued with a Traditionist. Since the two would not agree on the rules of the discussion, the argument would never take off. The inability to maintain a dialogue erected a barrier between the Traditionists and the *mutakallimūn* and created two discursive communities.

The createdness of the Qur'an and Islamic articles of faith

According to Ibn Ḥanbal's account of his interrogation, he was taken into a crowded room, dragging along his shackles.[1] The caliph, al-Mu'taṣim, was seated and Ibn Abī Du'ād and his companions were present. As Ibn Ḥanbal drew closer to the caliph, al-Mu'taṣim asked, somewhat annoyed: 'Didn't you allege (*za'amtum*) that he is a young man? Is he not a middle-aged shaykh?'[2] In his recollection of these events, Ibn Ḥanbal implies that the caliph was unhappy with the interrogators who had misinformed him about Ibn Ḥanbal and had attempted to belittle his stature. Ibn Ḥanbal greeted the caliph and was told to sit down. After a while he asked the caliph for permission to speak which he was given.

'To what,' Ibn Ḥanbal asked, 'did your cousin the messenger of Allah P.B.U.H. call?'[3] Ibn Ḥanbal addressed the caliph respectfully, referring to his noble lineage which goes back to the Prophet's family.

The caliph replied, 'To the testimony [that] there is no God but Allah.'[4]

Ibn Ḥanbal retorted, 'And I testify that there is no God but Allah.'[5]

In his opening remark, Ibn Ḥanbal did not even mention the createdness of the Qur'an and his second comment gets no closer to the inquisitorial question. After agreeing with the caliph about the importance of the statement, 'there is no God but Allah,' he went on to mention a dialogue between the Prophet and a party from the 'Abd al-Qays. According to the tradition that relates the contents of this conversation, the Prophet commanded the members of the party to believe in Allah and the testimony that there is no God but Allah, to pray, to donate *zakāt*, and to give a fifth of the booty. Ibn Ḥanbal concluded his comments by pointing out that he abides to the appeals of the Prophet and embraces the concept of Allah's oneness.[6]

The caliph remained quiet and the initiative was assumed by Ibn Abī Du'ād, who raised a number of theological arguments. Ibn Ḥanbal admitted that he was not familiar with these arguments and said that he had no intention of inquiring about them.

How can we make sense of this conversation, in which the participants seem to be talking past one other rather than to one other? Why did Ibn Ḥanbal ignore the inquisitorial question? Why did his opening statement deal with the oneness and uniqueness of Allah? Why did he remark so nonchalantly that he will not even try to answer Ibn Abī Du'ād's arguments?

In avoiding the issue of the Qur'an's createdness Ibn Ḥanbal made a statement about what he considers legitimate and illegitimate doctrinal discussions. He addressed the issue of Allah's oneness because it appears in the Qur'an. The reference to the Prophet's remarks to the 'Abd al-Qays about belief and ritual is likewise legitimate because it is sanctioned by the Prophet himself. In contrast the question about the createdns of the Qur'an is not mentioned in the Qur'an or Prophetic traditions, and therefore cannot be taken as part of doctrine. The implicit meaning of Ibn Ḥanbal's seemingly irrelevant remarks was that the inquisitorial question did not belong to the sphere of Islamic doctrine.[7]

When Ibn Ḥanbal chose to raise the issue of the oneness of Allah and ignore the question of the createdness of the Qur'an, he was conveying his opinion about the theological enterprise. Ibn Ḥanbal's position was that once a disagreement has arisen over a theological problem, and sanctified sources such as the Qur'an and Prophetic traditions do not furnish a clearly stated answer then any solution that comes up cannot be considered as an article of faith. His criticism of theological disputations is stated very clearly: 'Refrain from arguments (*khuṣūmāt*), avoid the company (*al-julūs*) of sectarians, and avoid quarrel (*al-mirā'*), dispute (*al-jidāl*) and arguments (*al-khuṣūmāt*) pertaining to creed (*dīn*).'[8] According to this outlook, the very definition of creed precludes arguments. Once there is disagreement over a theological matter, it cannot be raised to the level of doctrine.

Ibn Ḥanbal's aversion to the theological dispute over the Qur'an has been presented convincingly by Madelung in a study that traces the history of this controversy.[9] Apparently, Ibn Ḥanbal spoke explicitly about his reluctance to voice his opinion on the matter: 'We used to order silence and refrain from discussion about theology and the Qur'an. But since we were called to a doctrine, it was unavoidable that we refute it and clarify the matter as it ought to be clarified.'[10] Ibn Ḥanbal and the Traditionists were predisposed to avoid theological discussions in general and the question of the Qur'an more specifically because such activities generate disagreements and controversy.

When Ibn Ḥanbal chose to ignore the inquisitorial question and Ibn Abī Du'ād's remarks, he was undermining the legitimacy of the *miḥna*. His decision to avoid the issue signaled to his interrogators that the answer to the inquisitorial question should not be considered part of Islamic doctrine. In other words, the *miḥna* interrogation cannot lead to an answer that would be part of Islamic doctrine because it does not have the sanction of the holy sources. This criticism, which came up implicitly in Ibn Ḥanbal's dialogue with the caliph, was stated explicitly in one of Ibn Ḥanbal's exchanges with Ibn Abī Du'ād: 'You have presented an interpretation (*ta'wīlan*) and you are most knowledgeable, [however] what you have interpreted (*ta'awwalta*) does not warrant jailing and binding (*yuqayyadu 'alayhi*).'[11] This, then, is Ibn Ḥanbal's opinion on the controversy over the createdness of the Qur'an. Be your position as it may, he says to his opponent, and even if you are very knowledgeable and are capable of marshaling important evidence, it remains your personal opinion. A personal opinion is not part of Islamic dogma and therefore cannot be used as a criterion for other people's faith, and obviously it 'does not warrant jailing or binding.'

Other Traditionists raised this criticism of the *miḥna* as well. When Ibn Ḥanbal's uncle, Isḥāq b. Ḥanbal, discussed Ibn Ḥanbal's fate with the governor of Baghdād, he alluded to the same point: 'Amīr, that which my nephew likes [the position he espouses] does not contradict the revelation, and the difference of opinion is only about interpretation.'[12] In this comment Isḥāq b. Ḥanbal removes the issue from the most sacred plane, that of revelation (*tanzīl*), and places it on a secondary level, that of human interpretation, which tolerates differences of opinion. Isḥāq b. Ḥanbal based his plea to free Ibn Ḥanbal on the assumption that there is a dichotomy which differentiates between tenets of faith that appear in the Qur'an, i.e., 'revelation,' and issues that are raised in later discussions, i.e., 'interpretation'. The second category cannot be used as an indication of a believer's status.

Principles of theological investigation

There is a fascinating act of deception in Ibn Ḥanbal's self-confessed ignorance. He described his performance in the interrogation: 'They began to say this and that, and I replied this and that, and when they brought up something of theology that was not in the Book of Allah nor the *sunna* of his Messenger (PBUH) and there was no reference [in their argument] to Prophetic tradition (*khabar*) nor precedent (*athar*), I said I do not know what that is.'[13]

According to Ibn Ḥanbal, when the discussion began it was not a theological investigation, however his adversaries later introduced theological arguments. At that point Ibn Ḥanbal acknowledged ignorance: 'I do not know what that is.' Ibn Ḥanbal's admission of ignorance is mentioned by al-Jāḥiẓ, a Mu'tazili who was on close terms with Ibn Abī Du'ād, who wrote an account of Ibn Ḥanbal's interrogation.[14] His version of the events, however, differs somewhat from the Ḥanbali sources. Al-Jāḥiẓ maintains that Ibn Ḥanbal did participate in theological discussions, but failed to present a convincing argument. When his adversaries pushed him to the wall he would not admit that they were right, but feigned ignorance.

Though the two accounts are at variance regarding important details, they both depict Ibn Ḥanbal as incompetent in theological investigations. From the Mu'tazili standpoint, this spelled victory. In Ḥanbali eyes, Ibn Ḥanbal's profession of ignorance was not a confession but an accusation. Ibn Ḥanbal's replies were not simply an admission of his lack of expertise in the sphere of theology; they were a statement that theology was not worth knowing. His low opinion of *kalām* was the consequence of his view that the forms of proof used in theological discussions are inadequate for revealing the truths that they seek. In a nutshell, Ibn Ḥanbal believed that the tools that theological investigations devise cannot uncover the nature of God.

In order to comprehend what Ibn Ḥanbal meant by his admission of ignorance, we must examine some of the other statements he made during his three-day-long interrogation. The most frequent challenge that Ibn Ḥanbal placed before his interrogators was 'give me anything from the Book of Allah or the *sunna* of his Messenger.'[15] This demand distinguished between legitimate sources of theological truths, namely the sanctified Islamic texts, and the process of theological investigation, whose fruits could never attain the status of theological truths.

Ibn Ḥanbal's self-righteous tenacity stretched Ibn Abī Du'ād's patience to its limits, and at a certain point he retorted: 'And do you limit yourself to [what is written in] the Book of Allah or the *sunna* of his Messenger?"[16] Ibn Ḥanbal replied: 'Of what is Islam made besides the Book and the *sunna* (*wa-hal yaqūm al-Islam illā bi-'l-kitāb wa-'l-sunna*), you have invented (*ikhtara'ta*) a [personal] opinion and interpreted an interpretation which you propagate (lit. to which you call) to the people.'[17]

Ibn Ḥanbal's reply does not address Ibn Abī Du'ād's question. He merely emphasizes the dichotomy of Scripture and personal opinion. According to Ibn Ḥanbal, theological investigation falls under the rubric of personal opinion. Ibn Ḥanbal is willing to accept theological truisms if, and only if, they are clearly stated in the Qur'an and *sunna*. He will not agree, however, to consider the result of theological investigation as a theological truth, precisely because it was not found in a sanctified text. If a particular theological problem has to be investigated, this means that it did not appear in a clear manner in the texts. As a result it cannot be considered a part of doctrine. From this point of view the human imagination which concocts theological questions, the human faculties of reason which answer them, and human vanity which embraces the answers and promotes them to the status of absolute truth cannot enjoy the authority of scripture. Ibn Ḥanbal was concerned with delineating the sphere of articles of faith, and not with proving that his own opinion is correct. As a result, he felt it irrelevant to address Ibn Abī Du'ād's impatient accusation. By definition, the whole discussion, including Ibn Ḥanbal's own opinion, cannot be treated as a component of faith.

The most explicit remark that Ibn Ḥanbal makes about his opponents' inability to reveal the truth about God is in the following appeal to al-Mu'taṣim:

> O Amīr al-Mu'minīn, they do not have [the ability of] distinction and clarification, and the knowledge to which they summon me is not of the Book of Allah nor the *sunna* of his Prophet, [but] interpretation which they interpreted and [personal] view which they held, and the Prophet (PBUH) prohibited disputation regarding the Qur'an, and said: 'Dispute about the Qur'an is heresy (*kufr*),' and I am not an adherent of dispute nor of *kalām*, I am solely an adherent of traditions (*āthār wa-akhbār*).'[18]

Ibn Ḥanbal reiterates the dichotomy of scripture and private opinion. He admits that he is not knowledgeable in those areas of 'interpretation and personal judgement,' which his opponents have developed. However, he accuses them of being incapable of living up to their promises: 'They don't have [the ability of] distinction and clarification ...' It is as if he is saying, I admit that I do not know the contents of *kalām*, but they do not know the limitations of *kalām*. One need not study *kalām* in order to realize what its limitations are. We need only to observe that its sources are not scripture and that its means of investigation is the fallible human mind to realize that it cannot possibly attain what it aspires to grasp, namely, divine truths.

Al-Ma'mūn and his entourage of *mutakallimūn* held an appropriate view of human reason. In his letter of instigation, al-Ma'mūn accuses his opponents (Ibn Ḥanbal included) of lacking the faculties and training to achieve theological knowledge. This criticism reveals his view that he and his partners did possess the skill to use reason to investigate theological problems. This theme will appear in al-Jāḥiẓ's epistle to Ibn Abī Du'ād's son. Like al-Ma'mūn, al-Jāḥiẓ noted the Traditionists' inability to use reason:

> And the Traditionists and the masses (*wa-'l-'awāmm*) are those who follow blindly (*yuqallidūn*) and do not infer (*wa-lā yuḥaṣṣilūn*), and they do not choose, [yet] blind acceptance is objectionable according to rational reasoning, and forbidden by the Qur'an (*manhī 'anhu fī al-Qur'an*), as you can see they [Traditioninsts] have reversed (*'akasū*) the matters, and violated the norms. We have no doubt that he who examines (*naẓara*) and investigates and compares is in the better [position] (*aḥaqqu*) to understand and arrive at the truer argument.[19]

According to al-Jāḥiẓ, a theological truth can only be realized through intellectual capacities. Interestingly enough, al-Jāḥiẓ is fully aware of the Traditionists' views on this matter, and therefore he accuses them of reversing matters.

Al-Jāḥiẓ's emphasis on reason contradicts Ibn Ḥanbal's position: 'The creed (*al-dīn*) is only [what is found] in Allah's book and the traditions (*āthār*) and the practices (*sunan*).'[20] Ibn Ḥanbal discusses the way this information came down to his generation and characterizes the righteous scholars who transmitted theological dogma from generation to generation. They 'are not followers (*aṣḥāb*) of analogy nor of personal opinion (*ra'y*).'[21] This observation about righteous scholars is based on a more general statement about theology, in which Ibn Ḥanbal denies the legitimacy of the use of reason in theological matters: 'Because analogy in [questions] of creed is futile (*li-'anna al-qiyās fī al-dīn bāṭil*), and likewise with personal opinion (*wa-'l-ra'y*) [which is] even more futile then it [analogy].'[22]

Ibn Ḥanbal's condemnation of the *mutakallimūn* was not limited to what he considered as unrealistic and naive belief that they had devised techniques to unravel the most difficult riddles of the universe. He also found fault with the fact that the *mutakallimūn*'s discussions of theology took on the nature of disputations. Ibn Ḥanbal apparently found any disagreement regarding the nature of God offensive. It seems clear that Ibn Ḥanbal believed that content (the discussion of God) and style (disputations) was interrelated. In the criticism he airs before al-Mu'taṣim, Ibn Ḥanbal mentions the two in one breath: 'I am not an adherent of dispute nor of *kalām*.'[23] His discussions with his disciples show how deeply disturbed he was by disputations regarding theology. He describes the way of the sunna as 'abandonment (*tark*) [of] disputes (*al-mirā'*) and argument (*al-jidāl*) and controversies (*al-khuṣūmāt*) in matters of creed (*al-dīn*).'[24]

Debates and disputations became a social activity for the *mutakallimūn*.[25] When Ibn Ḥanbal condemned disputations, he was no doubt aware that he was attacking the social practices of the *mutakallimūn*. Ibn Ḥanbal's criticism was a means of demarcating the boundaries between the two discursive communities. His words highlight how different perceptions of theology were transformed into different social practices, expressing and buttressing the unique nature of each community.

Qur'anic exegesis and *sunna*

Ibn Ḥanbal's oft-repeated demand that his adversaries furnish Qur'anic proof forced Ibn Abī Du'ād to quote scripture. The verses that Ibn Abī Du'ād cited as proof for his belief that the Qur'an was created, compelled Ibn Ḥanbal to reply directly to his arguments. In contrast to his intentional disregard of Ibn Abī Du'ād's points about *kalām*, Ibn Ḥanbal felt obliged to address Ibn Abī Du'ād's Qur'anic arguments. As a result, the interpretation of the Qur'an became the central arena for the debate between Ibn Ḥanbal and Ibn Abī Du'ād.

In the course of the interrogation, two Qur'anic verses were presented as proof that the Qur'an states that it was created. The first was cited by Shu'ayb, the infamous Baghdādī *qāḍī*: 'We have made it (*ja'alnāhu*) a Qur'an.' He continued and pressed the point, 'is not everything that is made (*maj'ūl*) [also]created (*makhlūq*).'[26] To this Ibn Ḥanbal replied, 'I said to him, Allah said 'Then he reduced them (*ja'alnāhum*) to fragments...'[27] 'Green crops devoured (by cattle),'[28] did he create them? Is every *maj'ūl makhlūq* [is the meaning of *maj'ūl* always identical to *makhlūq*]?'[29]

The implication of Ibn Ḥanbal's terse reply is that *maj'ūl* and *makhlūq* are not necessarily synonymous. The term *maj'ūl* can be synonymous to *makhlūq* when it indicates something that was made to come into being, but it can also mean ascribing or granting something a specific characteristic. In the passages that Ibn Ḥanbal introduces, the term *ja'ala* takes the second meaning.

The exchange between Shu'ayb and Ibn Ḥanbal was brief. In a refutation written on Ibn Ḥanbal's authority sometime after the interrogation, Ibn Ḥanbal presented a fuller explanation of his position regarding the term *ja'ala* and an explicit critique of his opponents' interpretation of the term:

> 'Ask a Jahmī where in Allah's book or in the Sunna he will find it said that the Qur'an was created. Unable to find, he will say that it is (inferred) from Allah's words: 'We have made it an Arabic Koran', Q. 43:2, alleging that *Ja'ala maj'ūl* is (synonymous with) *makhlūq*...
>
> *Ja'ala*, when referring to creatures, has two different meanings in the Qur'an: it may mean naming, *Tasmiya*, or doing...
>
> When *ja'ala* is used of Allah to signify creation it invariably means creation and nothing but creation; if used of Allah to signify something other than creation, it is not creation and never stands for creation...
>
> Now when Allah says, 'We have made it an Arabic Qur'an', He means He made it Arabic in the sense of an action performed by God, not in the sense of creation.'[30]

In this presentation Ibn Ḥanbal states clearly that the term *ja'ala* has two meanings. One of the meanings is to create; the other implies giving something that already exists a name or unique characteristic. Thus, a personal judgement is necessary in order to make the *mutakallimūn*'s argument that in this verse *ja'ala* takes the first meaning, and not the second. This in and of itself was problematic in Ibn Ḥanbal's eyes. He stated more than once that there is no place for personal opinion in matters of dogma. The truth must be stated explicitly in the Islamic sanctified texts and must be self-evident. In his interrogation Ibn Ḥanbal demonstrated that the second condition was not met because of the dual meaning of the term *ja'ala*.[31]

A second Qur'anic verse cited during Ibn Ḥanbal's interrogation was presented by 'Abd al-Raḥmān b. Isḥāq: 'Allah said: 'Never cometh there unto them a new reminder', can something be new (*muḥdath*) and not created (*makhlūqan*).'[32]

'I said to him' recounts Ibn Ḥanbal, 'Allah the Almighty said: Sad. By the renown Qur'an (*Ṣ wa-al-qur'an dhī al-dhikr*), and the renown is the Qur'an, and in that one [the verse you quote] there is no *alif* and no *lām*.'[33]

Let us unravel this obscure exchange. 'Abd al-Raḥman b. Isḥāq drew Ibn Ḥanbal's attention to a Qur'anic verse that mentioned 'a new reminder,' and understood the reminder to mean the Qur'an. Based on this assumption he asks, is it not clear that what is new is also created? In his reply, Ibn Ḥanbal notes that what 'Abd al-Raḥman b. Isḥāq takes to be the Qur'an is not the Qur'an. Ibn Ḥanbal argues that the Qur'an is the word *al-dhikr*. The term *dhikr* in itself, without the article *al*, does not refer to the Qur'an. To prove that the article '*al*' makes a difference, he quotes another verse in which *dhikr* appears with the article *al*, and states explicitly that in the verse that his interrogators used there is no '*alif* or *lām* [a or l],' meaning the article 'the' is missing. Here Ibn Ḥanbal distinguishes between '*al-dhikr*,' ('the reminder') and '*dhikr*'('a reminder'). This distinction separates between the term 'reminder' and the Qur'an. As a result, the adjective 'new' does not refer to the Qur'an but to something else, and as a consequence the quote loses its relevance to the controversy over the createdness of the Qur'an.

In the *Radd*, Ibn Ḥanbal gives a more elaborate refutation that focuses on a different part of the verse. His disagreement with his interrogators shifts from *dhikr* to 'new' (*muḥdath*). He goes through a lengthy explanation, the gist of which is 'this then is our proof from Allah's word that the 'fresh warning' from the Lord is fresh as far as the Prophet is concerned who did not know it until he learned it from Allah and in that sense is *muḥdath*.'[34] In other words, 'new' describes the Prophet's knowledge and not Allah's action.

Along with introducing Qur'anic citations, the interrogators made an effort to harness a tradition that would prove that the Qur'an was created. They argued that a certain tradition includes the statement 'created *al-dhikr*.'[35] Such a quote, if substantiated, would be a powerful response to Ibn Ḥanbal's distinction between *dhikr* and *al-dhikr*. The implication of this tradition is that the '*al-dhikr*' – a term that even Ibn Ḥanbal recognized as depicting the Qur'an – was created. Ibn Ḥanbal replied that the quote is inaccurate and that the correct wording is 'wrote *al-dhikr*.'[36]

The scriptural evidence the *mutakallimūn* presented was sufficient to make them feel that they had proven their point even by the standards that the Traditionists had demanded. In light of what they considered an intellectual achievement, the Traditionists' refusal to be persuaded frustrated the *mutakallimūn*. According to al-Jāḥiẓ, Ibn Abī Du'ād snapped at Ibn Ḥanbal 'and we recited to you (*talawnā 'alayka*) verses from the Book.'[37] The Ḥanbalis, however, contended that in the sphere of scripture they had neutralized all arguments. According to Ibn Ḥanbal and his followers, the *mutakallimūn* did not present a convincing scriptural line of reasoning.

Both sides claimed to have had the upper hand in the debate. This sort of self-promotion is to be expected. However, putting obvious motives of propaganda to the side, the claims to polemic victory made by each party grew from a genuine belief that they had outdone their adversaries. Both Traditionists and *mutakallimūn* truly believed that their stand was not shaken by their opponents' arguments. These contrasting perceptions of the interrogation stem from the profoundly different views that each side had of the nature and legitimacy of Qur'anic interpretation.

Ibn Ḥanbal's polemic strategy was to demonstrate that his opponents quoted problematic verses which had multiple meanings and therefore could not be used as proof in the debate over the createdness of the Qur'an. Thus, he sought to expose the multiple meanings or lack of clarity of these verses. In the interrogation his answers were terse and he did little more than point to the obscurity of the verses.

Why was Ibn Ḥanbal content with demonstrating the ambiguity of the Qur'anic verses? Why did he not feel compelled to present a convincing interpretation of these verses? To understand his approach, we must take into account that Ibn Ḥanbal was highly suspicious of Qur'anic exegesis. His reservations focused on two areas. The first was that more often than not, the interpretations did not rely on chains of transmission that linked them with the ultimate authority – the Prophet. Such a formal shortcoming was of crucial importance to a Traditionist like Ibn Ḥanbal, who came to expect that authoritative religious statements must come from the mouth of the Prophet.

Ibn Ḥanbal expressed his skepticism of Qur'anic exegesis when he said the following: 'Three books have no roots (*aṣl*): *al-maghāzī*, *al-malāḥim* and *al-tafsīr*.'[38] The problem at hand was the absence of sound chains of transmission that go back to the Prophet. This remark fits the intellectual climate of third-century A.H. Traditionists, who focused their criticism of traditions on their chains of transmitters and grew to expect that the chains would go back to the Prophet. Thus, it makes sense that Ibn Ḥanbal was not satisfied with Qur'anic exegesis because scholars could not apply the same criteria and standards to it that they did to Prophetic traditions.

A study of the opposition to Qur'anic interpretation underscores another factor that generated suspicion of Qur'anic interpretation in Traditionist circles. 'Towards the end of the first century, however, opposition against every interpretation of Allah's word started. Its basis was a stern religiosity found within circles of strict traditionalists. Against sound reasoning (*ra'y*) they maintained tradition (*ḥadīth, sunna*).'[39] This atmosphere of suspicion probably influenced Ibn Ḥanbal, who grew up and began his studies towards the end of the second century A.H. Though he did not completely reject Qur'anic exegesis, he questioned the authority of human interpretation particularly in the case of difficult verses.

Ibn Ḥanbal's reservations about the interpretation of obscure verses and his criticism of the manner in which his adversaries used these verses is made explicit in his polemic tract *al-Radd 'alā Zanādiqa wa-'l-Jahmīyya*: 'This is what my father published in refutation of the Zanādiqa and the Jahmīyya, concerning the ambiguous passages *mutashābih* in the Qur'an which they question and misinterpret.'[40] The *Radd* focuses on the verses and traditions that Ibn Ḥanbal's opponents harnessed to prove that the Qur'an itself states that it was created. Ibn Ḥanbal goes over these verses one by one and attempts to undermine his opponents' arguments by demonstrating that the verses do not have one unequivocal meaning. The *Radd* is studded with the accusation, 'Jahm found three ambiguous verses in the Qur'an.'[41] When conversing with a Jahmī about the Qur'an Ibn Ḥanbal argues, the former will base 'his claim on one of the ambiguous verses.'[42] He saw a Jahmī's use of the *dhikr* and *muḥdath* verses as an attempt to confuse people by 'using ambiguous verses for his purposes.'[43]

The function of holy scripture is to furnish the believer with absolute dogmas and behavioral prescriptions. The statements that appear in sanctified literature are the building blocks of faith. Being the word of Allah, they enjoy a unique status, and are beyond human comprehension. One condition must be met to attain this status: Their meaning must be self-evident and they cannot arouse multiple meanings. When scholars understand Qur'anic verses in different ways, the verses lose their authoritative status. In other words, whenever the interpretation of a verse hinges on human reason and choice, the verse ought to be classified as ambiguous and cannot serve as a doctrinal foundation of Islam.

According to Ibn Ḥanbal, the only means of interpreting the Qur'an is through the Prophet's sunna: 'and the sunna in our opinion are the traditions (*āthār*) of the Prophet (PBUH) and the sunna will explicate (*tufassiru*) the Qur'an.'[44] This position places Ibn Ḥanbal among the strict Traditionists who rejected personal opinion as a tool for explicating the Qur'an and limited Qur'anic interpretation to Prophetic traditions. If the meaning of the Qur'anic verse is not self-evident or if no Prophetic tradition clarifies its meaning, and humans must use their rational faculties to comprehend it, the verse is ambiguous and cannot be perceived as a part of doctrine.

The accusation that Ibn Ḥanbal's opponents base their doctrine and polemics on ambiguous verses takes us back to the fundamental discursive and conceptual differences between the two milieus. The *mutakallimūn* saw ambiguity as an invitation to use human reason and unravel the complications of meaning. When Ibn Ḥanbal questioned the clarity of certain verses, the *mutakallimūn* considered that as a point of departure. Now, argued the *mutakallimūn*, each side must interpret the verses in the most sensible manner, and the more sensible explanation should become the authoritative interpretation. In contrast, the Traditionists considered these verses impregnable. Thus, the *mutakallimūn*'s discursive point of departure, was the Traditionists' dead end.

With this in mind we can understand why both sides claimed victory. Ibn Ḥanbal demonstrated that the Qur'anic verses that the *mutakallimūn* raised were unclear and therefore disqualified them from being used in the debate. The *mutakallimūn*, considered these verses as a springboard for a presentation to justify why one particular interpretation was superior to the other. Ibn Ḥanbal's argument was completed once he exposed the ambiguity. The *mutakallimūn* felt Ibn Ḥanbal was evading the issue.

There is an interesting and important congruence between Ibn Ḥanbal's attitude towards theological inquiry and Qur'anic exegesis. In both cases Ibn Ḥanbal limited the use of human intellect. If the sanctified Islamic texts were not self-evident, he would not delve into their meaning. Be it the divine attributes that the theological enterprise brought to the surface or the divine utterances that Qur'anic exegesis clarified, if these activities entailed the development of independent ideas and solutions, Ibn Ḥanbal circumvented the problem. The *mutakallimūn*, by contrast, channeled their intellectual energies to the very problems that Ibn Ḥanbal avoided. The essence of the *mutakallimūn*'s self-view hinged upon their ability to resolve the hitherto unresolved questions of theology and the ambiguous verses of the Qur'an. The Traditionists' reservations about the uncertainties of such intellectual activities and the *mutakallimūn*'s attraction to them generated two discursive communities which, for all intents and purposes, could not communicate with one other. The *miḥna* was, first and foremost, the showdown between these two communities over the authority to define and set the course of Islam.

CHAPTER NINE

The Aftermath

Ibn Ḥanbal and the court

In the decade and a half following Ibn Ḥanbal's release, the courts' attitude towards him changed dramatically from outright harassment to excessive solicitousness with presents and invitations. When Ibn Ḥanbal was released from his interrogation, he and his family lived in constant fear that he would be assassinated or imprisoned. Their distrust of state officials was such that when Ibn Ḥanbal was recuperating from his torture, he avoided the doctor's medication for fear that Ibn Abī Du'ād would arrange to poison him.[1] Some time after his release, probably in the days of al-Wāthiq, Ibn Ḥanbal went into hiding.[2] This was probably a consequence of a letter that Isḥāq b. Ibrāhīm, the governor of Baghdād, sent Ibn Ḥanbal ordering him to avoid meetings with other people and to leave the city when the caliph was visiting.[3] After receiving this message, Ibn Ḥanbal is said to have disappeared,[4] staying in the homes of trusted friends such as Fūzān and confining himself secretly to his own house.[5]

The caliph's duress probably had to do with his fear that Ibn Ḥanbal would galvanize the masses and lead a rebellion. By the time al-Wāthiq came into power, and probably before that, Ibn Ḥanbal's fate and opinions had become potent forces in Baghdādi politics. According to al-Dhahabī, during Ibn Ḥanbal's interrogation, the participants considered the possible consequences of a Ibn Ḥanbal's death or serious deterioration in his physical condition, and some thought these might spark riots. Fearing the violent reaction of the masses, Ibn Abī Du'ād wanted to release Ibn Ḥanbal immediately following his torture.[6] Ibn Abī Du'ād had good reason to fear Ibn Ḥanbal's political clout. Sometime after his release, Ibn Ḥanbal was approached by a group 'of the *fuqahā'* of the people of Baghdād,' who tried to organize a rebellion against al-Wāthiq. Ibn Ḥanbal refused to cooperate and vehemently criticized the potential rebels.[7]

Ibn Ḥanbal's torments did not cease when al-Mutawakkil came to power. Even though a reversal of policy was already in the making in the last years of al-Wāthiq's reign,[8] some of Ibn Ḥanbal's old enemies and a handful of *mutakallimūn* still wielded power over al-Mutawakkil in his first years as caliph.[9] During the first two years of al-Mutawakkil's reign, as he reconsidered his religio-political policy, Ibn Ḥanbal's old enemies did all they could to tarnish his reputation. One Isḥāq b. Ibrāhīm al-Muṣ'ābī, the governor of Baghdād who interrogated Ibn Ḥanbal and witnessed his flogging, was instructed to bring Ibn Ḥanbal to the caliphal court. While Isḥāq b. Ibrāhīm al-Muṣ'ābī was staying in the caliph's court, word reached him that Ibn Ḥanbal had insulted his son Muḥammad by leaving Baghdād without paying his respects to him. Isḥāq b. Ibrāhīm al-Muṣ'ābī reported the incident to al-Mutawakkil, who instructed Ibn Ḥanbal to return to Baghdād.[10]

This embarrassment was followed by a more serious entanglement in which Ibn Ḥanbal was said to have harbored an 'Alawī in his home. Ḥanbali sources consider Muḥammad b. Shujā' b. al-Thalgī as the culprit.[11] A biographical sketch of Ibn al-Thalgī sheds light on his motive for trying to tarnish Ibn Ḥanbal's reputation. Ibn al-Thalgī was a Ḥanafi jurist who has been described as 'having sympathy for the Mu'tazili school (*wa-lahu mayl ilā madhhab al-Mu'tazila*).'[12] He was also well versed in traditions and was accused by the Traditionists of using his familiarity with this branch of religious knowledge to contrive (*yaḍa'u*) traditions related to anthropomorphism and attributing them to the Traditionists.[13] As for courtly politics, suffice it to say that he gained access to the court through the mediation of Isḥāq b. Ibrāhīm al-Muṣ'ābī, Ibn Ḥanbal's long-time enemy, who had persuaded the caliph to send Ibn Ḥanbal back to Baghdād before they even met.[14]

This short profile dove-tails with the above-stated observation that the main actors in the persecution of the Traditionists were Ḥanafi-Mu'tazilis. As the members of the Ḥanafi-Mu'tazili milieu watched their power decline, Ibn al-Thalgī, one of the last Mu'tazilis with leverage in the court, played upon al-Mutawakkil's animosity to the Shī'īs, in order to create a rift between the wavering caliph and Ibn Ḥanbal, the ascending moral leader of the Traditionists.

As a result of Ibn al-Thalgī's accusations, al-Mutawakkil ordered Muẓaffar b. al-Kalbī, who was in charge of intelligence (*ṣāḥib al-khabār*), to search Ibn Ḥanbal's house.[15] Muẓaffar appeared in front of Ibn

Ḥanbal's house one night with a group of aides, read Ibn Ḥanbal the caliph's letter, alleging that he was harboring an 'Alawī in his home, and asked for Ibn Ḥanbal's response. After Ibn Ḥanbal claimed that he knew nothing of this affair and swore that he was not hiding anyone, Ibn al-Kalbī ordered that the house be searched. The search was thorough and included the animal's den (*saraba*), cabinet (or rooms on the second floor *ghuraf*), roof (*suṭūḥ*), book chest (*tābūt al-kutub*) and the women's quarter. Ṣāliḥ reports that the party that carried out the search included two women (*imra'atān*) who went through the women's quarters in Ibn Ḥanbal's house. He adds that they even examined the well by lowering candles into it.[16] The party failed to find an Alawī in Ibn Ḥanbal's or his son's homes. They reported the results to al-Mutawakkil who, according to Ḥanbal, realized that Ibn Ḥanbal had been set up.[17]

After this episode al-Mutawakkil tried to appease Ibn Ḥanbal by offering him financial support. He sent one of his chamberlains (*ḥujjāb*) with a letter informing Ibn Ḥanbal that he had been acquitted.[18] The chamberlain also brought a large sum of money that the caliph put at Ibn Ḥanbal's disposal. Ibn Ḥanbal refused to accept this gift. The chamberlain responded by cautioning Ibn Ḥanbal that if he would refuse the caliph's offer their relationship would go sour. This warning apparently persuaded Ibn Ḥanbal to accept the money. At day-break after a sleepless night, he gathered his family and some trusted disciples such as 'Abdūs b. Mālik,[19] al-Ḥasan b. al-Bazzār,[20] Hārūn al-Ḥammal,[21] Aḥmad b. Manī'[22] and Ibn al-Dawraqī,[23] and together they organized the distribution of the money.[24] It went primarily to poor Traditionists who resided in Baghdād and Kūfa.[25] He also donated some of it to charity.

Three years after al-Mutawakkil began his reign, Isḥāq b. Ibrāhīm al-Muṣ'ābī died. Sometime after that al-Mutawakkil invited Ibn Ḥanbal to travel to Sāmarrā', where the caliph's court was located. Ibn Ḥanbal tried to avoid this meeting by describing himself as an old and sick shaykh, but this did not deter al-Mutawakkil.[26] As a result Ibn Ḥanbal left for Sāmarrā', escorted by his two sons, Ṣāliḥ and 'Abdallāh, and by his uncle Isḥāq b. Ḥanbal.[27]

The caliph's attention made Ibn Ḥanbal feel pestered and morally challenged. As a result of this attitude, Ibn Ḥanbal endowed every mundane detail with weighty moral proportions. Housing, food and clothing became arenas for Ibn Ḥanbal's battle against al-Mutawakkil's hospitality.[28] He asserted his independence and maintained his integrity by renting a room, rather than residing in an *amīr*'s (prince's) palace, and by fasting, ignoring the huge amounts of food sent to him. Yet his position was compromised by the conduct of his sons and uncle, who enjoyed these luxuries and were willing to accept the caliph's financial support.[29]

As a result of his refusal to eat the caliph's food, Ibn Ḥanbal's physical state deteriorated to such an extent that the caliph sent his physician to examine the 'old and sick shaykh.' The physician's diagnosis was that Ibn Ḥanbal's poor health was a result of fasting.[30] Ibn Ḥanbal's wretched condition did not go unnoticed by the caliph's mother, who saw him when Ibn Ḥanbal was forced to meet her grandson, al-Mu'tazz.[31] She told al-Mutawakkil that Ibn Ḥanbal was not the type of person who would want anything that the caliph had and that his physical condition was not very good. In short, the caliph's mother recognized the futility of keeping Ibn Ḥanbal in the court.

Ibn Ḥanbal did all he could to convey this message to the caliph. On his way to Baghdād he swore not to teach traditions, so as to justify his lack of cooperativeness.[32] Later, in Sāmarrā', he avoided contact with the caliph and his *amīr*s. This attitude became unmistakable in his encounter with al-Mu'tazz. When Ibn Ḥanbal entered, the young prince greeted him politely. Ibn Ḥanbal was so rude that he did not reply. Apparently one Ibrāhīm b. Isḥāq witnessed this incident and was so infuriated he said that he wanted to kill Ibn Ḥanbal because of his attitude towards the prince.[33]

It may be that Ibn Ḥanbal's awareness of the gravity of his own condition and his uncertainty as to how long he would be away from home prompted him to write a will.[34] The witnesses to the document were his two sons, 'Abdallāh and Ṣāliḥ, and a third person called Abū Yūsuf.[35] After a number of edifying clauses, Ibn Ḥanbal turned to his finances. He asked that his fifty-*dinar* debt will be paid back to 'Abdallāh b. Muḥammad Fūzān. Another interesting stipulation was that the sum remaining after the payment of this debt be divided equally between his grandchildren, the children of Ṣāliḥ and 'Abdallāh. Each grandchild was to receive ten *dirham*. The most noteworthy aspect of this request is that Ibn Ḥanbal specifies that an equal sum should be given to the males and the females.[36]

When after sixteen days al-Mutawakkil allowed Ibn Ḥanbal to return to Baghdād, Ibn Ḥanbal did his best to enter the city unnoticed. He saw to it that the robe of honor that the caliph gave him would be sold, and that the money distributed to the poor.[37] But this did not put an end to his relations with al-Mutawakkil. Every day the caliph inquired about his well-being, and occasionally asked for his opinion, as in the case of Ibn Abī Du'ād's money.[38] At times he inquired about the legitimacy of scholars, as with Yaḥyā b. Aktham and Muḥammad b. Shujā' b.

al-Thalgī.[39] The caliph also asked Ibn Ḥanbal, in a consciously apologetic tone, to write him about the createdness of the Qur'an.[40] Lastly, he tried to give him more money, but here he encountered Ibn Ḥanbal's adamant refusal.

Strains within the Traditionist milieu

The victorious outcome of the *miḥna* could not heal the wounds that had been inflicted on the Traditionist milieu. As Traditionist resistance to the court's coercion grew and scholars who refused to declare that the Qur'an was created died in jail, disappointment and disrespect towards Traditionist leaders who did collaborate with the court increased. The memory of Aḥmad b. Nuḥ (d. 218), Nu'aym b. Ḥammād (d. 228), al-Buwayṭī (d. 232) and others, who died in jail because they refused to abide to the interrogators' demands,[41] set a high moral standard which made scholars who had capitulated appear morally inferior. The division between those who compromised their beliefs and those who did not ripped the Traditionist milieu apart, disgracing some of its most respected leaders and humiliating exemplary figures who had been famous for their piety. After this episode, relations between scholars who had resisted and scholars who had succumbed could not revert to what they had been.

Ibn al-Jawzī, author of Ibn Ḥanbal's *Manāqib,* provides some insight into Ibn Ḥanbal's disappointment, sorrow and anger:

> None of the replies of any of those [who capitulated] embarrassed and grieved Ibn Ḥanbal as the replies of Abī Naṣr al-Tammār, Yaḥyā b. Ma'īn and Abī Khaythama, because they were of the highest stature in his eyes and he did not think they would be so quick to answer. As for Abū Naṣr al-Tammār, he was one of the pious, heard traditions from Mālik [b. Anas] and the Ḥammā-dayn and others. But he did not persevere in the interrogation and replied. Ibn Ḥanbal thought it is improper to write [tradition] on his authority and when he died he did not pray for him.[42]

The sense that some of the leaders of the Traditionist milieu did not measure up to their own expectations was also prevalent among the very scholars who had capitulated. They themselves did not take their own behavior lightly and came out of the interrogations stricken with guilt and remorse. Two, Abū Ma'mar (d. 236) and Sa'dawayh (d. 225), confessed that they had blasphemed.[43]

The general impression one gets from the sources is that the Traditionists never knew how to react to this humiliating episode. Few felt as righteous as Ibn Ḥanbal and allowed themselves to actually punish their failed leaders. We can imagine that the general public avoided passing judgement on so many of their teachers and spiritual guides, due to the judicious assumption that in cases such as these, it was wise not to judge someone until you yourself have gone through the experience. What is more, taking an active position towards so many of the elite would have probably generated a major crisis in fields such as teaching and passing judicial judgements. Therefore, the sources reveal little about sanctions and direct confrontations within the Traditionist milieu. The exception to this was Ibn Ḥanbal and a few of his students.

Ibn Ḥanbal's attitude towards those Traditionists who capitulated was nuanced, but he was uncompromising in his refusal to transmit traditions on their authority. 'Ibn Ḥanbal was of the opinion that one should not write [tradition] from Abū Naṣr al-Tammār, nor those of Yaḥyā b. Ma'īn nor those of anyone else who was interrogated and replied.'[44] An indirect affirmation of this position was made by Ibn Ḥanbal regarding the Traditionist Abū Kurayb (d. 248): 'If I were to transmit on [the authority] of anyone who replied during the *miḥna*, I would transmit on the authority of Abī Ma'mar and Abī Kurayb.'[45] It is not clear why Ibn Ḥanbal took such an extreme position towards his colleagues and to the best of my knowledge, he was the only Traditionist to express his disappointment so aggressively.

Ibn Ḥanbal's staunch position against transmitting traditions on the authority of Traditionists that capitulated did not accord with his relationship with these individuals. Ibn Ḥanbal socialized with and even consulted Aḥmad al-Dawraqī, who was one of the first seven Traditionists to be interrogated, and whose cooperation with the court Ibn Ḥanbal considered to be detrimental to the Traditionists, when he tried to rid himself of the caliph's donations.

After the *miḥna* Ibn Ḥanbal sent part of the money he had received from al-Mutawakkil to Ibn Kurayb, who succumbed during his interrogation.[46] This indicates that Ibn Ḥanbal kept in touch with some of the Traditionists who collaborated with the authorities during the *miḥna*. We also know that he forgave Bishr b. al-Walīd, Ibrāhīm b. al-Mahdī and 'Abbās al-Anbārī on the basis of their refusal to cooperate with the authorities until they were threatened.[47]

On the other hand, the *Manāqib* contains a moving passage in which Yaḥyā b. Ma'īn, a long-time friend and colleague of Ibn Ḥanbal, visited the ailing Ibn Ḥanbal, only to be humiliated.[48] As Yaḥyā b. Ma'īn entered the room, he greeted Ibn Ḥanbal, but the sick man refused to answer. At this point the narrator, Abū Bakr al-Marwadhī, explains that Ibn Ḥanbal swore that he would not speak to anyone who had replied in his interrogation (i.e. succumbed) until he met Allah (i.e. die). As a consequence, when Yaḥyā b. Ma'īn, one of the outstanding scholars of his age who was also a close colleague of Ibn Ḥanbal, repeatedly apologized to Ibn Ḥanbal, it was to no avail. Ibn Ḥanbal refused to forgive him.

One of the most knowledgeable and esteemed Traditionists of Ibn Ḥanbal's generation, 'Alī b. al-Madīnī, went beyond mere capitulation. This Baṣrian scholar went so far as to supply Ibn Abī Du'ād with information in support of the Mu'tazilis' position.[49] His colleagues considered this to be betrayal. The tragic downfall of Ibn al-Madīnī who was one of the senior scholars in Ibn Ḥanbal's generation, illustrates how the *miḥna* crushed the intellectual leadership of the Traditionists.

The outstanding scholarly status that Ibn al-Madīnī enjoyed before the *miḥna* is revealed by the following anecdote: 'When 'Alī b. al-Madīnī would come to Baghdād he would preside over (*taṣaddara*) a study group (*ḥalqa* – lit. circle) [to which] came Yaḥyā b. Ma'īn, Aḥmad b. Ḥanbal and al-Mu'ayti and people would contend each other (*wa-'l-nās yutanāẓarūn*) and if they would disagree over something 'Alī would comment about it.'[50] 'Alī's position as leader of these forums which Ibn Ḥanbal and Yaḥyā b. Ma'īn frequented, points to his relative standing. It also indicates that these scholars met quite often and were probably quite close to one other before the *miḥna*.[51] In another anecdote which sets before the reader a similar hierarchy, Ibn al-Madīnī is described as lying down and dictating traditions to Ibn Ḥanbal, who was on his right and Yaḥyā b. Ma'īn, who was on his left.[52]

The three of them, along with a few other Traditionists, such as Abū Khaythama, were thought of as the intellectual elite of the Traditionists of their generation. Biographical dictionaries often compare the leading figures of different generations, and this type of a comparison was usually made about the four of them.[53] As we would expect each was ascribed a specific sub-field of religious knowledge (traditions, jurisprudence, criticism of Traditionists), in which he was seen as the foremost expert. Before the *miḥna* Ibn al-Madīnī was apparently the most outstanding of this group of scholars; after the *miḥna* his career was in shambles.

All four of these Traditionists were interrogated. Ibn Ḥanbal, who was reputed to have withstood torture, came out of the *miḥna* as the unquestioned moral leader of the Traditionists. Yaḥyā b. Ma'īn and Abū Khaythama suffered some loss of prestige in the eyes of many of their colleagues. Ibn al-Madīnī provoked anger and dismay among the Traditionists. Scholars such as Abū Zur'a,[54] Ibrāhīm al-Ḥarbī[55] and Abū Khaythama refused to transmit on his authority, although Yaḥyā b. Ma'īn continued to do so.[56]

For many of the leaders of the victorious Traditionist milieu, the *miḥna* was a personal humiliation and catastrophe. Their colleagues and students shunned some of them, while others lost the esteem of their friends. Many of them experienced a personal sense of loss, as old friends and colleagues died in jail, which merged with disappointment in themselves and pangs of guilt. Confusion regarding the status of old leaders and embarrassment tore at the social fabric of this milieu. Nonetheless, perhaps the most far-reaching impact of the *miḥna* on the Traditionist milieu was not confined to the personal fates of that generation, but to a falling out over theological issues.

Lafẓ al-Qur'an – the unresolved problem of theology

In his study *The Formative Period of Islamic Thought*, Watt observes that Western scholarship from the pre-World War II period 'gives the impression that there was a rationalist movement (the Mu'tazilis) and an anti-rationalist party (men like Aḥmad b. Ḥanbal) but practically nothing else...'[57] According to Watt this was rectified in post-war scholarship, which recognized that 'the rationalist movement of Kalām was wider than the Mu'tazili sect in the strict sense,' and that 'throughout the ninth century there were a number of upholders of a conservative doctrinal position who engaged in Kalām to some extent.'[58] Watt continues this trend of studying the gray area between the two poles, revelationist and rationalist. He focuses on groups of thinkers that did not fit these two categories, such as the Sunni *mutakallimūn* and the Ḥanafis who opposed the court doctrines regarding the createdness of the Qur'an.[59] Watt's correct observation that there were Sunnis who espoused *kalām* should not mislead us into thinking that the question of the standing of *kalām* was not highly contested among the Sunnis.

Throughout the third century A.H., theological investigations touched a raw nerve in the Sunni camp. The *miḥna*, the political manifestation of the debate over the legitimacy of theology, aggravated the existing tensions. Even after the Traditionists won this battle, they felt the repercussions of the *miḥna* among themselves. While presenting a united front to their Mu'tazili enemies, they had to work out a more cohesive position towards theology. Yet, in the decades following the *miḥna*, tensions were running so high that the Sunni camp went through another internal crisis regarding this question of the legitimacy of theology. The anti-*lafẓiyya* campaign was a reopening of the old debate. After destroying their Mu'tazili rivals, certain elements in the Traditionist camp turned inward and tried to purge their own cadres. The question of the createdness of the utterances of the Qur'an, *lafẓ al-Qur'an*, was their excuse to rid themselves of Sunni *mutakallimūn*.

A fine example of how the debate over *lafẓ al-Qur'an* came to reflect the controversy over theology in Traditionist circles is given by al-Subkī, who describes an indirect exchange between al-Karābīsī and Ibn Ḥanbal. At the outset of this mediated conversation, al-Karābīsī states that the *lafẓ al-Qur'an* was created, and is informed that Ibn Ḥanbal said that such a position is *bid'a* (innovation). As a result, al-Karābīsī changed his mind and said that *lafẓ al-Qur'an* was not created.[60] Ibn Ḥanbal reacted to this new opinion as he did to the first, and accused al-Karābīsī's new opinion of being *bid'a* (innovation). Al-Subkī explains Ibn Ḥanbal's seemingly self-contradicting statements in the following manner: 'And this demonstrates what we said, that when Aḥmad said 'this is *bid'a* (innovation)' he was only alluding to the discussion of the foundations of the question; otherwise (and if not) how can he reject the affirmation of something and [at the same time reject] its rejection.'[61] Al-Subkī's interpretation of Ibn Ḥanbal's paradoxical position strikes me as correct. By labeling both positions innovations, Ibn Ḥanbal took aim at the process that led to either position rather than at the positions themselves. His criticism was directed at the theological discussion and he chastised the mere act of raising the issue.

Before the *miḥna* many of these Sunni *mutakallimūn* had managed to get along with the more conservative Traditionists in their milieu. But after the *miḥna*, the question of one's position towards *kalām* became a burning issue. The *miḥna* brought *kalām* to the forefront of individual and Sunni group identity, turning it into a mark of distinction within Traditionist circles. The blurred internal distinctions within the Traditionist milieu in the pre-*miḥna* days, now became lines of group demarcation. *Lafẓ al-Qur'an* served as a litmus test among the Traditionists, defining one's attitude towards *kalām*.

Ibn Ḥanbal's tactics resembled the manner that Traditionists did battle with their ideological foes in the past. One element was the articulation of a theological doctrine that denies the legitimacy of anyone who thinks differently. Hence, according to Ibn Ḥanbal, any person who believed that the *lafẓ al-Qur'an* was created was a Jahmī.[62] By claiming that the position of the *lafẓiyya* was part of Jahmī theology, Ibn Ḥanbal delegitimized the position itself.

The second component of this strategy was a personal onslaught on the believers themselves, aimed at ruining the reputation and scholarly careers of specific scholars. This is precisely the type of tactics to which al-Ma'mūn alluded to in his *miḥna* letter, when he wrote of the 'self styled Sunnis' accusations against their enemies.[63] Hence, the attack of the *lafẓiyya* indicates that after (or perhaps even during) they won the battle with their external rivals (Mu'tazili-Ḥanafis), the conservative Traditionists turned to the Sunni *mutakallimūn* and resorted to their old tactics of besmirching the reputations of their ideological enemies so as to gradually squeez them out of the Traditionist milieu.

Just as previous Traditionists had pressured their ideological rivals in the second century, Ibn Ḥanbal tried to erect social and religious barriers between supporters of the *lafẓiyya* and conservative Traditionists.[64] He declared a number of prohibitions regarding socializing with Jahmīs. He forbade praying behind them,[65] giving testimony to a Jahmī *qāḍī*,[66] and marrying their women.[67] When asked about one of the outspoken adherents of the *lafẓiyya*, al-Karābīsī, Ibn Ḥanbal stated that people should not speak to him, write on his authority, or keep his company.[68]

The anti-*lafẓiyya* campaign was not as successful as some of the previous purges. An examination of two outstanding proponents of the createdness of *lafẓ al-Qur'an* reveals the ambivalence of the Sunni community towards this specific issue. The first, al-Ḥusayn b. 'Alī al-Karābīsī (d. 245), was originally a highly respected scholar who leaned towards the school of Iraq (Ḥanafis), and whose legal judgements were sought after by the authorities.[69] Upon meeting and studying with al-Shāfi'ī, he transferred to his school (*intaqala ilā madhhabihi*).[70] He seems to have been close to some of the leaders of the milieu. Ibn Ḥajar al-'Asqalānī writes on the authority of Ibn 'Abd al-Barr (d. 463) that 'there was between him [al-Karābīsī] and Aḥmad [b. Ḥanbal] friendship (*ṣadāqa*) and ruse (*kayda*) but after he disagreed with him about the Qur'an this friendship turned into enmity and each accused the other (lit. his companion) and the Ḥanābila renounced Ḥusayn al-Karābīsī.'[71] Much like the debate over the createdness of the Qur'an, the controversy over *lafẓ al-Qur'an* destroyed friendships among the Traditionists. The Traditionist milieu began to tear at its ideological seams. Al-Karābīsī, a convert from the more rationally inclined Ḥanafism, could not transform his world-view to an extent that would please the growing inflexibility of Ibn Ḥanbal and his followers. Thus, differences of opinion that in the past were overlooked became thorny matters of contention and grounds for mutual accusations.

Al-Karābīsī, who had a following among the Shāfiʿītes, lost his influence among the Ḥanbalis. These newly made enemies exerted a heavy price from al-Karābīsī. Ibn Ḥajar al-ʿAsqalānī quotes al-Khaṭīb al-Baghdādī, who observes, 'his [al-Karābīsī's] [traditions] are very rare because Aḥmad b. Ḥanbal would speak [negatively] of him due to the question of the utterance (*al-lafẓ*), and he [al-Karābīsī] would also speak of Aḥmad, and the people did not rely on him [al-Karābīsī] and when Yaḥyā b. Maʿīn heard (lit. came to him, *balaghahu*) that he [al-Karābīsī] spoke of Aḥmad he cursed him [al-Karābīsī].'[72] This is a fine example of how a personal campaign, led by the Traditionists, ruined the reputations of their enemies and destroyed their posthumous careers. Apparently, after the *miḥna* it was imprudent to be an outspoken opponent of Ibn Ḥanbal.

No less dramatic, though with precisely the opposite result, was the fate of Muḥammad b. Ismāʿīl al-Bukhārī. Probably some time after Ibn Ḥanbal's death, it was reported that al-Bukhārī held the belief that the utterance (*lafẓ*) of the Qur'an was created. Upon learning of this theological deviation, such prominent Traditionists as Abū Zurʿa and Abū Ḥātim abstained from his traditions.[73] The information came from Muḥammad b. Yaḥyā al-Dhuhlī (d. 256), one of the most respected Traditionists of his age, who was frequently lauded by Ibn Ḥanbal himself.[74] This incident, again, reveals how the Traditionists' networks passed information and gradually built a consensus about its own members. It also demonstrates that in the first decades after the *miḥna* anyone reputed to believe in the createdness of *lafẓ al-Qur'an* was deemed to be a theological deviant. The case of al-Bukhārī is fascinating because the attempt to expel him from the community of Traditionists failed so miserably. Al-Bukhārī, of course, was the compiler of the most authoritative book of traditions in the Islamic canon.

The inability of the scholars to marginalize and reject al-Bukhārī's collections of traditions was, in part, the result of al-Bukhārī's behavior. Al-Bukhārī never entered into an exchange of accusations with anyone, let alone the major cultural hero of the age, Ibn Ḥanbal. Furthermore, the manner in which he articulated his answer when asked about the issue of *lafẓ al-Qur'an* reveals his awareness of the sensitivities of the more zealous strands of Traditionists.[75] As a result there was some controversy over the exact wordings in his remark about the *lafẓ al-Qur'an*, and he was not ostracized from the Traditionist milieu.

In a comparison between Ibn Ḥanbal's and al-Shāfiʿī's legal thought I concluded that al-Shāfiʿī was the more flexible of the two with regard to the use of human reason in judicial practice. The primary difference between them, which reflects their dissimilar views of the hierarchy of priorities regarding human reason, was Ibn Ḥanbal's tendency to rely on the precedents of the Companions and Successors and al-Shāfiʿī's dependance on *qiyās*. This in and of itself marked a fault line within the Traditionist camp, which separated between the followers of Ibn Ḥanbal and many other Shāfiʿīs.

This tendency of al-Shāfiʿī and certain Shāfiʿītes to view human reason as an acceptable and useful tool for reaching legal judgement, was applied by certain trends of Shāfiʿītes to doctrinal matters. Though this may be a break from al-Shāfiʿī's position,[76] his adherents included a core of Sunni *mutakallimūn* and a host of other disciples who were tolerant of the *mutakallimūn*'s endeavors. Though they themselves did not agree about everything and had slight differences in their attitudes towards *kalām*, they were perceived by the more conservative Traditionists as members of one intellectual trend. The Traditionists' attempts to marginalize and destroy the reputation of al-Karābīsī and al-Bukhārī, two adherents of the *lafẓiyya* who seem to have had subtly different approaches towards *kalām,* reveals that from the Traditionists' perspective there was no place for such distinctions.

When the debate over the *lafẓ al-Qur'an* was initiated, the sides that took part in it were more or less divided into conservative Traditionists and Sunni *mutakallimūn*. In essence, al-Karābīsī, Ibn Kullāb,[77] Dāwūd b. 'Alī[78] and their disciples accepted some type of theological inquiry into matters of doctrine. Other Traditionists, such as al-Bukhārī and Muḥammad b. Naṣr al-Marwadhī, might not have supported the *kalām* enterprise as strongly, but seemed to endorse the endeavor or its results to some extent.[79] Still others, like al-Muḥāsibī, apparently did not hold to the doctrine of *lafẓ al-Qur'an* but were nonetheless strong believers in *kalām*. All of these scholars were Shāfiʿīs and many were shunned by Ibn Ḥanbal or his followers.

The fault line that emerged as a result of jurisprudential differences of opinions cracked, and the Traditionist camp came apart. On one side were the Ḥanbali minimalists and on the other, more flexible side, were the Shāfiʿīs. The disagreements over the nature of Allah's revelation could be circumvented no longer. The Ḥanbalis and their close supporters, who were riding high after the *miḥna*, refused to tolerate different views on such matters. But deep down, the break up of the Traditionist camp reflected more than the Ḥanbalis' overconfidence. It was a legitimate parting of ways between two incompatible views of human reason and its place in the religious sciences.

Be this as it may, the two *madhāhib* that evolved out of the Traditionist milieu were not perfect reflections of an ideological divide. Whereas the Ḥanbalis constituted an ideologically homogenous unit in the third century, the Shāfiʿīs were much more heterogenic. Ḥanbali theological uniformity and Shāfiʿī diversity would by and large remain a basic characteristic of the two *madhāhib* in the centuries to come. With the exception of Abū Yaʿlā and Ibn ʿAqil and a few others, the Ḥanbali camp would not bring together scholars with stark ideological differences. By contrast, the Shāfiʿīs will assemble under the *madhhab* umbrella staunch Traditionists and Ashʿarī *mutakallimūn*.[80] Notwithstanding a number of important changes, primarily in the sphere of Ḥanbali jurisprudence, and several exceptional theologians, the intellectual structure of the mid-third-century Traditionist milieu, remained intact for many centuries to come.

Epilogue

The formation of a *madhhab* was a long process that spanned several generations. It was certainly not the creation of one individual or even one generation. The processes of doctrinal articulation and social dissemination depended upon many scholars and local leaders who could adapt ideas and modes of conduct to their community's changing needs. Thus, this inquiry into Ibn Ḥanbal's influence on Ḥanbalism should not be understood as an attempt to ignore the contributions of his disciples. It is rather an attempt to study one form of religious leadership and place it in a broad historical context.

It is worthwhile to begin this assessment by examining the pre-Islamic period. In the concluding remarks of his suggestive article 'The Holy Man in Late Antiquity,' Peter Brown observed that the predominance of holy men in Late Antiquity sets that period apart from the Classical period (Greek and Roman) and the Middle Ages. He also pointed out that the growing presence of holy men and their new social roles 'coincides ... with the erosion of classical institutions.'[1] Thus, holy men and the institutions of Late Antiquity moved in a see-saw fashion. As the holy men came on the scene and entered center stage, institutions faded into the background. Putting it in a wider context, Brown states that 'the victory of Christianity in late Roman society... was the victory of men over the institutions of their past.'[2]

This state of affairs, in which individuals are at the forefront of the religious order and institutions play lesser roles, is also typical of early Islam, the monotheistic faith that was founded and elaborated on the closing centuries of Late Antiquity.[3] Throughout the classical era of Islam, Muslims did not recognize the spiritual authority of any formal body, other than the community as a whole. They did not confer that authority upon a select group of officials that would manage the religious lives of their followers, nor did they set up judicial, theological, or educational hierarchies. The Islamic religious order was made up mainly of charismatic individuals and learned scholars, and had little space for formal institutions.

Since institutions constitute a matrix of power, Islamic societies whose social order is not based on institutions pose a fascinating problem for historians: How do we approach a society whose power structure is nearly invisible to us, yet its ability to maintain a social order and perpetuate it are evident. This situation – in which historians of Islamic societies cannot rely on the well charted maps of social order that historians of Western societies have at their disposal, while the societies themselves clearly have social mechanisms that sustain their social order – was noted by R. Mottahedeh: 'For without guilds, church, gentry of official rank, caste and the myriad other well defined divisions and groups familiar from the study of other cultures, this [Buyid] society managed both to reproduce its forms from generation to generation, and to export these forms to new groups of people in lands further to the east.'[4]

Mottahedeh's work points to an important insight for the study of pre-modern Islamic societies. Based on his assumption that social structure existed but was not formalized, he sought ways to make nearly invisible social links, visible. Tracing and sketching the thin cords that tie individuals to one another, he suggested new ways to identify social patterns and historical processes in these societies. One facet that reveals the mechanisms of a society, whether formal or informal, is leadership. The acquisition of such a position, its scope of influence, and its limitations reveal how individuals interact, how they cooperate with each other, and how movements are formed. Studies of leadership have the potential to bring into relief the contours of nearly hidden social entities and expose their dynamics.

Islamic and Late Antiquity notions of religious leadership are similar in some ways. In both periods the authority of spiritual leaders was based upon their prestige and the esteem in which they were held, and they lacked the formal authority to impose their will and decisions. In fact, Brown astutely characterized the holy men of Late Antiquity as possessors of 'non-coercive power.'[5] Mottahedeh made a similar remark about scholars in Buyid society: 'This kind of leader could have, at best, only very mild authority over his followers … such leaders could claim precedence, rather than authority or coercive power.'[6]

'Non-coercive power' is a key to understanding the kind of influence that Ibn Ḥanbal exerted over his disciples. The means that were at his disposal and defined the kind of authority he could exercise over his following fit the characterization. It was not coercive because he, as most Islamic scholars and founders of *madhāhib*, did not build institutions or create hierarchies of power within his circle. The Ḥanbali circle, and later the Ḥanbali *madhhab,* did not set up formal positions of leadership. It did not have recognized bodies of scholars that determined legal or theological doctrine nor leaders that decided on the collective values that all Ḥanbalis must embrace. Nor did it have formal mechanisms to impose beliefs or norms of conduct on its members.

Ibn Ḥanbal, and future leaders, were followed on a voluntary basis. His adherents turned to him for legal advice and told stories about his conduct because they admired him and thought that he was living up to the highest standards of behavior. Their relationship with Ibn Ḥanbal depended on the esteem they felt for him and not on his ability to punish or impose his will upon them. At any given moment his followers could ignore his opinions, and in fact in some instances they did. For example, although he considered the question of cooperation with the rulers to be an important ethical issue and thought that it was improper for one to work for them or receive money from them, his disciples and his children did cooperate with the rulers and were willing to accept their donations. In other instances we find him scolding disciples who apparently operated in a manner contrary to his instructions. We also have an account of a disciple arguing with him about the future spiritual leader of the Ḥanbalis. These few illustrations indicate that Ibn Ḥanbal did not have any formal way of forcing his followers to obey him or to live by his ideas and values.

In essence, all *madhāhib* lacked hierarchies and bureaucracies and so did not have the mechanisms to impose collective policies or beliefs. However, they did gradually develop different ways to help members financially and as a consequence the leading figures of the *madhhab* in each generation had a degree of leverage over some of the *madhhab*'s followers. A unique aspect of the Ḥanbali circle during Ibn Ḥanbal's life was his refusal to build any kind of power mechanism for himself. In this matter he did not just stand apart from other circles of his age; he also maintained a policy that future Ḥanbalis would change. When he rejected al-Mutawakkil's donations he gave up tremendous clout. The sums of money that were to be sent to him could have been distributed among his disciples, thus enhancing his status and creating the typical equation of loyalty in exchange for material benefits. The invitations that the caliph extended to Ibn Ḥanbal to visit the court and give him advice could have strengthened his position as mediator between the rulers and his adherents, which would have been an effective way of attracting many new supporters.

This was probably the case with the Ḥanafis. As N. Tsafrir points out, Ḥanafi connections at court were most helpful in procuring their followers positions of *qāḍī* and as a result attracted many scholars to their *madhhab*. It was these forms of patronage, which can be identified in other *madhāhib* and were subsequently found among the Ḥanbalis as well, that Ibn Ḥanbal tried to avoid.[7] The fact that Ibn Ḥanbal's biographies refer to several stories about his refusal to play the patronage game indicate that his desire to distance himself from widespread forms of power is an important element in their collective identity.

Yet despite his reluctance to create any mechanisms for imposing his will or even milder forms of leverage through patronage, Ibn Ḥanbal was a highly influential, even powerful, religious leader. His influence was not manifested in organizing cadres of obedient devotees or an organization that would await his instructions. This was not found in any scholarly circle. His influence was based on the receptivity of large segments of the population to his ideas and his way of life. He was surrounded by hundreds of admirers who recorded his opinions on legal problems; he was an exemplar of proper behavior in wide circles; and he came to symbolize Traditionist resistance to the *miḥna*. His impact on his society derived from the mark he left on his admirers' attitudes, way of life, and ideals.

Ibn Ḥanbal's life was the formative moment of Ḥanbalism and his thoughts and ideals were the basis of the Ḥanbali intellectual framework. Although Ḥanbalism was not fully developed in his lifetime and was modified in subsequent generations, he did lay down its basic principles. Many of the ideas and modes of conduct that Ḥanbalis embraced and practiced can be traced back to Ibn Ḥanbal. The most distinctive of these are Ḥanbali attitudes toward people they considered theological deviants. Their confrontations with Shīʿīs and Muʿtazilis reflect Ibn Ḥanbal's harsh criticism of these sects and the uncompromising nature of their approach is in line with his behavior during the *miḥna*. Other elements in Ibn Ḥanbal's legacy that survived in future generations are his legal decisions, which were the basis of Ḥanbali legal literature, as well as his conduct, which served as a highly respected model of behavior. But it was not merely the blend of legal, theological, and moral ideas and ideals that Ibn Ḥanbal articulated that constituted the formative moment. It was the dozen or so devoted disciples who dedicated their lives to collecting his opinions on a wide range of issues, transmitting them and grooming the next generation of Ḥanbalis. It was the power of Ibn Ḥanbal's personality and ideas that moved these disciples to follow his path and in so doing create the link between the founder and his movement.

Notes

Inroduction

1 Al-Khaṭīb al-Baghdādī, *Ta'rīkh Baghdād* (Beirut, 1966), IV, 418.
2 On the *miḥna* see *EI*[2], 'Miḥna,' M. Hinds.
3 A. Hourani, 'Ṣūfism and Modern Islam: Mawlana Khalid and the Naqshabandi Order,' *The Emergence of the Modern Middle East* (Berkeley, 1981), 80.
4 There are numerous examples of individuals whose reputations of piety and learning won them positions of social influence. For an insightful analysis of this phenomenon in the medieval period see R. Mottahedeh, *Loyalty and Leadership in an Early Islamic Society* (Princeton, 1980), 135–150. See also D. Talmon-Heller, 'The Shaykh and the Community Popular Ḥanbalite Islam in 12th–13th Century Jabal Nablūs and Jabal Qasyun,' *Studia Islamica*, 79 (1994), 103–120. For a discussion on the importance of scholarship and piety in the construction of social standing in modern societies see D.F. Eickelman, 'Traditional Islamic Learning and Ideas of the Person in the Twentieth Century,' in *Middle Eastern Lives*, ed., M. Kramer (Syracuse, 1991), 35–59.
5 On the nature of Ibn Ḥanbal's leadership, its limits and scope of influence, see 'Epilogue.'
6 Ṣāliḥ b. Ḥanbal, *Sīrat al-imām Aḥmad b. Ḥanbal* (Alexandria, 1981); Ḥanbal b. Isḥāq, *Dhikr miḥnat al-imām Aḥmad b. Ḥanbal* (Cairo, 1977); and Ibn al-Jawzī, *Manāqib al-imām Aḥmad b. Ḥanbal* (Beirut, 1973), 301– 302.
7 Quoted in later sources such as Ibn al-Jawzī, *Manāqib*, 20–21.
8 Ibn Sa'd, *Kitāb al-ṭabaqāt al-kubrā* (Beirut, 1990), VII, 253; al-Bukhārī, *al-Ta'rīkh al-kabīr* (Hyderabad, 1361), I, pt. 2, 6; idem., *al-Ta'rīkh al-saghīr* (Cairo, 1976), II, 375.
9 Al-Jāḥiẓ, 'Khalq al-Qur'an' in *Rasā'il al-Jāḥiẓ*, ed. A.M. Harun (Cairo, 1979), III, 291–300.
10 Ṣāliḥ, *Sīrat al-imām*; For an analysis of this biography see N. Hurvitz, 'Biographies and Mild Asceticism: A Study of Islamic Moral Imagination,' *Studia Islamica* (85) 1997, 44–50; idem, *Aḥmad b. Ḥanbal and the Formation of Islamic Orthodoxy* (Ph. D. thesis, Princeton University, 1994),12–16.

11 Ḥanbal, *Dhikr.*
12 The Ḥanbali account of the *miḥna* also appears in Ibn Sa'd, *Ṭabaqāt.* For a thorough examination of this account of the *miḥna*, see M.D. Cooperson, *The Heirs of the Prophets in Classical Arabic Biography* (Ph.D. thesis, Harvard University, 1994), 340–400.
13 On al-Jāḥiẓ see *EI*[2], 'al-Djāḥiẓ,' C. Pellat; idem., *The Life And Works of Jāḥiẓ*, tr. D.M. Hawke (London, 1969).
14 On Ibn Abī Du'ād see *EI*[2], 'Aḥmad b. Abī Du'ād,' K.V. Zettersteen Ch. Pellat; J. van Ess, *Theologie und Gesellschaft um 2. Und 3. Jahrhundert Hidschra* (Berlin and New York, 1992), III, 481–502.
15 For an account of the anti-Ḥanbali narrative see *EI*[2], 'Miḥna,' M. Hinds.
16 Aḥmad b. Ḥanbal, *Musnad* (Beirut, 1991); idem., *Kitāb al-'ilal wa-ma'rifat al-rijāl* (Beirut and Riyad, 1408/1988); idem., *Radd 'alā zanādiqa wa-'l-jahmiyya* (Cairo, 1393); idem., *Kitāb al-sunna* (Dumam, 1986).
17 Ibn Abī Ya'lā, *Ṭabaqāt al-Ḥanābila* (Cairo, 1371/1952).
18 The extant *masā'il* collections are 'Abdallāh b. Ḥanbal, *Masā'il al-imām Aḥmad b. Ḥanbal* (Beirut, 1981); Isḥāq b. Ibrāhīm b. Hāni', *Masā'il al-imām Aḥmad b. Ḥanbal* (Beirut, 1400); Abū Dāwūd al-Sijistānī, *Kitāb masā'il al-imām Aḥmad* (Beirut, 1353). On the central disciples that collected Ibn Ḥanbal's *masā'il*, see H. Laoust, 'Le Ḥanbalisme sous le Califat de Bagdād (241/855–656/1258),' *Revue des Etudes Islamiques*, 27 (1959), 74–79.
19 Details in Hurvitz, *Aḥmad b. Ḥanbal*, 22–23.
20 Ibid., 23–24.
21 Abū Nu'aym al-Iṣfahānī, *Ḥilyat al-awliyā' wa-ṭabaqāt al-aṣfiyā'* (Beirut, 1967), IX, 161–233; There are exceptions to this tendency and al-Khaṭīb al-Baghdādī, *Ta'rīkh al-Baghdād*, is a case in point. On al-Khaṭīb al-Baghdādī and his tensions with the Ḥanbalis, see F. Malti-Douglas, 'Controversy and its Effects in the Biographical Tradition of al-Khaṭīb al-Baghdādī,' *Studia Isamica*, 46 (1977), 115–131.
22 On al-Khallāl, see *EI*[2], 'al-Khallāl,' H. Laoust; Ziauddin Aḥmad, 'Abū Bakr al-Khallāl The Compiler of the Teachings of Imām Aḥmad b. Ḥanbal,' *Islamic Studies*, 9 (1970), 245–254; C. Melchert, *The Formation of the Sunni Schools of Law, 9th-10th Centuries C.E.* (Leiden, 1997), 137–155.
23 On this work which is not extant, see *EI*[2], 'al-Khallāl,' H. Laoust.
24 Abū Nu'aym al-Iṣfahānī, *Ḥilyat al-awliyā'*; Ibn al-Jawzī, *Manāqib*; al-Dhahabī, *Tarjamat al-imām Aḥmad min ta'rīkh al-Islam* (Cairo, 1365/1946), 9–82; 'Abd al-Wahhāb al-Subkī, *Ṭabaqāt al-Shāfi'iyya al-kubrā* (Cairo, 1964), II, 27–63; Ibn Kathīr, *al-Bidāya wa-'l-nihāya* (Beirut, 1966), X, 325–341.
25 Al-Dhahabī, *Ta'rīkh*, 81. On al-Warkānī see *Ṭabaqāt al-Ḥanābila*, I, 287, where he is mentioned as Ibn Ḥanbal's neighbor and source of the story about mass conversion.
26 Ibn al-Jawzī, *Manāqib*, 21.
27 Ibid. 20.
28 For criticism of this story see al-Dhahabī, *Ta'rīkh*, 51–53; On the miracle of the trousers see Cooperson, *The Heirs*, 382–383.
29 In certain cases the biographers made this distinction themselves. Abū Nu'aym al-Iṣfahānī, *Ḥilyat*, IX, 204, where he distinguishes between Ṣāliḥ's 'most accurate account (*aṣaḥḥ al-riwāya*')' and other accounts.
30 Ibn Abī Ya'lā, *Ṭabaqāt al-Ḥanābila.*

31 For a critique of the reliability of biographical sources see N. Calder, *Studies in Early Muslim Jurisprudence* (Oxford, 1993). Calder assumes that there is a disjuncture between information that is found in biographic literature and 'the historical development of social institutions or ideas in the third century' (171). For a critique of Calder's views see J.E. Brockopp, 'Early Islamic Jurisprudence in Egypt: Two Scholars and Their *Mukhtaṣars*,' *International Journal of Middle East Studies*, 30 (1998), 167–182. I tend to agree with Brockopp's assessment that it is possible to 'reveal a basically reliable framework of information' (169), if the historical data undergoes a critical reading.

32 On Ibn Ḥanbal's lists of teachers, see chapter 2.

33 On the construction oh Ibn Ḥanbal's pious image see chapter 3 and Hurvitz, 'Biography.'

34 This generalization requires modifications. The most obvious are the hagiographic elements that were inserted into Ibn Ḥanbal's entries in ṣūfī biographic dictionaries. A second body of anecdotes that does not fit this generalization are stories by anonymous contemporaries mentioned above.

35 G. Levi, 'On Microhistory,' in *New Perspectives On Historical Writing*, ed., P. Burke (Cambridge, 1991), 95. Other historians that have grappled with these questions are German historians of *Alltagsgeschichte*. See A. Ludtke, 'Introduction: What is the History of Everyday Life and Who are its Practitioners?' in *The History of Everyday Life, Reconstructing Historical Experiences and Ways of Life*, ed., A. Ludtke, tr. W. Templer (Princeton, 1995), 3–40.

36 Ibid. 'Microhistory,' 98.

37 The comparison between Sherlock Holmes and microhistorians was made by E. Muir, 'Introduction: Observing Trifles,' in *Microhistory and the Lost Peoples of Europe*, eds., E. Muir and G. Ruggiero (Baltimore, 1991), vii.

38 On 'mild asceticism' see N. Hurvitz, 'Biographies and Mild Asceticism: A Study of Islamic Moral Imagination,' *Studia Islamica*, 85 (1997), 41–65.

39 On Ḥanbali moral outlook and the formation of Ibn Ḥanbal's circle of disciples, see N. Hurvitz, '*Madhāhib* (Schools of Law) and Historical Context: Re-examining the Formation of the Ḥanbali *Madhhab*,' *Islamic Law and Society*, 7 (2000), 37–64.

40 Two classic works that made use of Inquisition protocols are C. Ginzburg, *The Cheese and the Worms* (Baltimore, 1980); E. Le Roy Ladurie, *Montaillou* (London, 1978).

41 R. Humphreys, *Islamic History, A Framework of Inquiry* (Princeton, 1991), 193.

42 Levi, 'Microhistory,' 98.

43 A.A. Duri, *The Rise of Historical Writing Among the Arabs*, tr. L.I. Conrad (Princeton, 1983), 40; Hurvitz, 'Biographies,' 57–64.

44 G. Makdisi, 'Ethics in Islamic Traditionalist Doctrine' in *Ethics in Islam*, ed., R.G. Hovanissian (Malibu, 1985), 47–63; M. Fakhry, *Ethical Theories in Islam* (Leiden, 1991), 151–157.

45 Dwight M. Donaldson, *Studies in Muslim Ethics* (London, 1953), 194–212; A. Schimmel, *Mystical Dimensions of Islam* (Chapel Hill, 1975), 98–186.

46 Margaret Smith, *Rābi'a the Mystic and Her Fellow-Saints in Islam* (Cambridge, 1928, 1984), 10.

47 Tor Andrae, *In the Garden of the Myrtles, Studies in Early Islamic Mysticism*, tr. B. Sharpe (Albany, 1987), 46–47.

48 G. Bowering, *The Mystical Vision of Existence in Classical Islam* (Berlin, 1980), 56.
49 The ideology and practices of the extreme ascetics are dealt with in a number of works, such as Schimmel, *Mystical Dimensions*; Andrae, *Garden of Myrtles*, 33–54.
50 For a partial description of the Ḥanbali school's development see N. Hurvitz, '*Madhāhib*'.
51 There are different chronologies of this development. W. Madelung, *Religious Trends in Early Islamic Iran* (Albany, 1988), 19–20, discusses the spread of Ḥanafism and its mass following in Iran during the third century; this is corroborated by N. Tsafrir, 'The Beginnings of the Ḥanafi School of Iṣfahān,' *Islamic Law and Society*, 5 (1998), 1; M.G.S. Hodgson, *The Venture of Islam* (Chicago, 1974), I, 535, refers to the popular following of *madhāhib* in the second century; other historians such as Mottahedeh, *Loyalty and Leadership*, 25; R. Bulliet, *Patricians of Nishapur* (Cambridge, 1972), 31; I. Lapidus, *A History of Islamic Societies* (Cambridge, 1988), 167, refer to the *madhāhib* of the fourth century as mass movements.
52 J. Schacht, *An Introduction to Islamic Law* (Oxford, 1964), 62–63; S.A. Spectorsky, 'Aḥmad b. Ḥanbal's *Fiqh*,' *Journal of American Oriental Society*, 102 (1982), 462; idem., *Chapters on Marriage and Divorce, Responses of Ibn Ḥanbal and Ibn Rāhwayh* (Austin, 1993), ix.
53 Schacht, *Introduction*, 62.
54 This characterization of Ibn Ḥanbal's jurisprudential outlook has been made by M. Abū Zahra, *Ibn Ḥanbal* (Cairo, 1949), 273 where he states explicitly that Ibn Ḥanbal followed the legal path of al-Shāfi'ī and accepted the legitimacy of *qiyās*. H. Laoust also remarked on Ibn Ḥanbal's jurisprudential outlook in his article in *EI*^{2}, 'Aḥmad b. Ḥanbal,' 276: 'He [Ibn Ḥanbal] does not reject analogical reasoning (*kiyās*)'; for a similar assessment of Ibn Ḥanbal's attitude towards *qiyās* see W. Hallaq, 'Al-Shafi'i, Architect of Islamic Jurisprudence?' *International Journal of Middle Eastern Studies*, 25 (1993), 597.
55 I. Lapidus, 'State and Religion in Islamic Societies,' *Past and Present*, 151 (1996), 11; For a similar observation see W. Madelung 'The Vigilante Movement of Sahl b. Salāma al-Khurāsānī and the Origins of Ḥanbalism Reconsidered,' *Journal of Turkish Studies*, 14 (1990), 331: 'In these volunteer movements and Ḥanbalism, according to Lapidus' interpretation, the permanent separation of state and religion in Islam took shape.'
56 Lapidus, *Islamic Societies*, 166. While disagreeing with Lapidus over the identity and motives of these soldiers, Madelung accepts the basic premise that the Ḥanbalis built their following among soldiers. See 'Vigilante,' 337.
57 For a different view, one that agrees with Lapidus, see Madelung 'Vigilante,' 336. See also M. Cook, *Commanding Right and Forbidding Wrong in Islamic Thought* (Cambridge, 2001), 106, in which he emphasises that Ibn Ḥanbal was not involved in these political activities. I would like to thank Prof. M. Cook for sending me the drafts of the relevant chapters from this study.
58 Ibn Abī Ya'lā, *Ṭabaqāt al-Ḥanābila* (Cairo, 1371), I, 80–82.
59 S. Sabari, *Mouvements Populaires a Baghdad a l'epoque 'Abbaside ix-xi Siecles* (Paris, 1981), 102–103. See also M. Cook, *Commanding*, 101–105.
60 Ḥanbal, *Dhikr*, 81–82.

61 Ibid. 101–104.
62 G. Makdisi, *The Rise of Colleges* (Edinburgh, 1981), 8.
63 *EI*², 'Ḥanābila,' H. Laoust.
64 Laoust, 'Les Ḥanbalisme,' 70–71.
65 Sabari, *Mouvements*,101–103.
66 Ibid., 101.
67 Ibid., 103.
68 The most comprehensive statement of this view is C. Melchert, *The Formation of the Sunni Schools of Law, 9th-10th Centuries C.E.* (Leiden, 1997).
69 The exceptions to this statement are Spectorsky, 'Ibn Ḥanbal's *Fiqh*,'; idem., *Marriage and Divorce*; *EI*², 'Ḥanābila,' Laoust; idem., 'Le Ḥanbalisme.'
70 W.M. Patton, *Aḥmed Ibn Ḥanbal and the Miḥna* (Leiden, 1897).
71 Lapidus, 'State and Religion,' 11.
72 *EI*², 'Miḥna,' M. Hinds.
73 P. Crone and M. Hinds, *God's Caliph: Religious Authority in the First Centuries of Islam*, (Cambridge, 1986), 93.
74 J.A. Nawas, 'A Reexamination of Three Current Explanations for Al-Ma'mūn's Introduction of the *Miḥna*,' *International Journal of Middle Eastern Studies*, 24 (1994), 622.
75 Hurvitz, *Aḥmad b. Ḥanbal*; M. W. Zaman, *Religion and Politics Under the Early 'Abbasids* (Leiden, 1997), 106–118.
76 Zaman, 11.
77 Ibid.
78 Ibid., 108. This broad statement is not absolutely clear, since Zaman does point out that after al-Ma'mūn's death the 'claims to religious authority were neglected,' 112.
79 *EI*², 'Miḥna,' M. Hinds.
80 Nawas, 'Reexamination,' 624.
81 For a thorough source analysis of later Ḥanbali accounts of the *miḥna*, see Cooperson, *Heirs*, 340–400. Whereas Cooperson's caution regarding the reliability of these accounts is well placed, it is well worth remembering that they do reflect the Ḥanbali view of events.
82 Such a reading of the *miḥna* protocols is alluded to in Zaman, *Religion and Politics*, 113, where he observes: 'this caliph comes across as utterly convinced of the scholar's authority, and the only question is whose authority, among the scholars, he would defer to.'
83 Al-Ṭabarī, *Ta'rīkh al-rusul wa-'l-mulūk* (Leiden, 1879–1901), III, 1114.

Part One
Chapter One

1 Introduction, sources and methodology
2 Ṣāliḥ, *Sīrat al-imām*, 27; For variants of Ibn Ḥanbal's geneology see Abu Nu'aym al-Iṣfahānī, *Ḥilyat al-awliyā'*, IX, 162; *Ṭabaqāt al-Ḥanābila*, I, 4; Ismā'īl b. 'Umar Ibn Kathīr, *al-Bidāya wa-'l-nihāya*, (Cairo, 1932) X, 325
3 *Ṭabaqāt al-Ḥanābila*, I, 5.
4 Ibid.

5 Ibid.
6 Ibid.
7 Ibid.
8 *Ta'rīkh Baghdād*, IV, 413–414; al-Subkī, *Ṭabaqāt al-Shāfi'iyya*, II, 27; *Ta'rīkh al-Islam*, 9; *Ḥilyat al-awliyā'*, IX, 162.
9 *Ta'rīkh Baghdād*, IV, 414.
10 Ibid.
11 Muḥammad b. Mukarram b. Manẓūr, *Mukhtaṣar ta'rīkh Dimashq li-Ibn 'Asākir* (Damascus, 1984), III, 241.
12 This conversation took place some time before al-Ma'mūn and al-Mu'taṣim 'embarked on a policy of ousting the Arabs from the Diwan on an unprecedented scale.' D. Ayalon 'Preliminary Remarks on the Mamluk Military Institution in Islam,' in *War, Technology and Society in the Middle East*, eds., V.J. Parry and M.E. Yapp (London, 1975), 48, 53. On this change in policy see also D. Pipes, *Slave Soldiers and Islam* (New Haven, 1981), 150. An example of stopping payments to Arabs can be found in Muḥammad b. Yūsuf al-Kindī, *Kitāb al-wulā' wa kitāb al-quḍā'* (Leiden, 1912), 193.
13 Ibn Manẓūr, *Mukhtaṣar*, III, 241.
14 On 'Abdallāh b. Muḥammad b. al-Rūmī, see Aḥmad b. 'Alī, Ibn Ḥajar al-'Asqalānī *Tahdhīb al-tahdhīb* (Beirut, 1994), VI, 21–22.
15 Ibn al-Jawzī, *Manāqib*,19.
16 Ibn Manẓūr, *Mukhtaṣar*, III, 241.
17 *Manāqib*, 19–20.
18 *EI*[2], 'Marw al-Shahidjan,' A. Yu. Yakubovski [C.E. Bosworth].
19 Ibn Manẓūr, *Mukhtaṣar*, III, 241; *Ta'rīkh Baghdād*, IV, 415.
20 *EI*[2], 'Māzin,' G. Levi Della Vida.
21 Ibn Manẓūr, *Mukhtaṣar*, III, 241; *Ta'rīkh Baghdād*, IV, 415.
22 On Musayyab see H. Kennedy, *The Early Abbasid Caliphate* (Totowa, 1981), 79; and P. Crone, *Slaves on Horses*, 186–187.
23 Isḥāq, the father of Ḥanbal b. Isḥāq, is well known. 'Umar was the father of Rayḥana, Ibn Ḥanbal's second wife; see *Ṭabaqāt al-Ḥanābila*, I, 429. We read about 'Abdallāh b. Ḥanbal in Ṣāliḥ, 37, on the occasion of his funeral.
24 *Ta'rīkh al-Islam*, 34–35.
25 *Manāqib*, 21.
26 Ibid.
27 On Ibn Ḥanbal's interrogation, see pp. 131–144.
28 Ḥanbal, *Dhikr*, 55. A short survey of 'Abd al-Raḥmān's career appears in 'Abd al-Qādir b. Abī al-Wafā', *Jawāhir al-muḍīyya fī ṭabaqāt al-Ḥanafiyya*, (Hyderabad, 1933), I, 299, 300.
29 Ibid.
30 For a terse sketch of Ibn Ḥanbal's family and its comparison to the Barmacids, see P. Crone, *Slaves on Horses* (Cambridge, 1980) 70.
31 *Manāqib*, 298; *Ṭabaqāt al-Ḥanābila*, I, 429, were she is named 'Abāsa bint al-Faḍl.
32 Ibid., 299.
33 On *kafā'a* see F. Ziadeh, 'Equality (Kafā'ah) in the Muslim Law of Marriage,' *The American Journal of Comparative Law* 6 (1957), 503–517; M.M. Bravmann, *The Spiritual Background of Early Islam* (Leiden, 1972), 301–310; Of its place in Islamic social thought see L. Marlow, *Hierarchy and*

Egalitarianism in Islamic Thought, Cambridge, 1997), 30–34; On Ibn Ḥanbal's understanding of *kafā'a* see Spectorsky, *Marriage and Divorce*, 14–16. For a different interpretation of Ibn Ḥanbal's view see N. Hurvitz, review of S. Spectorsky, *Marriage and Divorce*, in *Islamic Law and Society*, 3 (1996).

34 Abū Dāwūd al-Sijistānī, *Masā'il*, 159, trans. S. Spectorsky, *Marriage and Divorce*, 61.

35 Isḥāq b. Ibrāhīm b. Hāni', *Masā'il*, I, 200.

36 On Shu'ūbiyya see I. Goldziher, *Muslim Studies* (London, 1967–1971), I, 137–198; H.A.R. Gibb, 'The Social Significance of the Shu'ūbiya,' in *Studies on the Civilization of Islam* (Boston, 1962), 62–73; R. Mottahedeh, 'The Shu'ūbiyyah Controversy and the Social History of Early Islamic Iran,' *International Journal of Middle East Studies*, 7 (1976), 161–182; H.T. Norris, 'The Shu'ūbiyyah in Arabic Literature,' in *The Cambridge History of Arabic Literature* (Cambridge, 1990), 31–47.

37 *Ṭabaqāt al-Ḥanābila*, I, 30. *Faḍl* can be translated as superiority or merit. *Sābiqa* can be translated as precedent or previous actions. In both cases the choice of the first option would give Ibn Ḥanbal's outlook a more extreme quality.

38 *EI*[2], 'Aḥmad b. Ḥanbal,' H. Laoust.

39 *Manāqib*, 298.

40 Information about her can be found in *Manāqib*, 298–299; *Ṭabaqāt al-Ḥanābila*, I, 428, 429, where she appears as 'Abāsa.

41 *Manāqib*, 299.

42 For a critical remark on Ibn Ḥanbal's account of the number of years that he was married to each of his wives see *Manāqib*, 300.

43 *Manāqib*, 299. This is not very clear; the mediator is referred to as a 'woman from among them' (*imra'at 'indahum*).

44 *Manāqib*, 299–300; *Ṭabaqāt al-Ḥanābila*, I, 429, where she appears in her full name, Rayḥāna bint 'Umar.

45 *Ṭabaqāt al-Ḥanābila*, I, 152.

46 *Manāqib*, 299–300; *Ṭabaqāt al-Ḥanābila*, I, 429.

47 Ibid., 300.

48 Ibid.

49 *Manāqib*, 301–302. *Ṭabaqāt al-Ḥanābila*, I, 429–430.

50 *Manāqib*, 301; Ya'qūb b. Isḥāq b. Bukhtān, Abū Yūsuf, described in *Ṭabaqāt al-Ḥanābila*, I, 415 as a neighbor and friend of Ibn Ḥanbal.

51 *Manāqib*, 301.

52 Ibid. On Sa'id's death, see *Manāqib*, 306.

53 Ibid.

54 Ibid.

55 Ibid., 302.

56 Ṣāliḥ, 40.

57 Ṣāliḥ, 40–41.

58 *Manāqib*, 304; *Ṭabaqāt al-Ḥanābila*, I, 173.

59 Ibid.

60 Ibid., 304–305.

61 On Ṣāliḥ's standing in his father's eyes, see *Manāqib*, 304; *Ṭabaqāt al-Ḥanābila*, I, 173.

62 *Manāqib*, 306.

63 Ṣāliḥ, 39.
64 The accepted principle of division was two-to-one ratio in favor of the grandsons.
65 *Manāqib*, 306.
66 Ibid.
67 *Manāqib*, 223.
68 On Muḥammad b. 'Ubaydallāh, see *Ṭabaqāt al-Ḥanābila*, I, 302–304.
69 *Manāqib*, 224.
70 Ibid.
71 Ibid.
72 Ibn Kathīr, *al-Bidāya*, X, 337.
73 *Ḥilyat al-awliyā'*, IX, 179.
74 On Ibn Ḥanbal's respect to such ascetics, see Ṣāliḥ, 46.
75 Ṣāliḥ, 40.
76 Ḥanbal, 43.
77 Ibid.
78 On *jiwār* see E. Lane, *An Arab-English Lexicon* (Cambridge, 1984), 484.
79 Ḥanbal was governor in Sarakhs and participated in the 'Abbāsid revolution. On al-Ḥusayn see Kennedy, *Early 'Abbasid*, 182.
80 Ḥanbal, 43.
81 Ibid., 43.
82 Ibid., 44.
83 Ibid., 43.
84 On al-Mutawakkil's religious policy see S. Miah, *The Reign of Mutawakkil* (Dacca, 1969), 75–103. On his attitude towards Ibn Ḥanbal see 81–83.
85 Ḥanbal, 101–107.
86 *Ta'rīkh al-Islam*, 68.
87 Ḥanbal, 104.
88 Ibid.
89 Ibid.
90 Ibid., 105.
91 *Ta'rīkh al-Islam*, 69.
92 Ibid.
93 Ibid.
94 Ṣāliḥ, 40.
95 *Manāqib*, 302.

Chapter Two

1 On Ṣafiya bint Maymūna, see *Manāqib*, 19, and *Ta'rīkh Baghdād*, IV, 412.
2 On foundation and history of Baghdād see EI^2, 'Baghdād,' A.A. Duri; J. Lassner, *The Topography of Baghdād in the Early Middle Ages* (Detroit, 1970); Charles Wendell, 'Baghdad, *Imago Mundi*, and Other Foundation-Lore,' *International Journal of Middle East Studies*, 2 (1970), 99–128.
3 On the city and its inhabitants as they are reflected in *The Thousand and One Nights* see R.C. Hovannisian and G. Sabagh, *The Thousand and One Nights in Arabic Literature and Society*, (Cambridge, 1997).

4 On *zanādiqa* see *EI*[1], 'Zindīḳ,' L. Massignon.
5 Al-Ṭabarī, III, 519; trans. H. Kennedy, vol. 29, 237.
6 Al-Ṭabarī, III, 520; trans. H. Kennedy, vol. 29, 238.
7 Ṣāliḥ, 30; *Manāqib*, 26.
8 *Manāqib*, 21. On official networks of supervision, intrusion of neighbors into each other's affairs, and management of neighborhoods, as was described in later sources, see E. Toledano, *State and Society in Mid-Nineteenth-Century Egypt* (Cambridge, 1990), 222–225; also A. Marcus, 'Privacy in Eighteenth-Century Aleppo: The Limits of Cultural Ideals,' *International Journal of Middle East Studies,* 18 (1986), 165–183.
9 This is precisely the dilemma that arose in the days of al-Mutawakkil. The similarity of the situations is reason enough to suspect the veracity of the anecdote. The story is sketched along the lines of events that took place half a century later.
10 The caliph was probably Hārūn al-Rashīd, who turned Raqqa into his headquarters in 180 A.H. If this identification is correct, the event took place when Ibn Ḥanbal was sixteen years old.
11 *Manāqib*, 20.
12 Ṣāliḥ, 28.
13 See for example Ibn Ḥajar al-'Asqalānī, *Tahdhīb*, or Khaṭīb al-Baghdādī, *Ta'rīkh al-Baghdād.*
14 On the potential and limits of biographical dictionaries as sources see H.A.R. Gibb, 'Islamic Biographical Literature,' in *Historians of the Middle East*, eds., B. Lewis and P.M. Holt (London, 1962), 54–58; R. Bulliet, 'A Quantitative Approach to Medieval Muslim Biographical Dictionaries,' *Journal of the Economic and Social History of the Orient*, 13 (1970), 195–211; H. Cohen, 'The Economic Background of the Secular Occupations of Muslim Jurisprudents and Traditionists in the Classical Period of Islam (Until the Middle of the Eleventh Century),' *Journal of the Economic and Social History of the Orient*, 13 (1970), 16–61; Humphreys, *Islamic History*, 187–208.
15 For a literary analysis of how the formal features of biographic entries serve ideological ends, see Kilpatrick, 'Autobiography'
16 Although I assume that the general atmosphere of tolerance or intolerance that surrounded Ibn Ḥanbal influenced his choice, it is difficult to pinpoint when these changes occurred and what mark they left on Ibn Ḥanbal.
17 *EI*[2], 'Abū Yūsuf, Ibrāhīm b. Ya'qūb,' J. Schacht.
18 Ibn Ḥanbal's encounters with Abū Yūsuf are ignored in *Ḥilyat al-awliyā'*, IX, 161–233. Abū Yūsuf is mentioned in passing in *Ta'rīkh al-Islam*, 10 and al-Subkī, II, 30. Ibn al-Jawzī is the only one to explicitly mention his studies with Abū Yūsuf, in *Manāqib*, 23. This statement does not go back to one of Ibn Ḥanbal's children or intimate friends, but to the relatively unknown Ya'qūb [b. Shayba?].
19 *Ta'rīkh Baghdād*, XIV, 259. More remarks to this effect made by other experts of *rijāl* can be found on this page for example, Ibn Ma'īn's 'Abū Yūsuf is the most noble from those that lie.'
20 *Ta'rīkh Baghdād*, XIV, 259, 260. *Ṣadūq* is a term that denotes the second level of trustworthiness. For the terminology that describes the hierarchy of transmitters see 'Uthmān b. 'Abd al-Raḥmān b. Ṣalāḥ al-Shahrazūrī, *'Ulūm al-ḥadīth*, (Halab, 1966) 109–114. 'Abd al-Raḥmān b. Abī Ḥātim, *Kitāb*

al-jarḥ wa-'l-ta'dīl, (Hyderabad, 1952) IV, pt. 2, 201; Ibn Ḥanbal, *Kitāb al-'ilal wa-ma'rifat al-rijāl*, (Beirut and Riyadh, 1408), III, 300.

21 *Ta'rīkh Baghdād*, XIV, 253, 255, 259; *al-Jarḥ*, XIV, pt. 2, 202. These references contain assessments of Abū Yūsuf. Though their contents differ, they all reflect the tensions of the period.

22 *Ta'rīkh Baghdād*, XII, 117; Ibn 'Adī al-Jurjānī, *al-Kāmil fī ḍu'afā' al-rijāl*, (Beirut, 1984) V, 1828.

23 Ibn Ḥibbān, *Kitāb al-majrūḥīn*, (Haleb, 1975), II, 110.

24 Ibn Ḥanbal, *'Ilal*, II, 345.

25 'Abd al-Raḥmān ibn al-Mahdī said he preferred him to Hushaym, Ibn Ḥanbal's first long-term teacher, mentioned above. Ibn Abī Ḥātim, *Jarḥ wa-'l-ta'dīl*, I, 153; *Ta'rīkh Baghdād*, VI, 232.

26 *Ta'rīkh Baghdād*, VI, 234. Mālik and Ḥammād passed away in 179, and Ibn 'Ulayya in 193.

27 *Ta'rīkh Baghdād*, VI, 238. A comparison appears in Wuhayb's entry in Ibn Ḥajar al-'Asqalānī, *Tahdhīb*, XI, 149, in which he states that Wuhayb was *laysa bihi ba's*, the second-highest category of transmitters, whereas Ibn 'Ulayya was *thābit*, the highest level a transmitter can reach. Hence, when Ibn Ḥanbal says he prefers Wuhayb over Ibn 'Ulayya, it demonstrates how a theological position can detract from the reputation of a transmitter.

28 There are several accounts of *kalām*, its origins and practitioners. The most comprehensive is J.van Ess, *Theologie*, vols. I-VI; On its origins see M. Cook, 'The Origins of Kalām,' *Bulletin of the School of Oriental and African Studies*, 43 (1980), 32–43; J. van Ess, 'The Beginnings of Islamic Theology,' in *The Cultural Context of Medieval Learning*, eds., J.E. Murdoch and E. D. Sylla, (Dordrecht, 1975), 87–111; For an overview of the topic see M. Abdel Haleem, 'Early *Kalām*,' in *History of Islamic Philosophy*, eds., S.H. Nasr and O. Leaman, (London, 1996), 71–88; On tensions between *mutakallimūn* and *muḥaddithūn* see J. Pavlin, 'Sunni *kalām* and Theological Controversies,' in *History of Islamic Philosophy*, eds., S.H. Nasr and O. Leaman (London, 1996), 105–118.

29 *Ta'rīkh Baghdād*, VI, 238; *Ṭabaqāt al-Ḥanābila*, I, 101.

30 'A. Mahmud, *Ittijāhāt al-fiqhiyya 'ind aṣḥāb al-ḥadīth*, (1979), 105–112.

31 *Ṭabaqāt al-Ḥanābila*, I, 36. For an interesting study of the term which links the Ḥashwiyya to the *aṣḥāb al-ḥadīth* and Ḥanbalis, see A. S. Halkin, 'The Ḥashwiyya,' *Journal of the American Oriental Society*, 54, (1934), 1–28. On Nābita, see Wadad al-Qadi, 'The Earliest 'Nābita' and the Paradigmatic 'Nawābit'', *Studia Islamica*, 78 (1993), 27–61.

32 Al-Ṭabarī, III, 1112–1113; tr. Bosworth, XXXII, 200. On the use of this term and its possible Persian influence, see F. Steppat, 'From *'Ahd Ardashīr* to Al-Ma'mūn: A Persian Element in the Policy of the *Miḥna*,' in *Studies in Arabica and Islamica*, ed., W. al-Qadi (Beirut, 1981), 451–454.

33 *Ta'rīkh Baghdād*, XI, 123.

34 Ibn Ḥajar al-'Asqalānī, *Lisān al-Mīzān* (Hyderabad, 1330), IV, 76.

35 Ibn Ḥajar al-'Asqalānī, *Tahdhīb*, VII, 319.

36 Ibid. *Ta'rīkh Baghdād*, XII, 107.

37 Ṣāliḥ, 28, 29, 31. The only variant to this periodization appears in *Ḥilyat al-awliyā'*, IX, 164, in which he tells Ṣāliḥ he started his studies with Hushaym in 177.

38 Abu Zahra, *Ibn Ḥanbal*, 94–96.
39 A partial list is found in Ibn Ḥanbal, *'Ilal*, IV, 342. On *tadlīs* see *EI*², 'Tadlīs,' G.H.A. Juynboll.
40 Ibn Ḥanbal, *'Ilal*, II, 98.
41 Ibn Ḥanbal, *'Ilal*, II, 322.
42 For a different chronology see Abu Zahra, *Ibn Ḥanbal*, 23. In his view, Ibn Ḥanbal's first destination was Baṣra, and the trip took place in 186 A.H. This contradicts the earliest source, Ṣāliḥ, 29.
43 Ibn Abī Ḥātim, *al-Jarḥ wa-'l-ta'dīl*, Introduction, 32–54.
44 Ibn Ḥanbal performed the *ḥajj* in 187, 191, 196–198.
45 Ibn Ḥanbal, *'Ilal*, I, 192, 384.
46 Ibn Ḥanbal, *'Ilal*, II, 261. For the same content with different transmitters, see Ibn Adī al-Jurjānī, *al-Kāmil*, VII, 2596 and Aḥmad b. 'Alī b. Ḥajar al-'Asqalānī, *Kitāb al-mudallisīn*, (Misr, 1913) 9–10.
47 The linkage to Shī'īsm was made by Ibn 'Adī al-Jurjānī in Ibn Ḥajar al-'Asqalānī, *Tahdhīb*, IV, 109. Ibn 'Adī does not include Ibn 'Uyayna in the *Kāmil*. However, in Ibn 'Adī al-Jurjānī, *al-Kāmil*, V, 1951, he is mentioned as having transmitted an anti-Mu'āwiya tradition. His association with Ḥanafism is indicated by his appearance in 'Abd al-Qādir b. Abī al-Wafā', *al-Jawāhir al-muḍīyya fī ṭabaqāt al-Ḥanafiyya*, (Hyderabad, 1332), I, 250.
48 Ibn Ḥajar al-'Asqalānī, *Tahdhīb*, XI, 134.
49 Ibid., 135.
50 *Ta'rīkh Baghdād*, IV, 413. On 'Abd al-A'lā, see Ibn Ḥajar al-'Asqalānī, *Tahdhīb*, VI 6, 90–92.
51 On their ages see Muḥammad b. Aḥmad al-Dhahabī, *Siyar a'lām al-nubalā'* (Beirut, 1994), IX, 561, 546; X, 124, 396, 242.
52 *Ta'rīkh Baghdād*, XIV, 56; XIII, 70; Ibn Ḥajar al-'Asqalānī, *Tahdhīb*, X, 168; Ibn Ḥanbal, *'Ilal*, III, 72.
53 *Ta'rīkh Baghdād*, XIII, 70.
54 Ibn Ḥajar al-'Asqalānī, *Tahdhīb*, X, 168; *Ta'rīkh Baghdād*, XIII, 70; Ibn Ḥajar al-'Asqalānī, *Tahdhīb*, X, 275. One of them, Abū Salama, taught Ibn Ma'īn and Ibn Ḥanbal about various Traditionists.
55 Ibn Ḥajar al-'Asqalānī, *Tahdhīb*, XI, 189–192.
56 Ibn Abī al-Wafā', *Jawāhir*, II, 212, 213.
57 Ibn Ḥanbal, *'Ilal*, I, 429.
58 *Ta'rīkh Baghdād*, X, 243. 'Alī b. al-Madīnī remarked that if 'Abd al-Raḥmān and Yaḥyā b. Sa'īd al-Qaṭṭān disagreed regarding the proficiency of a transmitter, he preferred 'Abd al-Raḥmān because Yaḥyā al-Qaṭṭān was harsh (*kāna fī Yaḥyā tashaddud*).
59 Ibn Abī al-Wafā', *Jawāhir*, II, 208–209; Ibn Ḥajar al-'Asqalānī, *Tahdhīb*, XI, 112.
60 Ibn Ḥajar al-'Asqalānī, *Tahdhīb*, VI, 277.
61 Ibid., 276.
62 W.B. Hallaq, 'Was al-Shafi'i the Master Architect of Islamic Jurisprudence,' *International Journal of Middle East Studies*, 25 (1993), 587–605. In (590), Hallaq raises doubts about Ibn Ḥanbal's respect to al-Shāfi'ī's achievement. Hallaq argues that Ibn Ḥanbal considered the *Risāla* 'religiously dubious.' I tend to understand Ibn Ḥanbal's remarks in the *Ṭabaqāt al-Ḥanābila*, I, 57 in a more moderate manner. The context of the discussion is writing the *Risāla*

and it is this writing that Ibn Ḥanbal opposes. Furthermore, on that same page he remarks against writing the words of Mālik b. Anas and Sufyān al-Thawrī, both of whom Ibn Ḥanbal respected as individuals and scholars.

63 'Abd al-Raḥmān b. Abī Ḥātim, *Ādāb al-Shāfi'ī* (Cairo, 1953), 43.

64 Yūsuf b. 'Abd al-Barr, *Al-Intiqā' fī faḍā'il al-thalātha al-a'imma al-fuqahā'* (Cairo, 1350), 76.

65 Ibn Abī Ḥātim, *Ādāb al-Shāfi'ī*, 55–56; Ibn 'Abd al-Barr, *al-Intiqā'*, 76.

66 *Ḥilyat al-awliyā'*, IX, 170; Similar opinion in Ibn Abī Ḥātim, *Ādāb al-Shāfi'ī*, 96.

67 Ibn Abī Ḥātim, *Ādāb al-Shāfi'ī*, 94–96.

68 Al-Subkī, II, 30. For a discussion of al-Subkī's relations with tradition-minded Shāfi'īs, see Makdisi, 'Ḥanbalite Islam' in *Studies on Islam*, ed., M. L. Swartz (New York, 1981), 224–228.

69 Ibn Kathīr, *al-Bidāya*, X, 327; Ibn 'Abd al-Barr, *Al-Intiqā'*, 75; *Ḥilyat al-awliyā'*, IX, 170. This is also found in Ibn Ḥanbal's *'Ilal*, I, 462.

70 Ibn Kathīr, *al-Bidāya*, X, 327.

71 On al-Shāfi'ī's criticism of local customs and the need to substitute them with Prophetic traditions see J. Schacht, *Origins of Muḥammadan Jurisprudence* (Oxford, 1950). On the connection between Ḥanbalism, Prophetic traditions and criticism of locally sponsored traditions, see Madelung, *Religious Trends*, 22.

72 For a theory of the development of Islamic jurisprudence that relies heavily on the shift from local to universal validity, see Schacht, *Origins*, 1–137.

73 Ibn Kathīr, *al-Bidāya*, X, 327.

74 Ibn Ḥanbal, *'Ilal*, I, 462. Other Shāfi'īs also include this humbling statement in their accounts. See *Ḥilyat al-awliyā'*, IX, 170; Ibn 'Abd al-Barr, *al-Intiqā'*, 75.

75 *Ṭabaqāt al-Ḥanābila*, I, 6.

76 *Manāqib*, 32; a similar anecdote is found, 31.

77 *Ḥilyat al-awliyā'*, IX, 169; *Manāqib*, 27.

78 On Yazīd b. Hārūn, see Ibn Ḥajar al-'Asqalānī, *Tahdhīb* (Beirut, 1984), XI, 319–321.

79 *Ḥilyat al-Awliyā'*, IX, 165.

80 Ibid., 164.

81 On Yaḥyā, see *Manāqib*, 30; on Isḥāq's travel's with Ibn Ḥanbal in 198, see *Manāqib*, 69.

82 *Manāqib*, 79–80.

83 *Ṭabaqāt al-Ḥanābila*, I, 346.

84 *Ḥilyat al-awliyā'*, IX, 164.

Chapter Three

1 *Manāqib*, 255.

2 Ibid. On the use of *'imāma* by the Prophet, see Ibn Sa'd, *al-Ṭabaqāt*, I, 455.

3 Ibid. Compare to the anecdote in which the Prophet protects himself from the cold with a blanket, as well as avoiding clothes that caused him to perspire Ibn Sa'd, *al-Ṭabaqāt*, I, 453.

4 *Manāqib*, 255.
5 Al-Washshā', *Al-Muwashshā* (Beirut, 1965), 178. Note the Prophet's refusal to wear silk cloak and his remark that it 'does not befit pious men.' Ibn Sa'd, *al-Ṭabaqāt*, I, 457.
6 *Manāqib*, 254.
7 Ibid.
8 Ibid.
9 On the importance of this principle see Schimmel, *Mystical Dimensions*, 117.
10 *Manāqib*, 249–250.
11 Ibid., 249. Suwayd's house is described in Ibn Ḥajar 'Asqalānī, *Tahdhīb*, IV, 244. His biography is discussed in Ibn Sa'd, *al-Ṭabaqāt*, VI, 45.
12 Ṣāliḥ, 40–41.
13 See, for example, Schimmel, *Mystical Dimensions*, 116: 'Like the early Christian monks who lived exclusively on the host, the Muslim saints considered hunger the best way to reach spirituality. To be empty of worldly food is the precondition for enlightenment. 'Could the reedflute sing if its stomach were filled?' Rumi asks repeatedly. Man can receive the divine breath of inspiration only when he keeps himself hungry and empty.'
14 T. Andrae, *Garden of the Myrtles*, 52.
15 Ibid.
16 Partial exceptions to this are Ibn Ḥanbal's decisions to avoid al-Mutawakkil's food when he visited his court as well as his son's food after they began to accept al-Mutawakkil's stipends.
17 Andrae, *Garden of Myrtles*, 53. One example of this 'art,' the *ṣaum dā'ūdī*, is mentioned in Schimmel, *Mystical Dimensions*, 115: '[The Ṣūfīs] would eat one day and fast one day, so that their bodies would not become accustomed to either of the two states.' Some ascetics famous for their fasting are Shaqīq al-Balkhī, who was 'the first mystic to speak of the 'alchemy of hunger' and 'claimed that forty days of constant hunger could transform the darkness of the heart into light . . .' Another famous ṣūfī who managed some incredible feats of 'systematic starvation of the body' was Sahl al-Tustarī. According to some anecdotes, he could abstain 'from food for seventy days.' Al-Tustarī's virtuosic acts of fasting were an inspiration to al-Ghazzālī, who quoted the ṣūfī master's aphorisms about hunger 'and illustrated them with al-Tustarī's practice' in his *Iḥyā 'Ulūm al-Dīn*. For anecdotes about al-Tustarī's fasts, see G. Bowering, *The Mystic Vision of Existence in Classical Islam* (New York, 1980), 55–57.
18 Ṣāliḥ, 40; *Manāqib*, 251.
19 Ṣāliḥ 40; *Manāqib*, 251.On the purchase of meat see, *Manāqib*, 302.
20 Bowering, *Mystic Vision*, 56.
21 The watermelon appears as a violation of elitistic etiquette in al-Washshā', *Muwashshā*, 194.
22 On 'alchemy of hunger,' see Schimmel, *Mystical Dimensions*, 115.
23 On self-mortification, sexual renunciation and castration in early Christianity, see P. Brown, *The Body and Society* (New York, 1988).
24 Many pious Muslims shared Ibn Ḥanbal's moderate ascetic practices. His ambivalence towards ascetic practices heralds one of the most widespread forms of behavior in Islam. Three or four centuries after his death the ascetics began to form ṣūfī orders (*ṭarīqa*). Most Muslims thought highly of

its members but would not go so far as to join them. These *muḥibbūn* or *mutashābbihūn*, whose ambivalence towards sufism is so well understood by Abū al-Najīb al-Suhrawardī, *A Sufi Rule for the Novice*, trans. M. Milson (Cambridge, 1975) seem to have gone down Ibn Ḥanbal's path. They respected the ways of the ṣūfīs, yet were reluctant to practice them to the hilt. Though many sufis looked down upon these 'lay members,' the inner tension of the 'lay members' had its precedent in the actions of one of the foremost figures in the Islamic pantheon.

25 Ibn Ḥanbal, *Kitāb al-wara'* (Beirut, 1983), 19.
26 It would be interesting to compare the moral attributes of different sorts of work, trade, manual labor, religious professions etc.
27 Ibn Ḥanbal, *Kitāb al-wara'*, 17.
28 *Manāqib*, 223.
29 Ṣāliḥ, 30.
30 *Manāqib*, 226.
31 Ibid.
32 On self-criticism among the ṣūfīs, see Schimmel, *Mystical Dimensions*, 112–114.
33 *Ḥilyat al-awliyā'*, IX, 177.
34 Ṣāliḥ, 43; *Manāqib*, 232.
35 Ibid. This is the opening anecdote in Ṣāliḥ's chapter on Ibn Ḥanbal's *zuhd*.
36 *Manāqib*, 232–235.
37 *Ḥilyat al-awliyā'*, IX, 181.
38 Ibid.
39 Al-Ṭabarī, III, 1125–1131; Bosworth, XXXII, 214–220.
40 Ibn Kathīr, *Al-Bidāya*, X, 328; *Manāqib*, 270.
41 *Manāqib*, 373, 377; *Ḥilyat al-awliyā'*, IX, 211, where he refers to them as *fitnat al-dunyā* and *fitnat al-dīn*.
42 Ṣāliḥ, 29, 31; See reference to 'Abdallāh b. al-Mubārak in Ibn Ḥanbal, *Kitāb al-wara'*, 121.
43 On Fuḍayl b. 'Iyāḍ, see *EI*[2], 'al-Fuḍayl b. 'Iyāḍ,' M. Smith; 'Alī b. 'Uthmān al-Hujwīrī, *al-Kashf al-Mahjūb*, trans. R.A. Nicholson (London, 1976), 97–100. See also the article by Jacqueline Chabbi 'Fuḍayl b. 'Iyāḍ, Un Precursor Du Ḥanbalisme,' in *Bulletin D'Etudes Orientales*, 30 (1978), 331–345, where she notes the ideological affinity between Ibn Ḥanbal and Fuḍayl b. 'Iyāḍ, particularly, on pages 340–342. Note, also, her distinction between asceticism and sufism. While the latter advocates an ideology of 'rupture sociale,' the former does not (343). I would like to thank Prof. M. Cook for referring me to this article.
On 'Abdallāh b. al-Mubārak, see *Encyclopedia Iranica*, "Abdallāh b. Mobārak,' P. Nwyia. See also, Hujwīrī, *Kashf*, 95–97.
Another important Traditionist in this line of mild ascetics was Fuḍayl b. 'Iyāḍ's teacher Sufyān al-Thawrī. Like other mild ascetics, Sufyān al-Thawrī merged social involvement with social criticism. For a summary of his life, see *EI*[1], 'Sufyān al-Thawrī,' M. Plessner.
44 M. Weber, *Economy and Society* (New York, 1968) II, 541–544, highlights some of the differences between mild and extreme asceticism. If we go along with Weber's distinction between 'inner worldly asceticism' and 'world rejecting asceticism,' Ibn Ḥanbal's views can be labeled 'inner

worldly' and those of the more extreme ascetics 'world rejecting.' We should, of course, be careful in the usage that we make with Weber's terminology. The historical and cultural contexts of classical Islam and early-modern Europe are far apart. The economic behavior that Protestant 'inner worldly asceticism' prescribes is almost the opposite of Ibn Ḥanbal's, because of their different attitudes regarding the accumulation of capital. Nonetheless, Weber's terminology and generalizations touch upon an important characteristic of Islamic asceticism. Like its Christian counterpart, Islamic asceticism can be divided by the criterion of worldly activities. In both Islam and Christianity, we come across individuals and movements, which aspire to express their discontent with the world and worldliness through worldly activities, while other individuals and movements express their discontent by avoiding any worldly activity, whatsoever.

Weber has given us another, more specific, insight into the mindset of ascetics. He argues that one of the features that characterizes 'inner worldly asceticism' is a sense of responsibility towards worldly affairs: 'In this case [that of 'inner worldly asceticism'] the world is presented to the religious virtuoso as his responsibility.' Thus, the ascetic is not just merely involved in worldly affairs. He has an ideological stake in it, and acts upon it. In Weber's words: 'He ['inner worldly ascetic'] may have the obligation to transform the world in accordance with his ascetic ideals.' II, 542. This observation carries us into the sphere of social criticism. Interestingly enough, social criticism was part of the agenda of the more moderate ascetics precisely because they did not reject the world in as complete a manner as the zealous ascetics. Their very moderation in worldly denial opened channels of communication with the world which they used to convey their criticism.

45 *Manāqib*, 305.

46 Ṣāliḥ, 47–48.

47 Ibn Kathīr, *al-Bidāya*, X, 328.

48 For a comprehensive study of *al-amr bi-'l ma'rūf* is see Cook, *Commanding*. For some interesting references to this phenomenon among Ḥanbalis in Baghdad, see George Makdisi, 'Autograph Diary of an Eleventh-Century Historian of Baghdad,' *Bulletin of the School of Oriental and African Studies*, XVIII, XIX (1956, 1957), parts I-V, 9–31, 239–260, 13–48, 281–303, 426–443.

49 *Ḥilyat al-Awliyā'*, IX, 177. A similar story occurs with 'Abdallāh, *Manāqib*, 302.

50 C. Bynum, *Holy Feast and Holy Fast* (Berkeley, 1987), 227.

Part II
Chapter Four

1 Muhannā b. Yaḥyā claimed that after they met in 198 A.H., he adhered (*lazimtu*) to Ibn Ḥanbal for forty-three years, i. e., until the end of Ibn Ḥanbal's life. See *Ṭabaqāt al-Ḥanābila*, I, 346. In his entry in Ibn Manẓūr, *Mukhtaṣar*, XXVI, 49, there is no mention of his Ḥanbali affiliation.

2 *Ṭabaqāt al-Ḥanābila*, I, 213; Ibn Ḥajar al-'Asqalānī, *Tahdhīb*, VI, 351. According to the *Tahdhīb*, Maymūnī began studying with Ibn Ḥanbal in 200 A.H.
3 Ibn Ḥajar al-'Asqalānī, *Tahdhīb*, VI, 351; *Ṭabaqāt al-Ḥanābila*, I, 213. He appears as '*ṣāḥib Aḥmad b. Ḥanbal*' in Yūsuf b. al-Zakī al-Mizzī, *Tahdhīb al-kamāl fī al-rijāl* (Beirut, 1992), XVIII, 334.
4 *Ṭabaqāt al-Ḥanābila*, I, 213.
5 For anecdotes about Ibn Ḥanbal's hiring himself out as a porter and camel driver, see *Ḥilyat al-awliyā'*, IX, 174–175; *Manāqib*, 226. For anecdotes about his going on the *ḥajj* on foot, see Ṣāliḥ, 30; *Ḥilyat al-awliyā'*, IX, 183.
6 On Muhannā, see *Ṭabaqāt al-Ḥanābila*, I, 346; on al-Maymūnī, see *Ṭabaqāt al-Ḥanābila*, I, 213.
7 'Abbās b. Muḥammad b. Mūsā, appears as '*min aṣḥāb Abī 'Abdallāh al-awwalīn*,' *Ṭabaqāt al-Ḥanābila*, I, 239; al-Faḍl b. Ziyād, appears as '*min al-mutaqaddimīn 'inda Abī 'Abdallāh*,' *Ṭabaqāt al-Ḥanābila*, I, 251; Qāsim b. Muḥammad, appears as '*min aṣḥāb Abī 'Abdallāh al-mutaqaddimīn*' *Ṭabaqāt al-Ḥanābila*, I, 258.
8 On the Khurāsāni background of Ḥanbalis see Madelung, *Religious Trends*, 22.
9 For Abū Bakr al-Marwadhī see *Ṭabaqāt al-Ḥanābila*, I, 56. He is depicted as '*ṣāḥib Ibn Ḥanbal*,' in *Ta'rīkh Baghdād*, IV, 423; for Ibrāhīm b. Isḥāq, see *Ṭabaqāt al-Ḥanābila*, I, 86.
10 *Ṭabaqāt al-Ḥanābila*, I, 56.
11 *Ṭabaqāt al-Ḥanābila*, I, 86; *Manāqib*, 509. A similar point was also made about Abū Bakr al-Marwadhī in *Manāqib*, 506.
12 *Ṭabaqāt al-Ḥanābila*, I, 195–196. See also *Ta'rīkh Baghdād*, X, 79, where he is labeled '*min aṣḥāb Abī 'Abdallāh*'.
13 *Ṭabaqāt al-Ḥanābila*, I, 195.
14 *Ṭabaqāt al-Ḥanābila*, I, 323. He is also mentioned as Ibn Ḥanbal's neighbor in *Manāqib*, 511, and as a conveyor of his jurisprudence in 7.
15 *Ḥilyat al-awliyā'*, IX, 213; *Manāqib*, 510; *Ta'rīkh Baghdād*, X, 79. The other is an anonymous Marwadhī who was a friend of Ibn Ḥanbal. See *Ḥilyat al-awliyā'*, IX, 175.
16 *Ḥilyat al-awliyā'*, IX, 197. Referred to as Buran.
17 *Ṭabaqāt al-Ḥanābila*, I, 97. Ibn Hāni' is also mentioned as one of the *abdāl* in *Ta'rīkh Baghdād*, VI, 204. In addition, he is also described as transmitter of many of Ibn Ḥanbal's *masā'il*.
18 *Ṭabaqāt al-Ḥanābila*, I, 108. On his special relations with Ibn Ḥanbal, see *Ta'rīkh Baghdād*, VI, 376.
19 *Ṭabaqāt al-Ḥanābila*, I, 323.
20 Ibid., 97.
21 Ibid., 56.
22 Ibid., 195.
23 A thorough exposition of the moral issue will be found in the next chapter.
24 For example, none appears in Ibn Ḥajar al-'Asqalānī's *Tahdhīb*. Their dates of death span from 256 A.H. to 275 A.H. and are borderline insofar as inclusion in the *Tahdhīb* is concerned. However, Ibn Ḥanbal's other distinguished disciples [Sijistānī (d. 275), Kawsaj (d. 261) and Athram (d. 251)] were of a similar age, and they do appear in the *Tahdhīb*.

25 Abū Bakr al-Marwadhī, *Kitāb al-wara'*; Ibn Hāni', *Masā'il.*
26 Al-Shāfi'ī's son Muḥammad b. al-Shāfi'ī appears in al-Subkī, *Ṭabaqāt al-Shāfi'iyya*, II, 71–74. Shāfi'ī's grandson through his daughter Zaynab, Aḥmad b. Muḥammad b. 'Abdallāh, appears in Subkī, *Ṭabaqāt al-Shāfi'iyya*, II, 186. Among the Ḥanafīs Ḥammād b. al-Nu'mān [Abū Ḥanīfa] appears in Ibn Abī al-Wafā', *Jawāhir*, I, 226–227. His son, Abū Ḥanīfa's grandson, Ismā'īl b. Ḥammād, appears in Ibn Abī al-Wafā', *Jawāhir*, I, 148–149.
27 On 'Abdallāh's contribution see Patton, *Aḥmed ibn Ḥanbal*, 20–21, 24; *EI*[2], 'Ḥanābila,' H. Laoust; Laoust, 'Le Ḥanbalisme,' 77.
28 Ibn Ḥajar al-'Asqalānī, *Tahdhīb*, V, 127.
29 *EI*[2], 'Aḥmad b. Ḥanbal,' H. Laoust.
30 There is a short entry on Marwadhī in *EI*[2], 'Marwazī,' ed.
31 For Abū Bakr al-Khallāl, see *EI*[2], 'Khallāl,' H. Laoust and *Ṭabaqāt al-Ḥanābila*, II,12–15; for Barbahārī, see *EI*[2], 'Barbahārī,' H. Laoust and *Ṭabaqāt al-Ḥanābila*, II, 18–45.
32 On Abū Bakr al-Khallāl see p. 4, fn. 22.
33 Asceticism as a key concept in Ibn Ḥanbal's behavioral code will be taken up in the next chapter. On *wara'* see Ibn Ḥanbal, *Kitāb al-wara'*.
34 *EI*[2], 'Barbahārī,' H. Laoust.
35 Laoust, 'Le Ḥanbalisme,' 81–84.
36 On al-Athram, who was compared favorably with the renowned Traditionist Abū Zur'a, see Ibn Ḥajar al-'Asqalānī, *Tahdhīb*, I, 71. For al-Kawsaj see Ibn Ḥajar al'Asqalānī, *Tahdhīb*, I, 227, where he is labeled 'one of the leaders among the Traditionists.' Al-Kawsaj was mentioned in a number of sources as a disciple of Ibn Ḥanbal and Isḥāq b. Rāhawayh (a prominent Shāfi'ī, who was introduced to al-Shāfi'ī by Ibn Ḥanbal). See Ibn Ḥajar al-'Asqalānī, *Tahdhīb*, I, 226 and 'Abd al-Hayy b. 'Imād, *Shadharāt al-dhahab fī akhbār man dhahab*, (Beirut, 1986), III, 234. On al-Kawsaj and his collection of Ibn Ḥanbal's *masā'il*, as well as their translation, see Spectorsky, *Marriage and Divorce*, 143–254.
37 *Ṭabaqāt al-Ḥanābila*, I, 72.
38 I cannot at this point explain why what they wrote angered Ibn Ḥanbal while what other prominent students wrote went unmentioned.
39 Ibn Ḥajar al-'Asqalānī, *Tahdhīb*, I, 71; *Ta'rīkh Baghdād*, V, 111.
40 *Ṭabaqāt al-Ḥanābila*, I, 43, 44, 114. See *Ta'rīkh Baghdād*, VI, 363. On this affair, see Spectorsky, *Marriage and Divorce*, 6, fn. 20.
41 *Ṭabaqāt al-Ḥanābila*, I, 86–93. On his attitude towards Ibn Ḥanbal see *Ta'rīkh Baghdād*, VI, 40; Ibn 'Imād, *Shadharāt al-dhahab*, III, 355. All three give the impression that Ibrāhīm al-Ḥarbī considered Ibn Ḥanbal as a role model.
42 *Ṭabaqāt al-Ḥanābila*, I, 159–162. On his attitude towards Ibn Ḥanbal, see *Ta'rīkh Baghdād*, IX, 58; al-Subkī, *Ṭabaqāt al-Shāfi'iyya*, II, 296; Ibn 'Imād, *Shadharāt al-dhahab*, III, 314. All of these sources point out his similarity with Ibn Ḥanbal, hence I have the impression that he took Ibn Ḥanbal as his role model.
43 Along with his outstanding professional reputation he was renowned for his piety, Ibn Ḥajar al-'Asqalānī, *Tahdhīb*, IV, 153–156.
44 Ibn Ḥajar al-'Asqalānī, *Tahdhīb*, IV, 154.
45 Abū Dāwūd al-Sijistānī, *Masā'il*, 262–326.

46 Ibn Ḥajar al-'Asqalānī, *Tahdhīb*, IV, 154. The information of Abū Dāwūd's writings appears in Ibn Ḥajar al-'Asqalānī, *Tahdhīb*, but not in the *Ṭabaqāt al-Ḥanābila*.
47 Al-Dhahabī, *Siyar a'lām al-nubalā'*, XIII, 364.
48 *Ṭabaqāt al-Ḥanābila*, I, 86. According to F. Sezgin, *Geschichte des Arabischen Schrifttums*, (Leiden, 1967), 507, both al-Ḥarbī and Abū Dāwūd transmitted *masā'il* on the authority of Ibn Ḥanbal.
49 *Ta'rīkh Baghdād*, VI, 40.
50 Al-Dhahabī, *Siyar a'lām al-nubalā'*, XIII, 369.
51 Abu Zahra, *Ibn Ḥanbal*, 174; *Ṭabaqāt al-Ḥanābila*, I, 7. The list is taken from al-'Ulaymī, *al-Manhaj al-Aḥmad fī tarājim aṣḥāb al-imām Aḥmad*, 338. It is found as a manuscript in the Dar al-Kutub, folio 4323.
52 It is certain that this rule of thumb which uses Ibn Ḥajar al-'Asqalānī's *Tahdhīb* as an indicator of a Traditionist's reputation has some exceptions, Ibrāhīm al-Ḥarbī being the first to come to mind. However, I still think that as a general indication it is useful.
53 Madelung, *Religious Trends*, 22.
54 For 'Abdallāh's comments that these were the only times that he was seen socializing, *Ḥilyat al-awliyā'*, IX, 184.
55 This factor will be examined in detail in Chapter V, '*Zuhd*.'
56 Al-Subkī, *Ṭabaqāt al-Shāfi'iyya*, II, 228; Ibn Ḥajar al-'Asqalānī, *Tahdhīb*, IX, 43; *EI*^{2}, 'Bukhārī,' J. Robson.
57 Ibid. 257.
58 Ibid. 296.
59 For an overview of this issue, see A.J. Wensinck, 'The Refused Dignity' in *A Volume of Oriental Studies Presentated to E.G. Browne*, eds. T.W. Arnold and R.A. Nicholson, 1922, 491–499. On resistance to this post specifically in the Islamic world see Khalil 'Athamina, 'The 'Ulama' in the Opposition: The 'Stick and Carrot' Policy in Early Islam,' *Islamic Quarterly*, 36 (1992), 153–178; N.J. Coulson, 'Doctrine And Practice In Islamic Law: One Aspect Of The Problem,' *Bulletin of the School of Oriental and African Studies*, 18 (1956).
60 Wensinck, *The Refused Dignity*, 499.
61 *Ṭabaqāt al-Ḥanābila*, I, 204.
62 Ibid. 196.
63 Ibn Kathīr, *al-Bidāya*, X, 328.
64 On the relations between the Ḥanafis and the state in this period, see N. Tsafrir, 'The Spread of the Ḥanafi School in the Western Regions of the Abbasid Caliphate up to the End of the Third Century A.H.' (Ph. D. thesis, Princeton University, 1993) One of Tsafrir's main arguments is that this cooperation contributed to the spread of the Ḥanafi school.
65 Ibn Abī al-Wafā', *Jawāhir*, I, 140–141.
66 Other scholars from Abū Ḥanīfa's closest circle who accepted the position: Zufar, 'Alī b. Mushir and al-Qāsim b. Ma'n.
67 *Manāqib*, 505. However, Ibn al-Jawzī himself was quite close to the caliphs of his time and was involved in politics. He was introduced to al-Muqtafī, the caliph, by Ibn Hubayra, a Ḥanbali vizir. See Laoust, 'Le Ḥanbalisme,' 112–113. On Ibn Hubayra's patronage of Ibn al-Jawzī see H. Mason, *Two Statesmen of Medieval Islam, Vizir Ibn Hubayra (499–560 AH / 1105–1165 AD)*

and Caliph an-Nāṣir li Dīn Allāh (553–622 AH / 1158–1225 AD) (The Hague, 1972), 34–35.

68 For a study of his views on *imān*, see W. Madelung, 'Early Sunni Doctrine Concerning Faith as Reflected in the Kitāb al-Imān of Abū 'Ubayd al-Qāsim b. Sallām (d. 224/839),' *Studia Islamica*, 32 (1970), 233–254. On his Shāfi'ī tendencies, see al-Subkī, *Ṭabaqāt al-Shāfi'iyya*, II, 154.

69 *Ta'rīkh Baghdād*, vol.12, 404–405.

70 *Ta'rīkh Baghdād*, XII, 407.

71 *Ta'rīkh Baghdād*, XII, 411; on 413, Ibrāhīm al-Ḥarbī makes a similar laudatory remark, with the exception of one field of knowledge, traditions.

72 Ibid., X, 266.

73 Ibid.

74 He does this with the somewhat apologetic comment, 'I read in '*al-sābiq wa-'l-lāḥiq*' by Ibn Thābit [al-Khaṭīb al-Baghdādi] [a remark that] said transmitted [presumably Duḥaym] on Aḥmad b.Ḥanbal.' *Ṭabaqāt al-Ḥanābila*, I, 204.

75 *Ṭabaqāt al-Ḥanābila*, I, 413.

76 Ibid. 410.

77 Ibn Abī al-Wafā', *Jawāhir*, II, 210–211.

78 Muḥammad b. Abī Bakr b. Khallikān, *Wafayāt al-a'yān wa-anbā' abnā' al-zamān*, (Cairo, 1948), V, 197.

79 Ibn Ḥajar al-'Asqalānī, *Tahdhīb*, XI, 160.

80 *Ṭabaqāt al-Ḥanābila*, I, 412; similar note in Ibn Abī al-Wafā', *Jawāhir*, II, 211.

81 Ibn Abī al-Wafā', *Jawāhir*, II, 211.

82 *Ṭabaqāt al-Ḥanābila*, I, 66; *Jawāhir*, I, 115.

83 *Ṭabaqāt al-Ḥanābila*, I, 63–64.

84 A short overview on ṣūfī activities in ninth-century Baghdād can be found in Ali Hasan Abdel-Kader, *The Life, Personality and Writings of Al-Junayd* (London, 1976). For references to the Baghdādi school of mysticism, see Schimmel, *Mystical Dimensions*, 47, 57–62.

85 The sisters of Bishr b. al-Ḥārith appear in the *Ṭabaqāt al-Ḥanābila*, I, 427–428.

86 Ibid., 127–129. On his standing and contribution to ṣūfī history see Schimmel, *Mystical Dimensions*, 47, 57; EI^2, 'al-Djunayd,' A.J. Arberry; J. S. Trimingham, *The Ṣūfī Orders of Islam*, (Oxford, 1971), 4.

87 *Ṭabaqāt al-Ḥanābila*, I, 268–269; see M. Smith, *An Early Mystic of Baghdād: A Study of the Life and Teaching of Ḥārith b. Asad al-Muḥāsibī* (London, 1935), 29.

88 On Ismā'īl b. Isḥāq, see *Ṭabaqāt al-Ḥanābila*, I, 103; On his relations with al-Muḥāsibī see Smith, *al-Muḥāsibī*, 35.

89 *Ṭabaqāt al-Ḥanābila*, I, 418.

90 Ibid., 268.

91 Ibid., 103.

92 Smith, *al-Muḥāsibī*, 36.

93 *Ṭabaqāt al-Ḥanābila*, I, 86.

94 Ibid., 128.

95 This term is used in EI^2, 'al-Djunayd,' A.J. Arberry and in Trimingham, *Ṣūfī Orders*, 4.

96 The celebrated ascetic and mystic of Baghdād. *Ṭabaqāt al-Ḥanābila*, 381–389; EI^1, 'al-Ma'rūf al-Karkhī,' R.A. Nicholson.

97 Ibn Ḥanbal considered Maʿrūf to be one of the *abdāl*, *Ṭabaqāt al-Ḥanābila*, I, 382.
98 Ibid.

Chapter Five

1 Ibn Ḥanbal, *Kitāb al-Zuhd* (Beirut, 1981).
2 In a survey by C.E. Farah, 'The Prose Literature of Ṣūfism,' in *Cambridge History of Arabic Literature, Religion, Learning and Science in the 'Abbasid Period*, eds. M.J.L. Young, J.D. Latham and R.B.Serjeant (Cambridge, 1990), the author refers to the use of biography as a means of conveying ṣūfī values and modes of behavior. Farah does not mention any such compendia before the third century.
3 Ascetic thought and values have been articulated since the appearance of Islam. These sentiments were elaborated both in prose and poetry. Ibn Ḥanbal's teacher, Wakīʿ b. al-Jarrāḥ and another scholar of Wakīʿ's generation with whom Ibn Ḥanbal wanted to learn, 'Abdallāh b. al-Mubārak, composed books under the title *Kitāb al-zuhd*. Ascetic poetry can be traced back to the closing decades of the first century A.H. See A. Hamori, 'Ascetic Poetry (Zuhdiyyat),' in *Cambridge History of Arabic Literature, 'Abbasid Belle-Lettres* (Cambridge, 1980), 268.
For a study on chains of spiritual masters see John Renard, *All the King's Falcons, Rumi on Prophets and Revelation* (New York, 1994), particularly 4–5.
4 Aḥmad b. Ḥanbal, *Kitāb al-zuhd*, 86–87.
5 Ibid., 98–99. The editor will argue that Ibrāhīm sacrificed Ismāʿīl, 99, n. 1.
6 Ibid., 164.
7 Ibid., 98.
8 Ibid., 85.
9 Ibid., 97.
10 Ibid.,162.
11 Aḥmad b. Ḥanbal, *Kitāb al-Zuhd*, 117.
12 Ibid., 118.
13 Ibid., 375.
14 Ibid.
15 On a similar concept in Judaism *Lamed Vav Tzadikim* see G. Scholem, 'The Tradition of the Thirty-Six Hidden Just Men' in *Messianic Idea in Judaism* (New York, 1971), 251–256, where Scholem contemplates the mutual influence of the *Lamed vav Tzadikim* and the *abdāl/awliyā'*, and quotes Rudolph Mach. 'As Rudolph Mach first noted, it [a special category of just men whose hidings is essential for the fulfillment of their function] appears in the Islamic mystical tradition, particularly in places which took over this Jewish conception and in their own way developed it further. According to this Jewish tradition God ordained that the saints direct the world [...] According to a treatise of the eleventh-century Persian mystic Hujwīrī they are not even aware of the special distinction of their rank ... For the present we cannot determine whether this conception originated in a Jewish tradition which had already taken on new form when it penetrated Islamic

circles or whether the metamorphosis occurred in Islam and then the tradition returned to Judaism in this new form at an as yet undermined time.' (254).

J. Chabbi, in her article 'Abdāl' in *Encyclopedia Iranica*, suggests that similar notions circulated among early Christians and that it might have been influenced by Manichaen ideas.

16 *Encyclopedia Iranica*, 'Abdāl,' J. Chabbi. On the concept and its literature see Lane, *Lexicon*, I, 168. For an interesting discussion of the *abdāl*, particularly in the ṣūfī and Shī'ī context, see Matti Moosa, *Extremist Shī'ītes* (Syracuse, 1988), 110–119.

17 *Encyclopedia Iranica*, 'Awliyā',' H. Algar.

18 Hujwīrī, *Kashf*, 212, 213.

19 *Ṭabaqāt al-Ḥanābila*, I, 97. The story of the anonymous traveler is found in *Manāqib*, 147. According to Chabbi, *Encyclopedia Iranica*, 'Abdāl", the term was used in the third century by Jāḥiẓ, *Kitab al-tarbī' wa-'l-tadwīr*, ed. C. Pellat (Damascus, 1955), 28.

20 *Encyclopedia Iranica*, 'Abdāl,' J. Chabbi.

21 Ibid.

22 *Ṭabaqāt al-Ḥanābila*, I, 209–212.

23 Ibid., 212.

24 Ibid.

25 Ibid., 210–211.

26 Ibn Ḥanbal, *Kitāb al-wara'*, 5.

27 Ibid.

28 Ibid.

29 Ibn Ḥanbal expresses a similar position in his remark about Ma'rūf al-Karkhī, *Ṭabaqāt al-Ḥanābila*, I, 382.

30 *Ṭabaqāt al-Ḥanābila*, I, 39.

31 Ibid.

32 Ibid. Ibn Ḥanbal's comment on asceticism is also conveyed by another renown ascetic, Ismā'īl b. Yusuf, *Ṭabaqāt al-Ḥanābila*, I, 107.

33 Ibid., 39.

34 Ibid., 78.

35 Ibid., 77.

36 Ibid., 230.

37 Ibid., 107.

38 Ibid., 124–125.

39 Ibid., 124.

40 Ibid.

41 *Manāqib*, 218.

42 Ibid.

43 *Ḥilyat al-awliyā'*, IX, 184.

44 On networks and patronage in that period see Mottahedeh, *Loyalty and Leadership* and Zaman, *Religion and Politics*, 119–166.

45 *Manāqib*, 218.

46 Laoust, 'Le Ḥanbalisme,' 74. This will be treated in the next chapter.

47 Ṣāliḥ, 39.

48 Mottahedeh, *Loyalty and Leadership*, 3.

49 Ibid., 57–60.

50 As the profiles in J. Kraemer, *Humanism in the Renaissance of Islam* (Leiden, 1986) bear witness.
51 Mottahedeh, *Loyalty and Leadership*, 158. In this case the flow of material benefits is reversed.
52 Ibid., 162.
53 On a fascinating patronage system in the Christian world see, P. Brown, *Power and Persuasion in Late Antiquity* (Wisconsin, 1988), 89–103.
54 An interesting remark on the complementary nature of self-control and criticism of society was made by M. Weber in his *Economy and Society*, II, 542: 'Religious virtuosity, in addition to subjecting the natural drives to a systematic patterning of life, always leads to a radical ethico-religious critique of the relationship to society...'
55 *Encyclopedia Iranica*, 'Amr Be Ma'rūf,' W. Madelung.
56 In article in *Encyclopedia Iranica*, 'Abū Ḥanīfa,' he is depicted as an active supporter of two 'Alīd revolts against the Umayyads.
57 *Encyclopedia Iranica*, 'Amr Be Ma'rūf,' W. Madelung.
58 Ibid.
59 Cook, *Commanding*, 101.
60 al-Khallāl, *Al-amr*, 158; One is reminded of Augustine's moral scruples regarding music and other sensual pleasures in Augustine, *Confessions*, (New York, 1952) 202: 'Thus I fluctuate between peril of pleasure and approved wholesomeness; inclined the rather (though not as pronouncing an irrevocable opinion) to approve of the usage of singing in the church; that so by the delight of the ears the weaker minds may rise to the feeling of devotion. Yet when it befalls me to be more moved with the voice than the words sung, I confess I have sinned penally, and then had rather not hear music.' On 'the allurements of smells' and food, see pp. 198–201.
61 Ibn Hāni', II, 174.
62 Discussions on these topics are found throughout al-Khallāl, *al-amr*.
63 On the issue of privacy, see Marcus, 'Privacy'.
64 For fascinating evidence about the Ḥanbali sense of group identity, asceticism and *al-amr bi-'l-ma'rūf*, see G. Makdisi's 'Autograph Diary.'

Chaper Six

1 On the impact of al-Shāfi'ī, see J. Schacht, *The Origins of Muhammadan Jurisprudence* (Oxford, 1950); For qualifying remarks about al-Shāfi'ī's contribution to Islamic legal thought see W. B. Hallaq, 'Was al-Shafi'i the Master Architect of Islamic Jurisprudence?' *International Journal of Middle East Studies*, 25 (1993), 587–605. Hallaq does not question al-Shāfi'ī's authorship or originality but his reception during the third century A.H. (601). Similar view appears in W.B. Hallaq, *A History of Islamic Legal Theories: An Introduction to Sunni Uṣūl al-Fiqh* (Cambridge, 1997), 18–19.
2 An example of such a rejection are the Ẓāhiris. See, I. Goldziher, *The Ẓāhiris, Their Doctrine and Their History* (Leiden: 1971). Note Hallaq's reference to the disappearance of the Ẓāhiris, and likeminded jurists, from

the legal scene as proof that *ijtihād* triumphed over *taqlīd*, W. Hallaq, 'Was the Gate of *Ijtihād* Closed?' 7–10.

3 Partial exception to this is the work of S.A. Spectorsky who examined certain principles of Ibn Ḥanbal's legal thought in her article 'Aḥmad b. Ḥanbal's *Fiqh*,' 461–465, and his substantive legal positions in her book *Marriage and Divorce*.

4 Goldziher, *Ẓāhiris*, 80; Schacht, *Introduction*, 62; Spectorsky, *Marriage and Divorce*, Preface, ix-x.

5 Spectorsky, *Marriage and Divorce*, Preface, x; Schacht, *Introduction*, 62–63; Goldziher, *Ẓāhiris*, 81.

6 Schacht, *Introduction*, 63. Similar description appears in F. Rahman, *Islam*, 2nd ed. (Chicago, 1979), 82.

7 N.J. Coulson, *A History of Islamic Law*, (Edinburgh, 1964), 71; The textbooks that refer to the Ḥanbalis are: H.A.R. Gibb, *Mohammedanism* (Oxford, 1962), 104; F.E. Peters, *Allah's Commonwealth* (New York, 1973) 244; R. Levy, *The Social Structure of Islam* (Cambridge, 1962), 179.

8 Coulson, 71.

9 Goldziher, *Ẓāhiris*, 80–84. Though Goldziher was ambiguous on this matter and at times created the impression that the distinction between the schools was miniscule.

10 EI^2, 'Aḥmad b. Ḥanbal,' H. Laoust.

11 Ibn Ḥāmid, *Tahdhīb al-ajwiba* (Beirut, 1988), 36–41.

12 Al-Sijistānī, *Masā'il*, 177; trans. Spectorsky, *Marriage and Divorce*, 78.

13 Ibn Hāni', II, 167.

14 Al-Sijistānī, *Masā'il*, 276.

15 'Abdallāh b. Aḥmad b. Ḥanbal, *Masā'il al-imām Aḥmad b. Ḥanbal* (Beirut, 1981), 5–6.

16 This presentation is taken from Ibn Rushd, *Bidāyat al-Mujtahid*, trans. Imran Ahsan Khan Nyazee , *The Distinguished Jurist's Primer* (Reading, 1994), 20–24.

17 Ibid., 90.

18 Al-Sijistānī, *Masā'il*, 79.

19 EI^2, 'Ṣaghīr,' A. Giladi.

20 Abu Zahra, 245–246.

21 Qur'an, trans. M. Pickthal, 5:6.

22 Ceremonies of ablution EI^2, 'Ghusl,' G.H. Bousqet; EI^1, 'Wuḍū',' J. Schacht and EI^1 'Ṭahāra,' A.S. Tritton. Some aspects regarding the attainment of the state of purity have become highly contested. This has been described 'as one of the most important external distinctions between Sunna and Shi'a .. among the Sunnis its recognition is an absolute essential of the profession of faith.' EI^1 'Wuḍū',' J. Schacht.

23 Ibn Rushd, *Bidāyat*, I, 26. He specifies: 'Allah will not receive (*lā yaqbalu*) prayer from one who is impure (*man aḥdatha*) until he will perform ablution.'

24 There is no record of a direct debate between the two: however, as will be seen in the exposition that follows, Ibn Ḥanbal makes a reference to those who employ *qiyās*, a method al-Shāfi'ī claims to use in this precise issue. For a translation of al-Shāfi'ī's position on this matter see Calder, *Early Muslim Jurisprudence*, 99–100.

25 Muḥammad b. Idris al-Shāfi'ī, *Kitāb al-umm* (Beirut, 1393), I, 34.
26 Ibid.
27 Ibid.
28 Ibid.
29 Ibid.
30 Ibid., 19.
31 Al-Sijistānī, *Masā'il*, 12.
32 Abu Zahra, *Ibn Ḥanbal*, 205. Compare this with al-Shāfi'ī's views as they are presented in Schacht, *Origins*, 19: 'Traditions from Companions are superseded not only by explicit traditions from the Prophet, but by analogical and other conclusions drawn from these last.'
33 See chapter 4, 21
34 Ibn 'Abd al-Barr, *al-Intiqā'*, 76.
35 Goldziher, *Ẓāhiris*, 23, where he quotes Nawawī, *Tahdhīb al-asmā'*, 63.
36 Goldziher, *Ẓāhiris*, 20–39.

Part III
Chapter Seven

1 For an inquiry into the use that Ibn Ḥanbal's biographers made of the *miḥna*, see Cooperson, *Heirs*, 329–506.
2 For a review of the scholarship on al-Ma'mūn's role as initiator of the *miḥna*, see J.A. Nawas, 'A Reexamination of Three Current Explanations for al-Ma'mūn's Introduction of the *miḥna*,' *International Journal of Middle East Studies*, 26 (1994) 615–629.
3 Ibn Khallikān, *Wafayāt*, I, 84. Similar story is found in Aḥmad b. Abī Ṭāhir Ṭayfur, *Kitāb Baghdād* (Leipzig, 1908), 56–57; Yaḥyā b. Aktham was introduced to al-Ma'mūn by the famous Mu'tazili, Thumāma al-Ashrath.
4 D. Gutas, *Greek Thought, Arabic Culture* (Routledge, 1998), 77–78.
5 Al-Ṭabarī, III, 1039; trans. Bosworth, XXXII, 100.
6 Al-Ṭabarī, III, 1040; trans. Bosworth, XXXII, 100–101.
7 Hodgson, *The Venture of Islam* (Chicago, 1974), I, 298; Peters, *Allah's Commonwealth*, 169; al-Nadim, *The Fihrist of al-Nadim*, trans. B. Dodge (New York, 1970), 583–584. For a revision that argues that earlier caliphs took an interest in the sciences and supported translators see Gutas, *Greek Thought.*
8 *Ḥilyat al-awliyā'*, IX, 181. On caliphal efforts to get involved in Islamic scholarship and support the *muḥaddithūn*, see Zaman, 119–166.
9 On Isḥāq b. Mūsā al-Anṣārī, see *Ta'rīkh Baghdād*, VI, 355–356.
10 Ḥanbal, 77.
11 Ibid.
12 Al-Ṭabarī, III, 1114; trans. Bosworth, XXXII, 201.
13 Al-Ṭabarī, III, 1112–1113; trans. Bosworth, XXXII, 200.
14 Al-Ṭabarī, III, 1114; trans. Bosworth, XXXII, 202.
15 Ibid.
16 Ibid.
17 Al-Ṭabarī, III, 1115; trans. Bosworth, XXXII, 203.
18 Ibid.

19 On Ibn Abī Du'ād see fn. 14 in introduction.
20 Al-Ṭabarī, III, 1139; trans. Bosworth, XXXII, 229– 230.
21 On al-Faḍl b. Marwān, see al-Ṭabarī, III, 1181–1186; trans. Bosworth, XXXIII, 28–35, and footnotes 107–109.
22 Al-Ṭabarī, III, 1186; trans. Bosworth, XXXIII, 34.
23 Ibid.; trans. Bosworth, XXXIII, 35.
24 Al-Ṭabarī, III, 1313–1314; trans. Bosworth, XXXIII, 194, 195.
25 Al-Ṭabarī, III, 1254; trans. Bosworth, XXXIII, 117.
26 Al-Ṭabarī, III, 1326; trans. Bosworth, XXXIII, 212.
27 Muḥammad b. Khalaf al-Wakī', *Akhbār al-quḍāt* (Cairo, 1369), III, 297, 298; 'Abd al-Raḥmān b. 'Alī b. Al-Jawzī, *al-Muntaẓam fī Ta'rīkh al-umam wa-'l-mulūk*, (Beirut, 1412), XI, 99; J. van Ess, *Theologie*, III, 490.
28 Wakī', III, 298.
29 *Ta'rīkh Baghdād*, IV, 149.
30 Miah, *Mutawakkil*, 19.
31 For the Ḥanbali position on the Jahmīyya see Abū Bakr al-Khallāl, *Musnad*, 420–428.
32 *Ta'rīkh Baghdād*, IX, 243.
33 *EI*[2], 'Miḥna,' M. Hinds.
34 *Ta'rīkh Baghdād*, X, 73.
35 Ibid.
36 *Ta'rīkh Baghdād*, VII, 364.
37 On *thughūr*, see al-Ṭabarī, III, 1352; trans. J.L. Kraemer, XXXIV, 38.
38 For an early and thorough study of this event see Patton, *Aḥmed*. Patton, however, does not utilize or examine any Mu'tazili source; A modern and more comprehensive study of the sources, which makes use of Mu'tazili accounts such as al-Jāḥiẓ's *Rasā'il*, appears in van Ess, *Theologie*, III, 460–473.
39 This will be explored in chapter 8.
40 Ḥanbal, 48; Ṣāliḥ, 56. On Mu'taṣim's lack of interest in the *miḥna* and his lenient attitude towards its interrogations, see *EI*[2], 'Miḥna,' M. Hinds.
41 Ḥanbal, 49, There is a similar exchange in Ṣāliḥ, 57.
42 On 'Abd al-Raḥmān b. Isḥāq, see *Ta'rīkh Baghdd*, X, 260–261.
43 Ḥanbal, 48.
44 Ḥanbal, 52, 55.
45 On Ibn Samā'a's affiliation with the *ahl al-ra'y*, see *Ta'rīkh Baghdād*, V, 341; on his Ḥanafi connections, see al-Dhahabī, *Siyar a'lām al-nubalā'*, X, 646.
46 On Ibn Samā'a's position see Ḥanbal, 55.
47 Ibid.
48 *Ta'rīkh Baghdād*, IX, 243.
49 Al-Dhahabī, *Siyar a'lām al-nubalā'*, X, 554.
50 *Fihrist*, 430. See also 397, 413, 427.
51 Abū Manṣūr 'Abd al-Qāhir b. Ṭāhir al-Baghdādi, *Al-Farq bain al-Firaq*, trans. A.S. Halkin, *Moslem Schisms and Sects* (Philadelphia, 1978), 11. In *EI*[2], 'Al-Nadjdjāriyya,' K. 'Athamina, the Najjāriyya are described as 'followers of al-Ḥusayn al-Nadjdjār, an early, specifically Ḥanafi sect of kalām.' See also Madelung, *Religious Trends*, 29.
52 *Al-Farq*, 9.
53 Ibid., 11.

54 Ibid., 9.
55 Ḥanbal, 66.

Chaper Eight

1 Ḥanbal, 47; Ṣāliḥ, 55.
2 Ḥanbal, 46.
3 Ibid., 47.
4 Ibid.
5 Ibid.
6 Ibid.
7 On the Traditionists tendency to avoid the question of the Qur'an's createdness see W. Madelung, 'The Origins of the Controversy Concerning the Creation of the Koran,' in *Orientalia Hispanica sive Studia F.M. Pareja Octogenario dicata*, ed. J.M. Barral, vol. I/1 (Leiden, 1974), 518–521.
8 *Ṭabaqāt al-Ḥanābila*, I, 241.
9 Madelung 'Controversy,' 513–525.
10 Ibid., 521, where he quotes al-Khallāl, *Musnad*, folio 156v.
11 Ṣāliḥ, 56.
12 Ḥanbal, 43.
13 Ṣāliḥ, 60.
14 Al-Jāḥiẓ, *Rasā'il*, III, 293.
15 Ṣāliḥ, 56, 59.
16 Ibid., 56; Ḥanbal, 51.
17 Ḥanbal, 51. For a similar argument see Ṣāliḥ, 56.
18 Ḥanbal, 60.
19 Al-Jāḥiẓ, *Rasā'il*, III, 298.
20 *Ṭabaqāt al-Ḥanābila*, I, 31.
21 Ibid.
22 Ibid.; A similar statement is found in 241.
23 Ḥanbal, 60.
24 *Ṭabaqāt al-Ḥanābila*, I, 241; there is a similar warning in *Ṭabaqāt al-Ḥanābila*, I, 130.
25 Gutas, 82.
26 Ḥanbal, 59. In Ṣāliḥ, 54, the verse appears in a more complete form, 'we have made it an Arabic Qur'an' (With the addition of 'an Arabic'). However, according to Ṣāliḥ, this quote was mentioned before Ibn Ḥanbal was taken into the caliphal interrogation, by Isḥāq b. Ibrāhīm, in whose house he was detained.
27 Qur'an, al-anbiyā', 58.
28 Qur'an, al-fīl, 5. This verse opens with '*fa-ja'alnāhum*' translated by Pickthal 'and made them like.'
29 Ḥanbal, 59.
30 Ibn Ḥanbal, *Radd 'alā al-Zanādiqa wa-'l Jahmīyya* (Cairo, 1393), 22–24; trans. Seale, *Muslim Theology* (London, 1964), 99–101.
31 In his polemic tract, *Radd 'alā Zanādiqa wa-'l-Jahmīyya*, Ibn Ḥanbal was even more explicit about the problems of the verse.

32 Ḥanbal, 49. The same argument is found in Ṣāliḥ, 57.
33 Ibid., 49. See the similar argument in Ṣāliḥ, 57.
34 Ibn Ḥanbal, *Radd*, 31; trans. Seale, 110.
35 Ṣāliḥ, 58.
36 Ibid.
37 Al-Jāḥiẓ, '*Khalq al-Qur'an*', III, 295.
38 Jalāl al-Dīn 'Abd al-Raḥmān al-Suyūṭī, *al-Itqān fī 'ulūm al-Qur'an*, IV, 178, 180. I would like to thank Adrien Leites for referring me to this quote.
39 H. Birkeland, *Old Opposition to the Interpretation of the Koran* (Uppsala, 1956), 42.
40 Ibn Ḥanbal, *Radd*, 5,6; trans. Seale, 96.
41 Ibid., 20; trans. Seale, 98.
42 Ibid., 22; trans. Seale, 99.
43 Ibid., 30; trans. Seale, 108.
44 *Ṭabaqāt al-Ḥanābila*, I, 241; similar comment, 252.

Chapter Nine

1 *Ta'rīkh al-Islam*, 55.
2 Ibid., 56–57.
3 Ḥanbal, 83–84; *Ta'rīkh al-Islam*, 56.
4 Ḥanbal, 84.
5 Ibid., 84.
6 *Tarīkh al-Islam*, 53; in Ḥanbal, 66 we come across a different opinion that is ascribed to Ibn Abī Du'ād, according to which he wanted to keep Ibn Ḥanbal in jail.
7 Ḥanbal, 81–82; *Ta'rīkh al-Islam*, 56.
8 *Manāqib*, 350.
9 On Mutawakkil's gradual change of policy see EI^2, 'Miḥna,' M. Hinds.
10 *Ta'rīkh al-Islam*, 58; Ibn Kathīr, *al-Bidāya*, X, 337.
11 Ḥanbal, 86–88; *Ta'rīkh al-Islam*, 59.
12 Ibn Abī al-Wafā', *Jawāhir*, II, 61. He is also mentioned in 'Abd al-Jabbār Asadābādī, *Faḍl al-I'tizāl* (Tunis, 1974), 344 and in Aḥmad b. Yaḥyā b. al-Murtaḍā, *Kitāb ṭabaqāt al-Mu'tazila* (Beirut, 1961), 128–129, 140. He appears in the *Fihrist*, 510–511, in the chapter on the Ḥanafis. Short biographical sketches of Ibn al-Thalgī can be found in Watt, *Formative Period*, 203, 282.
13 Ibn al-Murtaḍā, *Ṭabaqāt al-Mu'tazila*, 129; See also Ibn Ḥajar al-'Asqalānī, *Tahdhīb*, IX, 189.
14 *Fihrist*, 510–511.
15 *Ta'rīkh al-Islam*, 59. In Ḥanbal, 87, Muẓaffar and Ibn Kalbī are mentioned as two different people.
16 Ḥanbal, 88; *Ḥilyat al-awliyā'*, IX, 207.
17 Ḥanbal, 88; *Ta'rīkh al-Islam*, 59.
18 *Ta'rīkh al-Islam*, 60; Ḥanbal, 99–100.
19 *Ṭabaqāt al-Ḥanābila*, I, 241. Appears as al-'Aṭṭār.
20 Ibid., 140. Appears as Ḥasan b. al-Haytham al-Bazzār.

21 Ibid., 396. Also appears as al-Bazzāz.
22 Ibid., 76.
23 One of two brothers, Aḥmad al-Dawraqī, appears in *Ṭabaqāt al-Ḥanābila*, I, 21. He was one of the first interogees to reply in the *miḥna*. His brother, Ya'qūb b. Ibrāhīm al-Dawraqī, see *Ṭabaqāt al-Ḥanābila*, I, 414.
24 Ḥanbal, 101; *Ta'rīkh al-Islam*, 60.
25 *Ta'rīkh al-Islam*, 60. This includes 'Abdallāh b. Sa'īd Abī Sa'īd al-Ashajj (d. 252) who was of somewhat mediocre standing in Traditionist circles, Ibn Ḥajar al-'Asqalānī, *Tahdhīb*, V, 211. Another benefactor was Muḥammad b. al-'Alā' Abū Kurayb (d. 248) who was considered a very knowledgeable Traditionist. Ibn Ḥanbal said of him, 'should I have transmitted of the authority of one of those that replied in the *miḥna*, I would transmit on Abī Mu'mar and Abī Kurayb.' Ibn Ḥajar al-'Asqalānī, *Tahdhīb*, IX, 334. He is mentioned as one of those who replied during the *miḥna* in *Manāqib*, 386.
26 Ḥanbal, 101; *Ta'rīkh al-Islam*, 60.
27 *Ta'rīkh al-Islam*, 61; Ḥanbal, 102. Ḥanbal explains that he also set out with them but that Ibn Ḥanbal told him to return.
28 Ḥanbal, 102–105.
29 Ibid., 104–05.
30 *Ta'rīkh al-Islam*, 62.
31 Ḥanbal, 107.
32 *Ḥilyat al-awliyā'*, IX, 211; Ḥanbal, 107–108.
33 It could not be al-Muṣ'ābī because he died before Ibn Ḥanbal came to Sāmarrā'.
34 *Ta'rīkh al-Islam*, 71; *Ḥilyat al-awliyā'*, IX, 212–213.
35 *Ta'rīkh al-Islam*, 71.
36 *Ta'rīkh al-Islam*, 71.
37 Ibn Kathīr, *al-Bidāya*, X, 339.
38 Ibid., 339–340.
39 Ibn Ḥajar al-'Asqalānī, *Tahdhīb*, IX, 189.
40 *Ḥilyat al-awliyā'*, IX, 216; Ṣāliḥ, 90.
41 *Manāqib*, 393–401.
42 Ibid., 386.
43 Ibid., 387.
44 Ibid., 388.
45 Ibn Ḥajar al-'Asqalānī, *Tahdhīb*, IX, 334.
46 Ḥanbal, 101.
47 Ibid., 78–79.
48 The story is told by Abū Bakr al-Marwadhī, *Manāqib*, 389.
49 Ibn Ḥajar al-'Asqalānī, *Tahdhīb*, VII, 298–299; *Manāqib*, 390–392.
50 Ibn Ḥajar al-'Asqalānī, *Tahdhīb*, VII, 298.
51 Al-Madīnī visited Ibn Ḥanbal's house and commented about its ascetic appearance.
52 Ibn Ḥajar al-'Asqalānī, *Tahdhīb*, VII, 308.
53 Ibid.
54 Ibid., 301.
55 Ibid., 299.
56 Ibid., 301.
57 Watt, *Formative Period*, 279.

58 Ibid.
59 Ibid., 286.
60 Al-Subkī, *Ṭabaqāt al-Shāfi'iyya*, II, 118–119.
61 Ibid.
62 *Ta'rīkh al-Islam*, 27.
63 See pp. 120–122.
64 Ibn Ḥanbal, *Kitāb al-Sunna* (Dumam, 1986), I, 163–166; Ibn Hāni', II, 154; al-Sijistānī, 264–265.
65 *Kitāb al-Sunna*, I, 103.
66 Ibid.
67 Ibid., 105.
68 Ibn Hāni', II, 154.
69 Ibn Ḥajar al-'Asqalānī, *Tahdhīb*, II, 325.
70 Ibid.
71 Ibid.
72 Ibn Ḥajar al-'Asqalānī, *Lisān*, II, 303.
73 Ibn Ḥajar al-'Asqalānī, *Tahdhīb*, IX, 43.
74 Ibid., IX, 441–444.
75 Al-Bukhārī's statement reveals that he was critical of the *kalām*-oriented discussion on the matter, while al-Karābīsī leaned towards that kind of debate. See Watt, *Formative Period*, 283.
76 For an interesting interpretation of Shāfi'īs's anti-*kalām* views and hostility towards *mutakallimūn* see G. Makdisi, 'The Juridical Theology of Shāfi'ī,' *Studia Islamica*, 59 (1984), 12. In essence Makdisi considers Shāfi'ī's enterprise in the Risāla to be an attempt 'to create for traditionalism a science which would be used as an antidote to kalām.' In his concluding remarks (p. 46), Makdisi states: 'Shāfi'ī's purpose in writing the Risāla was to counter any system of religious knowledge that pretends to go beyond the Koran and the Prophet's Sunna. In contrast to kalām, which went beyond the Scriptures to speculate about the author, God himself, Shāfi'ī's doctrine declared the Scriptures to be all that was needed for salvation.' See also 40. On *mutakallimūn*, see 17, 18, where Makdisi quotes *Shadharāt al-Dhahab*, II, 9. Also see Muwaffaq al-Dīn b. Qudāma, *Taḥrīm al-naẓar fī kutub ahl al-kalām* (London, 1962), 17.
77 J. Van Ess, 'Ibn Kullab et la *Miḥna*,' *Arabica*, 37 (1990), 188–193.
78 Goldziher, *Ẓāhiris*, 125–127.
79 Watt, *Formative Period*, 283.
80 On the internal division within the Shāfi'ī school of law and some of its repercussions, see G. Makdisi, 'Ash'ari and the Ash'arites in Islamic Religious History,' *Studia Islamica*, XVII, XVIII (1962, 1963), 37–80; 19–39.

Epilogue

1 Peter Brown, 'The Holy Man in Late Antiquity,' in *Society and the Holy in Late Antiquity* (Berkeley, 1982), 151.
2 Ibid., 152.

3 Several works and conferences have touched on the links between Late Antiquity and early Islam. A sample of these are P. Brown, *The World of Late Antiquity* (London, 1971); G. Morony, *Iraq After the Muslim Conquest* (Princeton, 1984); A. Cameron and L.I. Conrad eds., *The Byzantine and Early Islamic Near East* (Princeton, 1992).

4 Mottahadeh, 5.

5 P. Brown, 'Town, Village and Holy Man: The Case of Syria,' in *Society and the Holy in Late Antiquity* (Berkeley, 1982), 162.

6 Mottahedeh, 146.

7 On the Ḥanafis see Tsafrir, 'The Spread of the Hanafis'. On *madhāhib* as patronage systems see Mottahedeh, 135–150.

Bibliography

Primary Sources

'Abdallāh b. Aḥmad b. Ḥanbal, *Masā'il al-imām Aḥmad b. Ḥanbal*, Beirut, 1981.
'Abd al-Ḥayy b. 'Imād, *Shadharāt al-dhahab fī akhbār man dhahab*, Beirut, 1986.
'Abd al-Jabbār Asadābādī, *Faḍl al-i'tizāl*, Tunis, 1974.
'Abd al-Qādir b. Abī al-Wafā', *Jawāhir al-muḍiyya fī ṭabaqāt al-Ḥanafiyya*, Hyderabad, 1933.
'Abd al-Qāhir b. Ṭāhir al-Baghdādī, *al-Farq bain al-firaq*, tr. A.S. Halkin, *Muslim schisms and sects*, Philadelphia, 1978.
'Abd al-Raḥmān b. Abī Ḥātim, *Kitāb al-jarḥ wa-'l-ta'dīl*, Hyderabad, 1952.
—— *Ādāb al-Shāfi'ī*, Cairo, 1953.
Abū Bakr al-Khallāl, *al-Musnad min masāil Abī Abdallāh*, Dacca, 1971.
—— *al-Amr bi-'l-ma'rūf wa-'l-nahy 'an al-munkar*, Cairo, 1975.
Abū Dāwūd al-Sijistānī, *Kitāb masā'il al-imām Aḥmad*, Beirut, 1353.
Abū al-Najīb al-Suhrawardī, *A Sufi Rule for the Novice*, tr. M. Milson, Cambridge, 1975.
Abū Nu'aym al-Iṣfahānī, *Ḥilyat al-awliyā' wa-ṭabaqāt al-aṣfiyā'*, beirut, 1967.
Aḥmad b. Abī Ṭayfūr, *Kitāb Baghdād*, Leipzig, 1908.
Aḥmad b. Ḥanbal, *Kitāb al-zuhd*, Beirut, 1981.
—— *Kitāb al-wara'*, Beirut, 1983.
—— *Kitāb al-sunna*, Dumam, 1986.
—— *Kitāb al-'ilal wa-ma'rifat al-rijāl*, Beirut and Riyad, 1988.
—— *Radd 'alā Zanādiqa wa-'l-Jahmiyya*, Cairo, 1393.
—— *Musnad*, Beirut, 1991.
'Alī b. 'Abdallāh b. al-Madīnī, *al-'Ilal*, Beirut, 1972.
'Alī b. 'Uthmān al-Hujwīrī, *al-Kashf al-maḥjūb*, tr. R.A. Nicholson, London, 1976.
al-Bukhārī, *al-Ta'rīkh al-kabīr*, Hyderabad, 1361.
—— *al-Ta'rīkh al-ṣaghīr*, Cairo, 1976.
al-Dhahabī, *Tarjamat al-imām Aḥmad min ta'rīkh al-Islam*, Cairo, 1365/1946.
—— *Siyar a'lām al-nubalā'*, Beirut, 1994.
Ḥanbal b. Isḥāq, *Dhikr miḥnat al-imām Aḥmad b. Ḥanbal*, Cairo, 1977.
Hishām b. Muḥammad al-Kalbī, *Jamharāt al-nasab*, Beirut, 1986.

Ibn Abī Ya'lā, *Ṭabaqāt al-Ḥanābila*, Cairo, 1371/1952.
Ibn 'Adī al-Jurjānī, *al-Kāmil fī ḍu'afā' al-rijāl*, beirut, 1984.
Ibn Ḥajar al-'Asqalānī, *Kitāb al-mudallisīn*, Misr, 1913.
—— *Tahdhīb al-tahdhīb*, Beirut, 1994.
—— *Lisān al-mizan*, Hyderabad, 1330.
Ibn Ḥāmid, *Tahdhīb al-ajwiba*, Beirut, 1988.
Ibn Ḥibbān, *Kitāb al-majrūḥīn*, Haleb, 1975.
Ibn al-Jawzī, *Manāqib al-imām Aḥmad b. Ḥanbal*, Beirut, 1973.
—— *al-Muntaẓam fī ta'rīkh al-umam wa-'l-mulūk*, Beirut, 1412.
Ibn Kathīr, *al-Bidāya wa-'l-nihāya*, Beirut, 1966.
—— *Ṭabaqāt al-fuqahā' al-Shāfi'iyyīn*, Cairo, 1993.
Ibn al-Murtaḍā, *Kitāb ṭabaqāt al-Mu'tazila*, Beirut, 1961.
Ibn Qayyim al-Jawziyya, *I'lām al-muwaqqi'īn*, Beirut, 1973.
Ibn Rushd, *The Distinguished Jurist's Primer*, tr. I.A.K. Nyazee, Reading, 1994.
Ibn Sa'd, *Kitāb al-ṭabaqāt al-kubrā*, Beirut, 1990.
Isḥāq b. Ibrāhīm b. Hāni', *Masā'il al-imām Aḥmad b. Ḥanbal*, Beirut, 1400.
Al-Jāḥiẓ, *Rasā'il al-Jāḥiẓ*, Cairo, 1979.
al-Khaṭīb al-Baghdādī, *Ta'rīkh al-Baghdād*, Beirut, 1966.
Muḥammad b. Abī Bakr b. Khallikān, *Wafayāt al-a'yān wa-anbā' al-zamān*, Cairo, 1948.
Muḥammad b. Aḥmad al-'Abbādī, *Kitāb ṭabaqāt al-fuqahā' al-Shāfi'iyya*, Leiden, 1964.
Muḥammad b. Mukarram b. Manẓūr, *Mukhtaṣar ta'rīkh Dimashq li-Ibn 'Asākir*, Damascus, 1984.
Muḥammad b. Yūsuf b. al-Kindī, *Kitāb al-wulā' wa kitāb al-quḍā'*, Leiden, 1912.
Muwaffaq al-Dīn b. Qudāma, *Taḥrīm al-naẓar fī kutub ahl al-kalām*, London, 1962.
al-Nadim, *Fihrist*, tr. B. Dodge, New York, 1970.
Qur'an
Ṣāliḥ b. Aḥmad b. Ḥanbal, *Sīrat al-imām Aḥmad b. Ḥanbal*, Alexandria, 1981.
Al-Shāfi'ī, *al-Risāla*, Cairo, 1379/1979; tr. M. Khadduri, *Islamic Jurisprudence Shāfi'ī's Risāla*, Baltimore, 1961.
—— *Kitāb al-umm*, Beirut, 1993.
al-Subkī, *Ṭabaqāt al-Shāfi'iyya al-Kubrā*, Cairo, 1964.
al-Suyūṭī, *al-Itqān fī 'ulūm al-Qur'an*, Beirut, 1987.
al-Ṭabarī, *Ta'rīkh al-rusul wa-'l-mulūk*, Leiden, 1879–1901.
'Umar b. al-Ḥusayn al-Khiraqī, *Mukhtaṣar*, Beirut, 1964.
'Uthmān b. 'Abd al-Raḥmān b. Ṣalāḥ al-Shahrazūrī, *'Ulūm al-ḥadīth*, Halab, 1966.
—— *Ṭabaqāt al-fuqahā' al-Shāfi'iyya*, Beirut, 1992.
al-Wakī', *Akhbār al-quḍāt*, Cairo, 1369.
al-Washshā', *al-Muwashshā*, Cairo, 1965.
Yūsuf b. 'Abd al-Barr, *al-Intiqā' fī faḍā'il al-thalātha al-a'imma al-fuqahā'*, Cairo, 1350.
Yūsuf b. Zakī al-Mizzī, *Tahdhīb al-kamāl fī al-rijāl*, Beirut, 1992.
Secondary Sources
Abd al-Kader, A.H., *The Life, Personality and Writings of al-Junayd*, London, 1976.

Abu Zahra, M., *Ibn Ḥanbal*, Cairo, 1949.
Abdel Haleem, M., 'Early *Kalām*', in *History of Islamic Philosophy*, eds. S.H. Nasr and O. Leaman, London, 1996.
'Athamina, K., 'The 'Ulamā' in the Opposition: The 'Stick and Carrot' Policy in Early Islam', *Islamic Quarterly*, 36.3 (1992), 153–178.
Augustine, *Confessions*, New York, 1952.
Ayalon, D., 'Preliminary Remarks on the Mamluk Institution in Islam', in *War, Technology and Society in the Middle East*, eds. V.J. Parry and M.E. Yapp, London, 1975.
Birkeland, H., *Old Opposition to the Interpretation of the Koran*, Uppsala, 1956.
Bowering, G., *The Mystic Vision of Existence in Classical Islam*, Berlin and New York, 1980.
Bravmann, M.M., *The Spiritual Background of Early Islam*, Leiden, 1972.
Brockopp, J., 'Early Islamic Jurisprudence in Egypt: Two Scholars and Their *Mukhtaṣars*', *International Journal of Middle East Studies*, 30 (1998), 167–182.
Brown, P., *The World of Late Antiquity*, London, 1971.
—— 'The Holy Man in Late Antiquity', in *Society and the Holy in Late Antiquity*, Berkeley, 1982.
—— 'Town, Village and Holy Man: The Case of Syria', in *Society and the Holy in late Antiquity*, Berkeley, 1982.
—— *The Body and Society*, New York, 1988.
—— *Power and Persuasion in Late Antiquity*, Wisconsin, 1988.
Bulliet, R., 'A Quantitative Approach to Medieval Muslim Biographical Dictionaries', *Journal of the Economic and Social History of the Orient*, 13 (1970), 195–211.
—— *Patricians of Nishapur*, Cambridge, 1972.
Bynum, C., *Holy Feast and Holy Fast*, Berkeley, 1987.
Calder, N., *Studies in Early Muslim Jurisprudence*, Oxford, 1993.
Cameron, A., and Conrad L.I., eds., in *The Byzantine and Early Islamic Near East*, Princeton, 1992.
Chabbi, J., 'Fuḍayl b. 'Iyāḍ, Un Precursor Du Ḥanbalisme', *Bulletin D'Etudes Orientales*, 30 (1978), 331–345.
Cohen, H., 'The Economic Background of the Secular Occupations of Muslim Jurisprudents and Traditionists in the Classical Period of Islam (Until the Middle of the Eleventh Century)', *Journal of the Economic and Social History of the Orient*, 13 (1970).
Cook, M., 'The Origins of *Kalām*', *Bulletin of the School of Oriental and African Studies*, 43 (1980), 32–43.
—— *Commanding Right and Forbidding Wrong in Islamic Thought* (Cambridge, 2000).
Cooperson, M.D., 'The Heirs of the Prophets in Classical Arabic Biography', unpublished Ph.D. thesis, Harvard University, 1994.
Coulson, N.J., 'Doctrine and Practice in Islamic Law: One Aspect of the Problem', *Bulletin of the School of Oriental and African Studies*, 18 (1956), 211–226.
—— *A History of Islamic Law*, Edinburgh, 1964.
Crone, P., *Slaves on Horses: The Evolution of the Islamic Polity*, Cambridge, 1980.

—— and Hinds, M., *God's Caliph: Religious Authority in the First Centuries of Islam*, Cambridge, 1986.

Donaldson, D.M., *Studies in Muslim Ethics*, London, 1953.

Duri, A.A., *The Rise of Historical Writing Among the Arabs*, tr. L.I. Conrad, Princeton, 1983.

Eickelman, D., 'Traditional Islamic Learning and Ideas of the Person in the Twentieth Century', in *Middle Eastern Lives*, ed. M. Kramer, Syracuse, 1991, 35–59.

Encyclopaedia Iranica, London, 1982–.

Encyclopaedia of Islam, 1 st edn., Leiden/London, 1913–38, 2nd edn., Leiden, 1960–.

Ess, J. van, 'The Beginnings of Islamic Theology', in *The Cultural Context of Medieval Learning*, eds. J.E. Murdoch and E.D. Sylla, Dordrecht, 1975.

—— 'Ibn Kullāb et la Miḥna', *Arabica*, 37 (1990), 173–233.

—— *Theologie und Gesellschaft im 2. Und 3. Jahrhundert Hidschra: Eine Geschichte des Religiosen Denken im Fruhen Islam*, Berlin and New York, 1991–.

Fakhry, M., *Ethical Theories in Islam*, Leiden, 1991.

Farah, C.E., 'The Prose Literature of Sufism', *Cambridge History of Arabic Literature, Religion, Learning and Science in the 'Abbāsid Period*, eds. M.J.L. Young, J.D. Latham and R.B. Serjeant, Cambridge, 1990.

Gibb, H.A.R., 'The Social Significance of the Shu'ūbiyya', in *Studies on the Civilization of Islam*, Boston, 1962.

—— 'Islamic Biographical Literature', in *Historians of the Middle East*, eds. B. Lewis and P.M. Holt, London, 1962.

—— *Muhammedanism*, Oxford, 1962.

Ginzburg, C., *The Cheese and the Worms*, Baltimore, 1980.

Goldziher, I., *Muslim Studies*, tr. C.R. Barder and S.M. Stern, London, 1967–1971.

—— *The Ẓāhiris*, tr. W. Behn, Leiden, 1971.

Gutas, D., *Greek Thought, Arabic Culture*, London and New York, 1998.

Halkin, A.S., 'The Ḥashwiyya', *Journal of the American Oriental Society*, 54 (1934), 1–28.

Hallaq, W.B., 'Was the Gate of *Ijtihad* Closed?', *International Journal of Middle East Studies*, 16 (1984), 3–41.

—— 'Al-Shafi'i, Architect of Islamic Jurisprudence?', *International Journal of Middle Eastern Studies*, 25.4 (1993), 587–605.

—— *The History of Islamic Legal Theories: An Introduction to Sunni Uṣūl al-Fiqh*, Cambridge, 1997.

Hamori, A., 'Ascetic Poetry (Zuhudiyyat)', in *Cambridge History of Arabic Literature,'Abbāsid Belle-Lettres*, Cambridge, 1980.

Hodgson, M.G.S., *The Venture of Islam*, Chicago, 1974.

Hourani, A., 'Sufism and Modern Islam: Mawlana Khalid and the Naqshabandi Order', in *The Emergence of the Modern Middle East*, Berkeley, 1981.

Hovannisian, R.L., and Sabagh G., *The Thousand and One Nights in Arabic Literature and Society*, Cambridge, 1997.

Humphreys, R., *Islamic History, A Framework of Inquiry*, Princeton, 1991.

Hurvitz, N., 'Aḥmad b. Ḥanbal and the Formation of Islamic Orthodoxy', unpublished Ph.D. thesis, Princeton University, 1994.

—— Review of S.A. Spectorsky, *Chapters on Marriage and Divorce* in *Islamic Law and Society*, 3.3 (1996), 376–380.
—— 'Biographies and Mild Asceticism: A Study of Islamic Moral Imagination', *Studia Islamica*, 85 (1997), 41–65.
—— '*Madhāhib* (Schools of Law) and Historical Context: Re-examining the Formation of the Ḥanbali *Madhhab*', *Islamic Law and Society*, 7.1 (2000), 37–64.
Kennedy, H., *The Early Abbasid Caliphate*, Totowa, 1981.
Kraemer, J., *Humanism in the Renaissance*, Leiden, 1986.
Ladurie, Le Roy E., *Montaillou*, London, 1978.
Lane, E. W., *An Arabic-English Lexicon*, Cambridge, 1984.
Laoust, H., 'Le Ḥanbalisme sous le Califat de Bagdad, (214/855–656/1258)', *Revue des Etudes Islamiques*, 27 (1959), 67–128.
Lapidus, I., *A History of Islamic Societies*, Cambridge, 1988.
—— 'State and Religion in Islamic Societies', *Past and Present*, 151 (1996), 3–27.
Lassner, J., *The Topography of Baghdād in the Early Middle Ages*, Detroit, 1970.
Levy, G., 'On Microhistory', in *New Perspectives On Historical Writing*, ed. P. Burke, Cambridge, 1991.
Levy, R., *The Social Structure of Islam*, Cambridge, 1962.
Ludtke, A., 'What is the History of Everyday Life and Who are its Practitioners', in *The History of Everyday Life, Reconstructing Historical Experience and Ways of Life* ed. A. Ludtke, Princeton, 1995.
Madelung, W., 'Early Sunni Doctrine Concerning Faith as Reflected in the Kitāb al-Īmān of Abū 'Ubayd al-Qāsim b. Sallām (d. 224/839)', *Studia Islamica*, 32 (1970), 233–254.
—— 'The Origins of the Controversy concerning the Creation of the Koran', *Orientalia Hispanica sive Studia F.M. Pareja octogenario dicata*, ed. J.M. Barral, vol. I/1, Leiden, 1974.
—— *Religious Trends in Early Islamic Iran*, Albany, 1988.
—— 'The Vigilante Movement of Sahl b. Salāma al-Khurāsānī and the Origins of Ḥanbalism Reconsidered', *Journal of Turkish Studies*, 14 (1990), 331–337.
Mahmud, J., *Ittijāhāt al-fiqhiyya 'ind aṣḥāb al-ḥadīth*, 1979.
Makdisi, G., 'Autograph Diary of an Eleventh-Century Historian of Baghdād', *Bulletin of the School of Oriental and African Studies*, 18,19, (1956,1957).
—— 'Ash'ari and the Ash'arites in Islamic Religious Thought', *Studia Islamica*, 17, 18 (1962,1963), 37–80, 19–39.
—— *The Rise of Colleges*, Edinburgh, 1981.
—— 'Ḥanbalite Islam', in *Studies on Islam* ed. M.L. Schwartz, New York, 1981.
—— 'Ethics in Islamic Traditionalist Doctrine', in *Ethics in Islam*, ed. R.G. Hovannisian, Malibu, 1983.
—— 'the Juridical Theology of Shafi'i', *Studia Islamica*, 59 (1984), 5–47.
Malti-Douglas, F., 'Controversy and its Effects in the Biographical Tradition of al-Khatib al-Baghdadi', *Studia Islamica*, 46 (1977), 115–131.
Marcus, A., 'Privacy in Eighteenth Century Aleppo: The Limits of Cultural Ideals', *International Journal of Middle East Studies*, 18 (1986) 165–183.

Mason, H., *Two Statesmen of Medieval Islam*, The Hague, 1972.
Melchert, C., *The Formation of the Sunni Schools of Law, 9th-10th Centuries C.E.*, Leiden, 1977.
Miah, S., *The Reign of Mutawakkil*, Dacca, 1969.
Moosa, M., *Extremist Shi'ites*, Syracuse, 1988.
Morony, G., *Iraq After the Muslim Conquest*, Princeton, 1984.
Mottahedeh, R., 'The Shu'ūbiyyah Controversy and the Social History of Early Islamic Iran', *International Journal of Middle East Studies*, 7 (1976), 161–182.
—— *Loyalty and Leadership in an Early Islamic Society*, Princeton, 1980.
Muir, E., 'Introduction: Observing Trifles', in *Microhistory and the Lost Peoples of Europe*, eds. E. Muir and G. Ruggiero, Baltimore, 1991.
Nawas, J.A., 'A Reexamination of Three Current Explanations for Al-Ma'mūn's Introduction of the *Miḥna*', *International Journal of Middle Eastern Studies*, 24 (1994), 615–629.
Norris, H.T., 'The Shu'ūbiyyah in Arabic Literature', in *The Cambridge History of Arabic Literature*, Cambridge, 1990, 31–47.
Patton, W.M., *Aḥmed Ibn Ḥanbal and the Miḥna*, Leiden, 1897.
Pavlin, J., 'Sunni *kalām* and Theological Controversies', *History of Islamic Philosophy*, eds. S.H. Nasr and O. Leaman, London, 1996.
Pellat, C., *The Life and Works of Jāḥiẓ*, tr. D.M. Hawke, London, 1969.
Peters, F.E., *Allah's commonwealth*, New York, 1973.
Pipes, D., *Slave Soldiers and Islam*, New Haven, 1981.
al-Qadi, W., 'The Earliest 'Nābita' and the Paradigmatic 'Nawābit', *Studia Islamica*, 78 (1993) 27–61.
Rahman, F., *Islam*, Chicago, 1979.
Renard, J., *All the King's Falcons, Rumi on Prophets and Revelation*, New York, 1994.
Sabari, S., *Mouvements Populaires A Baghdad a l'epoque 'Abbaside ix-xi Siecles*, Paris, 1981.
Schacht, J., *Origins of Muhammadan Jurisprudence*, Oxford, 1950.
—— *An Introduction to Islamic Law*, Oxford, 1964.
Schimmel, A., *The Mystical Dimensions of Islam*, Chapel Hill, 1975.
Scholem, G., 'The Tradition of the Thirty-Six Hidden Just Men', in *Messianic Idea in Judaism*, New York, 1971.
Sezgin, F., *Geschichte des Arabischen Schrifttums*, Leiden, 1967.
Smith, M., *An Early Mystic of Baghdād: A Study of the Life and Teaching of Ḥārith b. Asad al-Muḥāsibī*, London, 1935.
—— *Rabī'a the Mystic and Her Fellow-Saints in Islam*, Cambridge, 1984.
Spectorsky, S.A., 'Aḥmad b. Ḥanbal's *Fiqh*', *Journal of American Oriental Society*, 102 (1982), 461–465.
—— *Chapters on Marriage and Divorce, Responses of Ibn Ḥanbal and Ibn Rāhwayh*, Austin, 1993.
Steppat, F., 'From *'Ahd Ardashīr* to Al-Ma'mūn: A Persian Element in the Policy of the *Miḥna*', in *Studies in Arabica and Islamica*, Beirut, 1981, 451–454.
Talmon-Heller, D., 'The Shaykh and the Community Popular Ḥanbalite Islam in 12th-13th Century Jabal Nablūs and Jabal Qaysun', *Studia Islamica*, 79 (1994), 103–120.

Toledano, E., *State and Society in Mid-Nineteenth-Century Egypt*, Cambridge, 1990.
Tor, A., *In the Garden of Myrtles, Studies in Early Islamic Mysticism*, tr. B. Sharpe, Albany, 1987.
Trimingham, J.S., *The Sufi Orders of Islam*, Oxford, 1971.
Tsafrir, N., 'The Spread of the Ḥanafi School in the Western Regions of the 'Abbāsid Caliphate up to the End of the Third Century A.H.', unpublished Ph.D. thesis, Princeton University, 1993.
—— 'The Beginnings of the Ḥanafi School of Iṣfahān', *Islamic Law and Society*, 5.1 (1998), 1–21.
Watt, W.M., *The Formative Period of Islamic Thought*, Edinburgh, 1973.
Weber, M., *Economy and Society*, New York, 1968.
Wendell, C., 'Baghdad; *Imago Mundi* and Other Foundation-Lore', *International Journal of Middle Eastern Studies*, 2 (1971), 99–128.
Wensinck, J., 'The Refused Dignity', in *A Volume of Oriental Studies presented to E.G. Browne*, eds. T.W. Arnold and R.A. Nicholson, 1922, 491–499.
Zaman, M.Q., *Religion and Politics Under the Early 'Abbasids*, Leiden, 1997.
Ziadeh, F., 'Equality (Kafā'ah) in the Muslim Law of Marriage', *The American Journal of Comparative Law*, 6 (1975), 503–517.
Ziauddin, A., 'Abū Bakr al-Khallāl The Compiler of the Teachings of Imam Aḥmad b. Ḥanbal', *Islamic Studies*, 9 (1970), 245–254.

Index

Name Index

For Product Safety Concerns and Information please contact our EU representative GPSR@taylorandfrancis.com
Taylor & Francis Verlag GmbH, Kaufingerstraße 24, 80331 München, Germany

www.ingramcontent.com/pod-product-compliance
Ingram Content Group UK Ltd.
Pitfield, Milton Keynes, MK11 3LW, UK
UKHW021955180926
475701UK00003B/46
* 9 7 8 0 4 1 5 6 1 6 4 1 6 *